THE
WISDOM
OF
CONFUCIUS

Edited and translated
with notes by
LIN YUTANG

THE MODERN LIBRARY · NEW YORK

COPYRIGHT, 1938, BY RANDOM HOUSE, INC.
COPYRIGHT RENEWED, 1966, BY RANDOM HOUSE, INC.

*Distributed in Canada
by Random House of Canada Limited, Toronto*

THE MODERN LIBRARY
is published by RANDOM HOUSE, INC.
New York, New York

Manufactured in the United States of America

TO TSUIFENG

IMPORTANT CHARACTERS
MENTIONED

CONFUCIUS: from K'ung Futse, meaning "Master K'ung"; known also as Chungni; 551–479 B.C.

MENCIUS: from Mengste; ranks next to Confucius in the Confucian Temples and represents Confucian moral idealism; author of the *Book of Mencius,* included in the *Four Books;* 372–289 B.C.

TSESZE: grandson of Confucius and teacher (?) of Mencius, author of *Central Harmony* and two or three chapters in *Liki;* known also as K'ung Ch'i; 492–431 B.C. and therefore could not have taught Mencius personally.

HSUNTSE or Hsun Ch'ing, or Hsun Huang: contemporary and rival of Mencius, representing another important development of Confucius' teachings, with emphasis on scholarship and rituals; his views often incorporated in *Liki;* his own books exist today; about 315–about 236 B.C.

SZEMA CH'IEN: author of the great Chinese work of history, the *Shiki;* master of Chinese prose; 145–85 (?) B.C.

CHENG HSUAN or Cheng K'angch'eng: most important commentator in Han Dynasty; 127–200 A.D.

CHU HSI: most important commentator of Sung Dynasty; through his influence the collection of *Four Books* came to be studied in all Chinese elementary schools; his commentary the only correct one recognized in civil examinations; 1130–1200 A.D.

CONFUCIUS' DISCIPLES AND IMMEDIATE CIRCLE

YEN HUEI or Yen Yuan: Confucius' favorite disciple, whom the Master praised only in superlative terms; 521–490 B.C.

K'UNG LI or Poyu: Confucius' only son, entirely undistinguished; 532–483 B.C.

TSELU: oldest of the regular disciples of Confucius; always protested against Confucius' conduct; received rough handling in the hands of the authors of the *Analects;* died in a fight because he insisted on adjusting the tassels on his cap "like a gentleman" during the fight and was therefore wounded; born 542 B.C.

TSEKUNG: the most devoted of Confucius' disciples; reputed to be a first-class diplomat; born 520 B.C.

TSEHSIA: pronounce as Tse Shia; the more scholarly type; became a great teacher after Confucius' death; born 507 B.C.

TSEYU: also a close disciple and a good diplomat; born 506 B.C.

TSENGTSE or Tseng Ts'an: noted for filial piety; the youngest and most philosophical of the disciples; teacher of Confucius' grandson; ranks next to Mencius in the Confucian Temples; born 505 B.C.

JAN CH'IU or Jan Yu: a practical and able man; became secretary to Baron K'ang Chi; later disowned by Confucius because he helped the Baron to tax the people; born 522 B.C.

DUKE AI OF LU, BARON K'ANG CHI OF LU (under the Duke), DUKE CHING OF CH'I, DUKE LING OF WEI: rulers of the time with whom Confucius had constant conversations.

QUEEN NANCIA: a notoriously beautiful and licentious queen, wife of DUKE LING OF WEI.

YANG HO: a powerful but corrupt official in Lu, whom Confucius heartily disliked.

THE PRONUNCIATION
OF CHINESE NAMES

1. Every vowel in the Romanized spelling of Chinese is pronounced.
2. The vowels have as their basis the usual Latin values:

a as in *father*
e as in *eight*
eh as in *burr*
erh as in a Scotch *burr*
i as in *machine* and *in*
o as in *old*
u as in *goose*
$ü$ as in German *lügen* (spelled merely as u in this book, but always occurs in the combination *hsu* and in most cases of *yu*)

3. The vowel sound in combinations like *tse, sze* does not exist in English. It is made with difficulty by Westerners, but is actually the vowel sound produced when the sound of z is prolonged and definitely vocalized

("buzzing" sound). In this instance, I depart from the Wade system, which renders it as *tzŭ*, because of its cumbersomeness. It frequently appears in names like *Laotse, Chuangtse, Tsengtse, Tsesze*.

4. The vowel sound indicated by the combination *ih* does not exist in English. It is made when the tongue and lip positions of the English *sh* are held unchanged and vocalized. For practical purposes, read the *ih* as *ee* (or if possible as a sound in between *she* and *shir*); there's no use trying to reproduce the sound exactly.

5. The important diphthongs are: *ia, ai, ou, uo, ei, ieh, ua* —all pronounced with their individual approximate Latin values (*h* in *ieh* is not pronounced).
   ao may be pronounced nearly as *aw*.

6. Combinations like *in, ing, an, ang* are pronounced with the usual Latin values for the sounds (*in, ing, ahn, ahng*). But *en, eng* are pronounced as *ern, erng*, or for practical purposes as *un, ung* (*sun, sung*) in English, whereas Chinese *un, ung* must be pronounced as *oon, oong*.

7. The distinction between *sh* and *hs* is a nuisance for English readers: read both as *sh* for practical purposes. Technically, the sound *hs* is different and comes invariably before *i* and *ü*. Since the two groups are clearly separated by the occurrence or absence of a following *i* or *ü*, that distinction in spelling between *sh* and *hs* is totally unnecessary for Chinese readers, and meaningless for Westerners.

8. The Chinese language distinctly differentiates between aspirated and unaspirated *p, t, k, ch, ts.* For practical purposes read *p, t, k, ch, ts,* as *b, d, g, j, dz,* and read *p', t', k', ch', ts'* like the regular English *p, t, k, ch, ts.*

9. Remember therefore to follow the Latin values for the vowels as a general principle, and for practical purposes read:

    hs as *sh*

    ih as *ee* (or *ir*)

   ieh as *y-ay*

    eh as *er*

    en as *un*

  eng as *ung*

CONTENTS

THE WISDOM OF CONFUCIUS

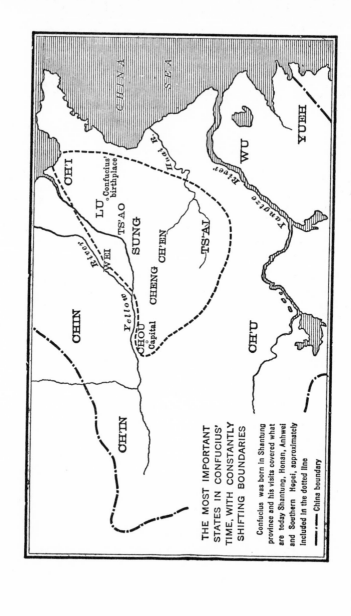

THE MOST IMPORTANT
STATES IN CONFUCIUS'
TIME, WITH CONSTANTLY
SHIFTING BOUNDARIES

Confucius was born in Shantung
province and his visits covered what
are today Shantung, Honan, Anhwei
and Southern Hopei, approximately
included in the dotted line

— · — · — China boundary

Chapter I

INTRODUCTION

I. THE CHARACTER OF CONFUCIAN IDEAS

CAN one be enthusiastic about Confucianism nowadays? I wonder. The answer seems to depend on whether one can be enthusiastic about sheer good sense, a thing which people usually cannot work up very much enthusiasm for. The more important question seems to be whether one can believe in Confucianism nowadays. This is especially important to the modern Chinese of today, a question that directly challenges their minds and cannot be brushed aside. For there is a centrality or, shall I say, universality, about the Confucian attitude and point of view, reflected in a joy in Confucian belief that I see even among maturing modern Chinese who have received a Western education. The centrality and basic appeal of its humanism have a strange strength of their own. During the political chaos and battle of ideas in the centuries immediately following Confucius, Confucianism won the victory over Taoism, Motianism, Naturalism, Legalism, Communism and a host of other philosophies. It maintained this supremacy over the Chinese people for the length of two thousand five hundred years,

3

with the exception of a few periods, and it always came back to its own stronger than ever. Apart from Taoism which was in fashion in the third to sixth centuries A.D., its strongest rival was Buddhism, which attained a great vogue with the Sung scholars. But with all its fine metaphysics, Buddhism succeeded only in modifying the interpretation of the method of arriving at knowledge and the aim of this humanist culture. It shifted the emphasis to certain ideas originally in the Confucian classics and directed a fuller attention to them, but did not replace Confucianism itself. Perhaps it was merely the old prestige of Confucius, but there was a great pride among the Confucian scholars, a belief in their own correctness, which made these scholars renounce Buddhism and look askance at it with toleration or contempt, as the case may have been. The same common sense that crushed the mysticism of Chuangtse also made them renounce the mysticism of Buddhism. Today Confucianism meets a still greater rival, not Christianity, but the entire system of Western thought and life and the coming of a new social order, brought about by the industrial age. As a political system aiming at the restoration of a feudal order, Confucianism will probably be put out of date by the developments of modern political science and economics. But as a system of humanist culture, as a fundamental viewpoint concerning the conduct of life and of society, I believe it will still hold its own. We have not yet progressed so far that, for instance, the doctrines of Karl Marx and Confucius no longer meet, or have no longer a common meeting point. Confucianism, as a live force in the Chinese people, is still going to shape our national conduct of affairs and modify Communism in China, if it is ever introduced. We will merely repeat the fight with Western Communism that Mencius fought with the early Chinese Communists and won. It is in this sense that a study of Confucianism and its fundamental beliefs will be of interest to people of the Western world, in helping them fundamentally to understand the Chinese *ethos* and Chinese *mores*.

To Western readers, Confucius is chiefly known as a wise man speaking in aphorisms or moral maxims, which hardly suffices to explain the depth of the influence of Confucianism. Without a deeper unity of belief or system of thought, no mere collection of aphorisms could dominate a nation's history as Confucianism has dominated China. The answer to the puzzle of Confucius' great prestige and influence has to be sought elsewhere. Without a fundamental system of beliefs which is accepted to be true, maxims and proverbs might easily grow stale and outworn. The *Analects*, the Confucian Bible, is such a collection of moral maxims, and it is chiefly through the *Analects* that Confucianism has been made known to the West. But the *Analects* after all is only a collection of the cream of Confucius' sayings, often torn apart from their contexts, which are found with a fuller elucidation in *The Book of Mencius, Liki* and other books. After all, Confucius did not talk the whole day in staccato sentences. It would be impossible, therefore, to arrive at a full appreciation of the influence and prestige of Confucius without an understanding of the system of Confucian ideas as a system.

To put it briefly, Confucianism stood for a rationalized social order through the ethical approach, based on personal cultivation. It aimed at political order by laying the basis for it in a moral order, and it sought political harmony by trying to achieve the moral harmony in man himself. Thus its most curious characteristic was the abolition of the distinction between politics and ethics. Its approach was definitely an ethical approach, differing from the Legalists who tried to bring about a strong nation by a rigid enforcement of the law. It was also a positive point of view, with a keen sense of responsibility toward one's fellow men and the general social order, as distinguished from the negative cynicism of Taoism. Fundamentally, it was a humanist attitude, brushing aside all futile metaphysics and mysticism, interested chiefly in the essential human relationships, and not in the world of spirits or in immortality. The strongest doctrine of this particular type of humanism, which accounts for its great enduring influence, is the doctrine that "the measure of man is man," a doctrine which makes it possible for the common man to begin somewhere as a follower of Confucianism by merely following the highest instincts of his own human nature, and not by looking for perfection in a divine ideal.

To be more specific, Confucianism was definitely aiming at the restoration of a rationalized feudal order, with clear gradations of rank, at a time when the feudal system of the Chou Dynasty was breaking down. In order to understand this, one has to go back to a conception of the collapse of the feudal system in Confucius' days and the centuries immediately following. There were hundreds of duchies, baronies, and townships, which had emerged as independent states, with the stronger states growing in power and territory and constantly warring with one another. The power of the Emperor, still holding a theoretic sovereignty over the Chinese Empire, had dwindled to nothing; in fact to such an extent that neither Confucius in his time nor Mencius later, who went about to persuade different kings to put their doctrines into practice, did not even bother to go and see the Emperor. This was a contradiction of his own theory of a rationalized social order, upholding loyalty to the highest authority. The situation was so bad that there was no point in either one of them trying to see the weak Emperor at all. There was, therefore, an international anarchy, resembling conditions in modern Europe. Treaties were scrapped, and there were alliances and big and little ententes, which never lasted very long. Taxation was frightful, in order to keep up the growing armies, and the smaller states were constantly worried about invasions by the powerful neighboring states. Conferences were constantly held, now with the ruler of one leading state and now with that of another sitting as the chairman. Philosophers began to develop the distinction between "offensive" and "defensive" warfare and between "aggressors" and "victims." Curiously, there developed a kind of intellectual internationalism; scholars moved about and switched their allegiance from one state to another. The ancient rites and insignias of rank had fallen into a terrible confusion; there was great inequality of wealth; and this moral and political chaos set every keen mind thinking about the best way of bringing about peace and order. In this atmosphere, the greatest intellectual activity, coupled with the greatest freedom of thought, brought about the greatest richness and variety in Chinese philosophy. Some repudiated civilization entirely, as Laotse and Chuangtse did; some became budding Communists, believing that every man should work for his living with his hands; some taught the oneness of God, the love of God, and a humanitarian, unselfish and even ascetic personal life, to the extent of repudiating music itself, as Motse did; and there were Sophists, Stoics, Hedonists, Epicureans and downright Naturalists. Many people, like modern Europeans, began to suspect civilization itself, and harked back to the primitive life, as some modern thinkers are harking back to the African jungle or the Island of Bali. Some others, like Confucius, were like the modern Christians, who believe in the force of moral ideals, in education, in the arts, in continuity with the past, and in maintaining some sort of international decencies and a high moral standard in human relationships, which were all part of the Confucian faith.

The chapter "On the Conduct of the Confucianists" in *Liki* (*Juhsing*, Ch. XLI) distinguishes this school of scholars from the rest. The term *Ju* (Confucianism is known in China as "the religion of the *Ju*" since Confucius' time) was already current in Confucius' day, and the scholars styled as *Ju* were probably a special set of people, conservative in point of view, backed by historical scholarshilp, and wearing a special *Ju* cap and *Ju* gown as symbols of their belief in the past. The following are a few extracts showing the high moral idealism of this group of followers of Confucius:

The Duke Ai of Lu asked Confucius, "Is the Master's dress that of the *Ju?*" Confucius replied, "I grew up in Lu and wore a gown with broad sleeves, and stayed later in Sung and therefore wore a cap of black cloth. I have heard it said that a gentleman is broad in his scholarship, but wears the gown of his own country. I do not know if this gown that I wear may be called a *Ju* gown." "What about the conduct of the *Ju?*" asked the Duke, and Confucius replied, "I shall not be able to finish it if I were to describe all the details, and if I did, I would have to stop over here and yet not be able to cover it all, even after you have changed the attendants several times." The Duke then asked Confucius to sit down on the mat, and Confucius sat in his company and said,

"A *Ju* is like one who has jewels in his keeping waiting for sale; he cultivates his knowledge morning and night to prepare himself for requests for advice; he cherishes integrity and honesty of character against the time when he is appointed; he endeavors to order his personal conduct against the time when he shall be in office. Such is his independence!

"A *Ju* is orderly in his dress and careful in his actions; his great refusals seem like lack of respect and his little refusals seem like false manners; when he appears on public occasions, he looks awe-inspiring, and on small occasions he appears self-retiring; his services are difficult to get and difficult to keep while he appears gentle and weak. Such is his appearance!

"A *Ju* may be approached by gentle manners but may not be cowed by force; he is affable but he cannot be made to do what he doesn't want; and he may be killed, but may not be humiliated. He is simple and frugal in his living, and his faults or mistakes may be gently explained but not abruptly pointed out to his face. Such is his strength of character!

"A *Ju* lives with the moderns but studies the ancients. What he does today will become an example for those in the generations to follow. When he lives in times of political chaos, he neither courts favors from those in authority, nor is boosted by those below. And when the petty politicians join hands to defame or injure him, his life may be threatened, but the course of his conduct may not be changed. Although he lives in danger, his soul remains his own, and even then he does not forget the sufferings of the people. Such is his sense of responsibility!

"A *Ju* is broad in his knowledge and not narrow-minded; he cultivates his conduct without cease; and in his private life he does not abandon himself. When he is successful, he does not depart from the truth. In his personal manners he values living in peace and harmony with others. He maintains the beauty of his inner character and is leisurely in his ways. He admires those cleverer than himself and is generous toward the masses, and is flexible in principle. Such is his ease of mind and generosity of character!"

Against this background of international anarchy and a collapsing ancient feudal order, the different essential tenents of Confucian teachings will be more readily understood and appreciated, particularly Confucius' efforts to restore an ancient feudal order through ritual and music. The characteristic ideas of this body of teachings are, to my mind, five in number, and since these are also the ideas constantly to be met with in the following translations, an examination of their exact import is essential to a true understanding of Confucianism.

1. The identification of politics and ethics:

The whole emphasis of Confucianism upon ritual and music and its apparent preoccupation with moral platitudes usually strikes the Western readers as queer and almost unintelligible. And yet, nothing is clearer than the fact that the so-called "ritual and music" embody better than any other phrase, the entire aim of the Confucian social order. It sounds almost childishly naive to hear Confucius say, in reply to a question about government by his disciple: "Ah Shih, didn't I tell you before? All that one needs to do is simply for the gentleman to fully understand ritual and music and then apply them to the government! (*Liki,* Ch. XXVIII)." This is easily understood, however, from the Confucian point of view, if we remember the Confucian definition of government as merely an effort to "put things right" or "put things in order." In other words, Confucius was aiming at the moral basis for peace in society, out of which political peace should naturally ensue. The *Analects* reports a conversation as follows: Someone asked Confucius, "Why don't you go into the government?" And Confucius replied, "Is it not said in the *Book of History* con-

cerning filial piety that the King of Chen was a good
son and a good brother and then he applied the principles to the government of things? This is also being in
the government. Why, therefore, should I go into the
government?" In other words, Confucius was almost an
anarchist, believing as his highest political ideal in a society of people living in moral harmony which should
make government itself unnecessary. This is implied in
his saying that "In acting as a judge at lawsuits, I am as
good as anyone. But the thing is, to aim so that there
should not be any lawsuits at all (*Analects,* XII)." How
this is to be achieved will be made clear in the following
paragraphs. But it is unmistakable that Confucius held
the final aim of government and the criminal law and
ritual and music to be identical: "The final goals of
ritual and music and the criminal law and government
are the same, namely, to bring about a community of the
people's aspirations and to result in social and political
order" (see Chapter X "On Music"). Confucius was
never quite satisfied with the kind of political order
achieved by a rigorous administration or enforcement of
the criminal law. "Guide the people by governmental
measures," he said, "and regulate them by the threat of
punishment, and the people will try to keep out of jail,
but will have no sense of honor or shame. Guide the
people by virtue and regulate them by *li* (sense of propriety) and the people will have a sense of honor and
respect." There are then two kinds of political order, and
it is in this sense that Confucius once said, "When the
kingdom Ch'i moves a step forward, it will have reached

the culture of the kingdom of Lu (his own country), *i.e.,* the first stage of peace that he spoke of; and when the kingdom of Lu moves a step forward, it will have reached the stage of true civilization, *i.e.,* the second stage."

2. *Li,* or the rationalized social order:

Confucianism, besides being known in China as "the religion of Confucius" and "the religion of the *Ju,*" is further known as "the religion of *li,* or ritual." It will at once be sensed by Western readers, that there is much more to this conception of *li* than merely ritualism itself, or the entire Confucian system is a sham and a fake. We have to meet this fact squarely, for the phrase "ritual and music" occurs again and again in the Confucian texts and seems to embody the entire Confucian system of outward social order, as the conception of "true manhood" seems to embody the essence of Confucian teachings regarding personal conduct. The importance and exact meaning of the phrase "ritual and music" will be made amply clear in the Three Confucian Discourses (Chs. VI, VII, VIII). Here it is only necessary to point out that Confucius' own definitions of government and of *li* exactly coincide. Government is defined as putting things or people in order, but *li* is also defined as "the order of things (*Liki,* XXVIII). The Chinese word *li* therefore cannot be rendered by an English word. On one extreme, it means "ritual," "propriety"; in a generalized sense, it simply means "good manners"; in its highest philosophic sense, it means an ideal social order with everything in its place, and particularly a rationalized feudal order, which was breaking down in Confucius' days, as I have already pointed out.

To adhere to the philosophic meaning, Confucius was trying to restore a social order, based on love for one's kind and respect for authority, of which the social rites of public worship and festivities in ritual and music should be the outward symbols. Of course, the rituals of worship lead straight back to primitive religious rites and ceremonies, and it is clear that this so-called "religion of *li*" was truly semi-religious in character, being related to God at one end in the sacrifice to heaven by the Emperor, and related to the common people at the other end by the teachings of affection and discipline and respect for authority in the home life. There have existed different religious sacrifices to heaven or God, to the ancestors of the rulers, to the spirits of the earth and the mountains and rivers. Confucius, as reported several times in the *Analects* and the *Liki,* said that he did not know of the meaning of these particular sacrifices to God and the Imperial Ancestors, known as *chiao* and *t'i,* and that if he did, it would be as easy to rule the world as to turn over one's hand. In this aspect, the body of Confucian thought resembles most the laws of Moses, and it is easier to compare Confucius in the *scope* of his teachings to Moses than to any other philosopher. The *li* of Confucius, like the laws of Moses, covers both religious laws and laws of civil life and considers the two as integrated parts of a whole. After all, Confucius was a product of his times, living in what Comte calls the "religious" era.

Furthermore, Confucius would undoubtedly have been a High Churchman in temperament, an Episcopalian or a Roman Catholic, if he were a Christian. He loved the rituals of worship, certainly not as merely ceremonial acts without meaning, but with his clear knowledge of human psychology, he saw that the proper rituals brought about in the worshipper a respectful or God-fearing state of mind. Furthermore, he was a conservative, like all Episcopalians or Roman Catholics, and believed in authority and in continuity with the past. Personally, his artistic sense was too keen for him to be moved by the appeal of ceremonies and music, of which we have sample evidence in the *Analects* (see Ch. V, Sec. 2, "The Emotional and Artistic Life of Confucius"). And as the worship of God and the ancestors of the rulers was to bring about a state of true piety, so the ceremonies of drinking festivals and archery contests in the villages, accompanied with song and dance and kowtowing, teaching the villagers to observe form and order in their festivities, were also to bring about a sense of general order and courtesy among the masses.

Psychologically, therefore, the functions of ritual and music are the same. Confucianism gave a sort of philosophic and even poetic meaning to ritual and music and dance. This is nothing surprising, considering that Confucius himself was a great lover of music, learned to play on musical instruments from a master of music at the age of twenty-nine, and constantly sang and played on the *ch'in* (a string instrument) even amidst his troubles. It is definitely stated that the six branches of study in Confucius' time were: ritual, music, archery, carriage driving, writing and mathematics. Confucius himself edited the *Book of Songs* at the age of sixty-four, and it is said that after this job of editing, the different songs were first shifted and properly classified with respect to their accompanying music. In fact, Confucius' own school, according to reports, seemed continually to echo with the sounds of song and music, and Tsekung, when placed in charge of a town, began to teach the people to sing, which induced a smile and a joike from Confucius (Ch. V, Sec. 3). The philosophic meaning of ritual and music is fully developed in Chapter X. The gist of it is: "when you see a nation's dance, you know the character of the people"; "music comes from the heart, while ritual comes from the outside"; "music is a sense of joy—what cannot be restrained or replaced from the human heart"; the different kinds of music in different countries are an indication of the different *mores* of the different peoples"; "music harmonizes the community, while ritual draws its social distinction"; "music represents heaven or the abstract, while ritual represents the earth or the concrete"; finally "therefore the ancient kings instituted ritual and music not only to satisfy our desires of the ear and the eye and the mouth and the stomach, but in order to teach the people to have the right taste or the right likes and dislikes and restore the human order to its normalcy."

Naturally, the whole system of *li* embodies also a concrete plan of a social hierarchy, concluding with a prodigious amount of scholarship regarding rules and ceremonies for the religious sacrifices, the festivities of drinking and archery and the conduct of men and women and children and the taking care of old people. This branch of Confucian historical scholarship was best developed by Hsuntse, a great philosopher whose books still exist and who was a contemporary and rival of Mencius, while its philosophic meaning is also fully developed in the *Liki* (see the Three Confucian Discourses, Chapters VI, VII, VIII), which largely reflect Hsuntse's interpretations.

This understanding of the importance of *li* helps us also to understand another corollary of Confucius' doctrines, the importance of terminology, that is, everything should be called by its right name. Therefore, when Confucius wrote the political annals of his time and the two preceding centuries, called the *ch'uch'iu* or *Spring and Autumn*, his intention was largely to restore the social order by sharp distinctions in terminology. A ruler killing a rebellious general would be called *sha*, while a prince or a minister killing his ruler would be called *shih*. When the Baron of Wu assumed the title of "king," Confucius merely wrote down "Baron Wu," thinking that he had degraded him by that single word in his Chronicles.

3. Humanism:

The finest philosophic perception of Confucius, it seems to me, is his recognition that "the measure of man is man." If it were not so, the whole system of Confucian ethics would fall to pieces, and would immediately become impracticable. The whole philosophy of ritual and music is but to "set the human heart right," and the kingdom of God is truly within the man himself. The problem for any man intending to cultivate his personal life is merely to start out on a hunt for the best in his human nature and steadfastly to keep to it. That is practically the essence of Confucian ethics. This results in the doctrine of the Golden Rule, and is best explained in Chapter III, "Central Harmony." Of course as a part of this humanism, there is a high and fine conception of *jen* or "true manhood," about which Confucius constantly talked, but which, as a qualification, he consistently refused to allow to all except two of his disciples and three great men in history. Confucius was constantly reluctant to fix this concept of a "true man," and when he was asked whether such and such a good man was a "true man," in nine cases out of ten he refused to apply that epithet to a living man. But, as is made clear in the chapter on "Central Harmony," Confucius also pointed out that in order to climb high, one had to begin from the low ground, and in order to reach a distant place, one had to begin by making a first step, and once he said, "Being a good son and a good younger brother provides already the basis for being a true man."

The conception *jen* (true manhood) is as difficult to translate as the conception of *li*. In Chinese writing, this character is composed of "two" and "man," signifying the relationship between men; in its present pronunciation, it is identical with the sound for "man," but in the ancient language it had a pronunciation which was identical to that of "man" in a particular phrase, quoted by a Han commentator, but unrecognizable today. In certain instances in Confucian books, the word for "true manhood" is actually used interchangeably with the common word for "man," the clearest instance of which occurs in the *Analects,* where a disciple speaks about "a man falling into a well," the word for "man" being written with the word for "true manhood," usually translated as "kindness" or "benevolence." Anyway the association of ideas is clear. In the English language in different words, such as *human, humane, humanitarian,* and *humanity,* the last word has a double meaning of "mankind" and "kindness." Both Confucius and Mencius also once defined "true manhood" as the "love of man." But the matter is not so simple. In the first place, as I have pointed out, Confucius refused to give a concrete example of a true man, whereas certainly he would not have refused to give a concrete example of merely "a kind man." In the second place, this "true manhood" is often described as a state of mind, a state that one "searches for," "attains," "feels at peace in," "departs from," "is based upon," and (Mencius) "dwells in," as in a house.

The essential idea of *jen* is therefore a conception of

the state when man is truly himself, and from this point on, Mencius starts out on his whole philosophy about the essence of human nature, and finds that "human nature is good," while Hsuntse, believing that human nature is bad and taking up the other end of Confucian teachings regarding education and music and the system of social order and outward forms of moral conduct, develops the idea of *li,* with emphasis on restraint. In common English phraseology, we speak of certain people among our acquaintances as "a real man" or "a real person," and this seems to come closest to the Confucian conception of *jen.* On the one hand, we begin to understand why Confucius refused to give so many good men of his day that label, as we can see today how many men or women we would be willing to call "a real person," in its most ideal sense. (Abraham Lincoln certainly was one.) On the other hand, we do find that the approach to being a real man is after all not so difficult, and that anyone can be a real person if he keeps his heart right and has some contempt for the artificialities of civilization—in other words, every common person can be a real man if he wants to. This fully fits in with the Confucian and Mencian statement that to be a real man, one merely needs to start out by being a good son or daughter or brother or sister, or a good citizen. I consider, therefore, my translation of *jen* as "true manhood" fully accurate and adequate. In certain places, it will have to be rendered merely as "kindness," just as the word *li* in certain places will have to be rendered merely as "ritual" or "ceremony" or "manners."

Actually, Mencius arrived at the position that men are all created equal in goodness of heart, and that "all men can be like the Emperors Yao and Shun" (the Confucian models of perfect virtue). It is this humanistic approach of climbing high from the low and reaching for the distance from the nearby, and of making an easy start in virtue or the development of character that accounts for the great fascination of Confucianism over the Chinese people, as distinguished from the much more idealistic doctrine of Motse, teaching actually the "fatherhood of God" and "universal love," so akin to Christianity. The humanistic idea of measuring man by man not only forces one to discover the true self, but naturally also results in the Golden Rule, known in Chinese as *shu,* namely, as Confucius repeatedly said, "Do not do unto others what you would not have others do unto you." Confucius not only gave this as a definition of the "true man," but also said that it was *the* central thread of all his teachings. The word for *shu* (meaning "reciprocity") is written in Chinese with the two elements "a heart" and "alike." In modern Chinese, it usually means "forgiveness," but the transition is easy to understand, for if you assume that all men's reactions are the same in a particular circumstance, and if you place yourself in the other man's position, you would naturally forgive. Confucianism, therefore, constantly reverted to the personal test of how would you feel yourself or "finding it in yourself." The best analogy, as given in Chapter III, is that of a carpenter trying to make an axe-handle—all he needs to do is to look at the handle of the axe in his own hand for a model. He will not have to go far. The measure of man is man.

4. Personal cultivation as the basis of a world order:

The ethical approach of Confucianism to the problems of politics has already been made clear. Put in the plainest terms, Confucius believed that a nation of good sons and good brothers could not help making an orderly, peaceful nation. Confucianism traced back the ordering of a national life to the regulation of the family life and the regulation of the family life to the cultivation of the personal life. That means very much about the same thing as when modern educators tell us that the reform of the present chaotic world after all must ultimately depend on education. The logical connections between a world order as the final aim and the cultivation of the personal life by individuals as a necessary start are made perfectly plain in the chapter, "Ethics and Politics" (Chapter IV) and also in Chapter III, Sec. 6, and throughout the Chapters VI, VII, VIII. The Chinese preoccupation with moral maxims and platitudes becomes then intelligible, for they are not detached aphorisms, but are part of a well-rounded political philosophy.

Interpreted in the light of modern psychology, this doctrine can be reduced easily to two theories, the theory of habit and the theory of imitation. The whole emphasis on "filial piety," more clearly translated by myself as "being a good son," is psychologically based on the theory of habit. Confucius and Mencius literally said that, having acquired the habits of love and respect in the home, one could not but extend this mental attitude of love and respect to other people's parents and elder brothers and to the authorities of the state. As stated in Chapter IV, "when the individual families have learned kindness, then the whole nation has learned kindness, and when the individual families have learned courtesy, then the whole nation has learned courtesy." The teaching of young children to love their parents and brothers and to be respectful to their superiors lays the foundation of right mental and moral attitudes for growing up to be good citizens.

5. The intellectual upper class:

The theory of imitation, or the power of example, results in the doctrine of the intellectual upper class and of "government by example." The intellectual upper class is at the same time a moral upper class, or it fails in its qualifications to be considered the upper class at all. This is the well-known conception of the Confucian "gentleman" or "superior man" or "princely man." This princely man is not at all a super man of the Nietzschean type. He is merely a kind and gentle man of moral principles, at the same time a man who loves learning, who is calm himself and perfectly at ease and is constantly careful of his own conduct, believing that by example he has a great influence over society in general. He is perfectly at ease in his own station of life and has a certain contempt for the mere luxuries of living. All the moral teachings of Confucius are practically grouped around this cultivated gentleman. The Chinese word for this, *chuntse,* was a current term given a new meaning by the usage of Confucius. In many places, it definitely meant "the sovereign" and could not be translated as "gentleman" and still make sense; in other places, it obviously meant only a cultivated "gentleman." With the existence of an intellectual upper class of rulers, the two meanings merged into one another, and formed a concept very similar to Plato's "philosopher king." The theory of the power of example is fully developed in Chapter XII of the *Analects* (see Chapter V of this book, Sec. 9). Confucius had an overweening confidence in the power of moral example. When a rapacious rich official, Chik'angtse, told Confucius that he was worried about the prevalence of robbers and thieves in his country, Confucius bluntly replied, "If you yourself don't love money, you can give the money to the thieves and they won't take it."

II. A BRIEF ESTIMATE OF THE CHARACTER OF CONFUCIUS

The great prestige of Confucius and Confucian teachings during the centuries immediately after his death, as well as in subsequent Chinese history, must be ascribed to three factors: first, the intrinsic appeal of Confucian ideas to the Chinese way of thinking; second, the enormous historical learning and scholarship accumulated and practically monopolized by the Confucianists, in contrast to the other schools which did not bother with historical learning (and this body of scholarship carried enough weight and prestige of its own); and thirdly, the evident charm of personality and prestige of the Master himself. There are in this world certain great teachers, whose personality seems to account for their influence more than their scholarship. We think of Socrates, or of St. Francis of Assisi, who themselves did not write any books of account, but who left such a tremendous impress on their generation that their influence persisted throughout the ages. The charm of Confucius was very much like the charm of Socrates; the very fact that the latter commanded the affection and respect of Plato is sufficient evidence of the power of his personality and his ideas. It is true Confucius edited the *Book of Songs,* and it is also true that he wrote the bare skeleton of events, chronicled in the *Spring and Autumn,* but after all the great tradition of his teachings was put down by his disciples and future followers.

There are, of course, many characterizations of Confucius' personality in the various Confucian books. We get a foretaste of it at the end of Chapter III, on "Central Harmony." His disciple Yen Huei also lauded him to the skies, comparing him to a great mysterious something: "You turn up your head and look at it and it seems so high; you try to drill through it and it seems so hard; it appears to be in front of you and all of a sudden it appears behind you." Some of the best characterizations, however, are the following: It was said that he was "gentle but dignified, austere, yet not harsh, polite and completely at ease." Confucius' self-characterizations were still better. Once a king asked one of his disciples about Confucius and the disciple could not make an answer. The disciple then returned to tell Confucius of the incident, and Confucius replied, "Why didn't you tell him that I am a man who forgets to eat when he is enthusiastic about something, who forgets all his worries when he is happy, and who is not aware that old age is coming on?" In this statement, we see something of the joy of life, the enthusiasm and the positive, persistent urge for doing something. He also said of himself several times that he was not a "saint," but that he admitted he was tireless in learning and in teaching other people. As an illustration of this positive urge in Confucius, there is also the following record. One of his disciples was putting up for the night at a place, and the gatekeeper asked him where he was from. Tselu replied that he was from Confucius and the gatekeeper remarked, *"Oh, is he the fellow who knows that a thing can't be done and still wants to do it?"* There was a high moral idealism in Confucius, a consciousness of a mission, that made him completely believe in himself.

The charm of Confucius' private character really lies in his gentility, as is so clearly shown in his conversational tone with his disciples. Many of the sayings of Confucius contained in the *Analects* can only be interpreted in the light of a leisurely discourse of a humorous teacher with his disciples, with an occasional shot of witticism. Read in this light, some of his most casual remarks become the best. I like, for instance, such perfectly casual sayings as the following: He remarked one day to two or three intimate disciples talking with him, "Do you think that I have hidden anything from the two or three of you? Really, I have hidden nothing from you. There is nothing that I do that I don't share with the two or three of you. That's I." Another instance: Tse-kung loved to criticize people and Confucius said, calling him by his intimate name, "Ah Sze, you are very clever, aren't you? I have no time for such things." Another instance: Confucius said, "I really admire a fellow who goes about the whole day with a well-fed stomach and a vacuous mind. How can one ever do it? I would rather that he play chess, which would seem to me to be better." In one instance, Confucius said something derisively about what one of his disciples was doing. The disciple was puzzled, and Confucius explained that he was merely pulling his leg, implying that really he approved. For Confucius was a gay old soul. His gentility and hospitality toward all desiring to learn are recorded in the following incident, resembling a story in the Bible when Jesus said, "Suffer the little children to come unto me." The people of a certain village were given to mischief, and one day some young people from that village came to see Confucius, and the disciples were surprised that Confucius saw them. Confucius remarked, "Why be so harsh on them? What concerns me is how they come and not what they do when they go away. When a man approaches me with pure intentions, I respect his pure intentions, although I cannot guarantee what he does afterwards."

But Confucius was not all gentility. For he was a "real man." He could sing and be extremely polite, but he also could hate and sneer with the hatred and contempt of a "real man," which was shared by Jesus in his hatred of the scribes. There was never a great man in this world who did not have some genuine good hatreds. Confucius could be extremely rude and there are recorded in the *Analects* four or five caustic remarks made about people in their presence. He could be rude in a way that no Confucianist dares to be rude today. There was no class of persons that Confucius hated more than the goody-goody hypocrites whom Confucius described as "the thieves of virtue." Once such a person, Ju Pei, wanted to see Confucius, and Confucius sent word to say he was not at home. When Ju Pei was just outside the door, Confucius took up a string instrument and sang "in order to let him hear it" and know that he was really at home. This passage in the *Analects* has confused all Confucian critics, who proceeded upon the assumption that Confucius was a saint and not a human being, and was always polite. Such orthodox criticism naturally completely dehumanized Confucius. Another passage in the *Analects,* recorded in *Mencius,* also puzzled the critics. A corrupt official, by the name of Yang Ho, presented Confucius with a leg of pork. As the two persons heartily disliked each other, Yang Ho found out when Confucius would not be at home and then presented the leg of pork at his home as a matter of courtesy. Confucius also took the trouble to find out when Yang Ho was not at home and then went to say thanks to him and leave his card. In reply to a question from his disciples concerning the rulers of his day, Confucius remarked, "Oh, those are rice bags!" (i.e., good only for filling themselves with rice). At another time he made this remark about a man who was reputed to have indulged in singing at his mother's death. "As a young boy, you were unruly; when grown up, you have accomplished nothing, and now in your old age you refuse to die. You are a thief!" And Confucius struck his shin with a walking stick.

There was, in fact, a lot of fun in Confucius. He led a full, joyous life, the full human life of feelings and artistic taste. For he was a man of deep emotionality and great sensitive taste. At the death of his favorite disciple, Confucius wept bitterly. When he was asked why he wept so and was so shaken, he replied, "If I don't weep bitterly at the death of such a person, for whom else shall I weep bitterly?" His curious sensitiveness and capacity for shedding tears was shown in an instance when he passed by casually a funeral of one of his old acquaintances. He went in, and moved by the weeping of others, he also wept. When he came out, he asked his disciple to take a part of the accoutrements on his horse as a funeral gift, and said, "Take it in as my formal present. I hated this weeping without reason."

This man, who sang and played musical instruments (*ch'in, seh,* and *hsuan*) and edited a book of songs with accompanying music, was an artist. As I have already pointed out, he was a lover of ritual and music. As an illustration of his Episcopalian temper, there was the following incident which contrasted him sharply with Jesus who had much less respect for the laws and the prophets and all the ritualism that went with them. Jesus allowed a person to save a cow out of a pit on the Sabbath. Confucius might have approved, or he might not. His disciple Tsekung once proposed to abolish the winter sacrifices of lambs, and Confucius replied, "Ah Sze, you love the lamb, but I love the ritual!" Anyway, he wasn't interested in animals. For on hearing that a stable was burnt down by fire, it was recorded that he asked whether any persons were hurt but "did not ask about the horses." The artist in him made him say that a man's education should begin with poetry, be strengthened by proper conduct, and "consummated in music." It was also recorded that when he heard another man sing and liked it, he would ask for an *encore* and then join in the refrain. The artist in him also made him very fastidious about his food and his dress. I have already pointed out elsewhere that his fastidiousness about food was most probably the cause of his wife's running away.* He refused to eat when anything was not in season, or not properly cooked, or not served with its proper sauce. And he had good taste in matching colors in his dress. A modern modiste could easily understand why he would match a black lamb coat with a black covering, a white faun coat with a white covering, and a fox coat with a yellow covering. (This "covering" corresponds to the "lining" in Western fur coats, for Chinese fur coats are

* See *Importance of Living*, Page 249

worn with the fur on the inside and the silk on the outside.) He was also something of an inventor in the matter of dress. His bedclothes were longer than his body by half, to avoid cold feet, and he struck upon the beautiful idea of making his right sleeve shorter than his left sleeve for convenience at work, which must have also exasperated his wife and caused this woman to run away from the crazy man. (For all these facts see Chapter X of the *Analects,* or Chapter V, Section 2, in this book. The aristocracy of his taste extended even to divorce. For three successive generations, the Master, his son, and his grandson were divorced or separated from their wives. On the intellectual lineage (the Master, his great disciple Tsengtse, and Tsengtse's disciple Tsesze), the record of divorce was also unbroken for three and a half generations, it being reported that the intellectual fourth generation, Mencius (who studied under Tsesze), *almost* divorced his wife. So, although none of them was particularly rich, they were undoubtedly aristocrats.

One of the most important characteristics of Confucius which really accounted for his great prestige was simply his scholarship and love of learning. Confucius said this repeatedly of himself. He admitted that he was not one of those "born to know the truth," but that he was an indefatigable reader and teacher, tireless in his search after knowledge and learning. He admitted that in every hamlet of ten families, there were some righteous and honest men as good as himself, but none who loved learning the way he did. He counted as one of the things that would trouble him "the neglect of his studies." In one of his sayings, I note a sigh of regret which is the regret of a modern research scholar. In his efforts to reconstruct the religious practices, ceremonies and customs of the ancient dynasties, he went to the city of Chi to search for survivals of the customs of Hsia Dynasty, and to the city of Sung to learn of the surviving religious practices of the ancient Dynasty of Shang. He said, "I should be able to talk about the religious customs of the Hsia Dynasty, but there are not enough evidences in the city of Chi. I should be able to talk about the religious customs of the Shang Dynasty, but there are not enough evidences in the city of Sung. There are not enough historical documents and evidences left. If there were, I should be able to reconstruct them with evidences." In other words, he was essentially a research scholar in history, trying to salvage from existing customs as well as historical documents the ancient social and religious practices which had decayed and the theocracy which had broken down. Nevertheless, he did his best, and the result of his labors was the collection of the Confucian *Five Classics* which were strictly history (dictum of a Ch'ing scholar, Chang Hsueh-ch'eng), as distinguished from the *Four Books*. I have no doubt that people were attracted to Confucius, less because he was the wisest man of his time, than because he was the most *learned* scholar, the only one of his day who could teach them about the ancient books and ancient scholarship. There was a great body of historical learning concerning the governmental systems of ancient times, and there was still a greater body of historical learning concerning the religious rites and ceremonies of a decaying or decayed theocracy, particularly that of the Shang Dynasty, as we can see from Confucius' *Five Classics*. He was reported to have had three thousand pupils in all, of which number seventy-two were accomplished in the *Book of Songs,* the *Book of History* and the theory and practice of rituals and music. He believed in history and the appeal of history, because he believed in continuity. It will be seen in the chapter on "Central Harmony" (Chapter III), that he regarded as the three essential requisites for governing the world: Character, position of authority, and the appeal to history, and that lacking any one of these things, no one could succeed with a governmental system and "command credence," however excellent it might be. The actual result was that there grew up within the Confucian school a great body of historical learning which the other schools entirely lacked, and personally I believe the victory of the Confucian school over the other schools of Laotse and Motse was as much due to its prestige in scholarship as to its intrinsic philosophic value. The Confucian teachers had something definite to teach and the Confucian pupils had something definite to learn, namely, historical learning, while the other schools were forced to air merely their own opinions, either on "universal love" or on "love of oneself."

A word must be said about the genial humor of Confucius, both because it supports and illustrates what I have said about his living a full, joyous life, so different from the conventional picture of Confucius presented to us by the killjoy Sung doctrinaires, and because it helps us to see his simplicity and greatness. Confucious was not a cheap wit, but occasionally he could not resist turning a clever line, such as the following: "A man who does not say to himself 'What to do? What to do?'—indeed I don't know what to do with such a person"; or this, "Know what you know and know that you don't know what you don't know—that is the characteristic of one who knows" (or in Chinese fashion, "Know, know; don't know, don't know—that is know"); or this, "A man who knows he has committed a mistake and doesn't correct it is committing another mistake." Sometimes he was also capable of a little bit of poetic humor or occasional license. There was a passage in the *Book of Songs,* in which the lover complained that it wasn't that she did not think of her sweetheart, but that "his house was so far away." Commenting upon this passage, Confucius remarked, "She really did not think of him at all; if she did, how could the house seem far away?"

But the most characteristic humor that we find in Confucius was also the best kind of humor generally, the humor of laughing at his own expense. He had plenty of chance to laugh at his own outward failures or of admitting that other people's criticisms of him were quite correct. Some of this humor was merely casual light raillery between the Master and his disciples. Once a man from a certain village remarked, "Great indeed is Confucius! He knows about everything and is expert at nothing." Hearing this comment, Confucius told his disciples, "What shall I specialize in? Shall I specialize in archery or in

driving a carriage?" (In this connection he once admitted jokingly that if wealth could be achieved entirely
by human effort, he would achieve it even if he had to be
a cab driver.) During the failure of his political career,
Tsekung once remarked, "Here is a piece of precious
jade, preserved in a casket and waiting for a good price
for sale." And Confucius replied, "For sale! For sale! I
am the one waiting for a good price to be sold!" Refusal
to see humor in Confucius would land the critics and
commentators in ridiculous difficulties over such a passage. But as a matter of fact, the Master and his disciples
constantly joked back and forth. Confucius was once in
difficulties while travelling. Being mistaken for a certain
other man who had maltreated the people, he was surrounded by troops. He finally escaped, his favorite disciple Yen Huei failed to turn up till later, and Confucius
said to him, "I thought you were killed." Yen replied,
"As long as you live, how dare I be killed!" In another
story, once the Master and his disciples had lost track of
each other. The disciples finally heard from the crowd
that there was a tall man standing at the East Gate with
a high forehead resembling some of the ancient emperors, but that he looked crestfallen like a homeless
wandering dog. The disciples finally found him and
told him about this remark and Confucius replied, "I
don't know about my resembling those ancient emperors, *but as for resembling a homeless, wandering dog,
he is quite right! He is quite right!*" This is the best type
of humor, and what appeals to me most is that passage
in *The Life of Confucius* (Chapter II, Section 5), where

Confucius was actually singing in the rain. There is a deep pathos about that group of wandering scholars, roaming for three years in the wilds between Ch'en and Ts'ai, having just escaped trouble, all dressed up in their tremendous scholarship and having nowhere to go. These last years of wandering became the turning point of Confucius' career, after which he admitted his full failure in seeking a political career and returned to his native country to devote himself to editing and authorship. He compared himself and his disciples to a nondescript band of animals, "neither buffalos, nor tigers" wandering in the wilds, and began to ask his disciples what was wrong with him. After the third answer, Confucius approved and said to the disciple who made that clever answer, smilingly, "Is that so? Oh, son of Yen, *if you were a rich man, I would be your butler!*" That is a passage that completely won me over to Confucius. Taken as a whole, that passage has a beauty and pathos comparable to Gethsemane, except that it ends on a cheerful note.

III. SOURCES AND PLAN OF THE PRESENT BOOK

I have remarked that the Confucian school practically monopolized the historic scholarship of those days, including the ability to read what was then already an archaic script, and this body of historic learning was handed down as the Confucian *Five Classics*. In the year 213 B.C., the "burning of books" (with the exception of books on medicine, astrology and horticulture) took

place, and in the following year, 212 B.C., 460 Confucian
scholars were buried alive for criticizing Ch'in Shih-
huang, the builder of the Great Wall. It happened, however, that this Emperor's Dynasty, founded for "ten
thousand generations," collapsed five years after the massacre and many old Confucian scholars who had committed the classics to memory had survived it. These old
scholars thus had salvaged the Confucian classics by an
oral tradition and by sheer memory, assisted, I suspect,
nevertheless by some inscribed pieces of bamboo that
they had hidden away. These people then taught their
disciples and had these classics written down in what
was then called the "modern script," for Chinese writing
went through a great process of simplification during the
reign of that great Emperor. In the century following
and afterwards, however, there came to light ancient
bamboo inscriptions, written in the "ancient script,"
which had been hidden away and had escaped destruc-
tion. The most notable instance was the discovery of
ancient texts by a "King of Lu," who had opened up the
walls of Confucius' own house and temple and found
these preserved. As they were in archaic script, scholars
set about to decipher them, a difficult but not impossible
job in those times. There grew up, therefore, a separate
tradition, known as the "ancient script" tradition, which
in part differed from the tradition of the "modern
script," notably in regard to the records of the ancient
forms of society and systems of government and concerning the mythological rulers. These two different traditions were noted already in the Han Dynasty, but the

greatest commentator, Cheng Hsuan, for instance, tried to harmonize the two. A compromise was effected. Thus throughout the succeeding dynasties, the orthodox version and interpretation of the *Book of Songs* and the *Spring and Autumn* were based upon the "ancient script," while the *Liki*, admitted as one of the *Five Classics*, decidedly belonged to the tradition of the "modern script." The distinction between the two traditions was not sharply drawn until the Ch'ing scholars of the 17th, 18th and 19th centuries set about with their scientific comparative method to restore the tradition of the "modern script." Every available scrap of evidence and every method of historical criticism and philological research was brought to bear upon this question, the most notable achievement being the conclusive proof of forgery of twenty-five out of fifty-eight existing chapters in the *Book of History,* thus restoring this classic to a collection of thirty-three chapters, representing the tradition of the "modern script." The general position is, not that the archaic script itself was a forgery, but that our present version of the so-called archaic script was a forgery.

The term "Confucian classics" today usually refers to the *Five Classics* and the *Four Books*. The *Five Classics* as I have pointed out formed the body of historical learning edited, taught and handed down by Confucius himself, while the *Four Books* on the whole represented the works of his followers, their records of Confucius' sayings and their interpretations or developments of Confucius' thoughts. Then at other times, we also speak of the *Thirteen Classics*. The contents of these different collec-

tions will be made plain by the Tables on pages 40 and
41. It should be remembered, however, that in Confucius' own day, there were *Six Classics* instead of *Five,* the
additional one being *The Book of Music,* the remaining
portions of which survive today as one of the chapters of
Liki (Chapter X of this book). The comparative Tables
on pages 40 and 41 will show the relationships. "*" indi-
cates the "ancient script" (*kuwen*) tradition; "#" indi-
cates the "modern script" (*chinwen*) tradition.

The usual approach to the study of Confucian wisdom
by directly attacking the *Analects* is a mistake, because it
leads nowhere. The *Analects* is a promiscuous and unedited collection of Confucius' sayings, often taken out
of their contexts in longer discourses recorded elsewhere,
which would make the meaning clearer. There are also
duplicate quotations existing in different chapters, of
which there are twenty, showing that the work grew by
itself in separate hands and was not edited by any one
man. Some of the chapters, evidently compiled by the
disciples of Tsengtse, would contain more sayings of
Tsengtse. The different sayings in any one chapter are
not arranged at all in sequence of ideas; sometimes one
can detect a main theme, but more often one cannot.
There are evident later additions at the end of some
chapters, and some lines in the text, for instance those at
the end of Chapter X, are clearly incomplete.

But the greatest difficulty for a Western reader in approaching the system of Confucian thought through the
Analects lies in the Western reader's habit of reading. He
demands a connected discourse, and is content to listen

while he expects the writer to talk on and on. There is no such thing as reading a line out of a book and taking a day or two to think about it, to chew and digest it mentally and have it verified by one's own reflections and experience. Actually, the *Analects* must be read, if it is to be read at all, by having the different aphorisms spread out on the separate days of a calendar block, and letting the reader ponder over one saying each day and no more. This is the orthodox method of studying the *Analects,* the method of taking a line or two and thoroughly mastering the thought and its implications. This evidently cannot be done with respect to modern readers. Besides, no one can get a well-rounded and consecutive view of the development of Confucius' thoughts by merely reading the *Analects*.

This is the reason why in the present plan, I am forced to select from the Confucian classics and the *Four Books* those chapters which represent connected essays or connected discourses on any one topic. In fact, there exist in the *Liki* connected Confucian dialogues, of which Chapters VI, VII and VIII are good examples. In Chapters III and IV, on "Central Harmony" and "Ethics and Politics," we find also a connected development of ideas in the form of essays. Actually, of the nine chapters of Confucian texts (i.e., excluding the *Life* by Szema Ch'ien) selected and translated by myself in this book, seven are chapters from the *Liki,* while the remaining two chapters consist of one selection from Mencius and one collection of "Aphorisms of Confucius," arranged or classified sayings selected from the *Analects,* with a few selections from other chapters of *Liki*. By looking at the above table, it will be seen that besides introducing five new chapters from the *Liki*, it covers in four chapters (III, IV, V, XI) the same field as the *Four Books,* which Chinese children were required to learn, in the elementary grades. This method is therefore orthodox. Two of the *Four Books,* "Central Harmony" and "Personal Cultivation," were taken from the *Liki* anyway and elevated into the position of parts of the *Four Books* together with the *Analects* and the *Book of Mencius* only by the Sung scholar Chu Hsi (1130–1200), and there is no reason why the other chapters of the *Liki* should not have equal authority with those two chapters which Chu Hsi selected.

There is the general question as to the validity and accuracy of records of Confucius' sayings in *Liki* and even in the *Analects*. This is the general question of what exactly Confucius or Buddha or Socrates said and to what extent we can believe, for instance, that Plato's accounts of the Socratic dialogue were literally accurate. A synoptic study of the Four Gospels of the Christian Bible reveals discrepancies enough. And we find the same variations of the sayings of Confucius, given in slightly different words in the *Analects,* the *Book of Mencius* and the *Liki*. It was inevitable that Plato colored the sayings of Socrates through his own pen, and the same was true of many of the chapters of the *Liki*. Modern politicians who have the occasion to be interviewed by reporters realize the practical impossibility of obtaining a literally accurate report of what they have

FIVE CLASSICS	THIRTEEN CLASSICS	COMMENTS
Book of Songs (*Shiking*)	Book of Songs (Mao*, Ch'i#, Han#, and Lu# versions)	Three hundred and five songs and sacred anthems besides six with music and title without texts, edited by Confucius.
Book of History (*Shuking*)	Book of History (33 chapters* and 28 chapters*)	Composed of early historic documents, chiefly king's proclamations, being the earliest of Chinese documents and most archaic in style of all the classics.
Book of Changes (*Yiking*)	Book of Changes (Pi*, Shih#, Meng#, Liang# and Ching# versions)	The philosophy of mutations of human events, originally a divination system based on changing arrangements of lines of an octogram (resembling the changing combinations of dots and dashes in the Morse system), but developed into a full philosophy for human conduct in varying circumstance.
Spring and Autumn (*Ch'unch'iu*)	Spring and Autumn (Cho*, Kungyang# and Kuliang# amplifications)	The Classic itself, a bare chronicle of events of two and a half centuries (722–481 B.C.), written by Confucius with a view to restoring correct terminology. The three *chuan* or amplifications narrate the events in detail, or elucidate the meaning of Confucius' text.
Book of Rites (*Liki*)	*Chouli** *Yili* (*Liking*)	Allegedly a record of governmental system of early Chou Dynasty. Different ceremonial rites.

Five Classics

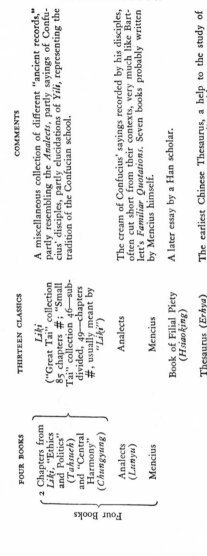

FOUR BOOKS	THIRTEEN CLASSICS	COMMENTS
Four Books { 2 Chapters from *Liki*, "Ethics and Politics" (*Tahsueh*) and "Central Harmony" (*Chungyung*)	*Liki* ("Great Tai" collection 85 chapters #; "Small Tai" collection 46—subdivided, 49—chapters divided, 49—chapters #, usually meant by "*Liki*")	A miscellaneous collection of different "ancient records," partly resembling the *Analects*, partly sayings of Confucius' disciples, partly elucidations of *Yili*, representing the tradition of the Confucian school.
Analects (*Lunyu*)	Analects	The cream of Confucius' sayings recorded by his disciples, often cut short from their contexts, very much like Bartlett's *Familiar Quotations*. Seven books probably written by Mencius himself.
Mencius	Mencius	
	Book of Filial Piety (*Hsiaoking*)	A later essay by a Han scholar.
	Thesaurus (*Erhya*)	The earliest Chinese Thesaurus, a help to the study of ancient classics, grouped according to ideas.

said. Nothing short of a dictaphone can convince the politicians of what they actually said themselves.

The *Liki* itself, as I have already said, is only a collection of various records in the possession of the Confucian school, and is definitely of extremely diverse origin. Some of these, including the essay on "Central Harmony" are ascribed to Tsesze, the grandson of Confucius, and some others, particularly a few in the "Great Tai" collection, are undoubtedly handed down by Tsengtse or his disciples. The chapters on education and music doubtless reflect the ideas of the Confucian philosopher Hsuntse, a contemporary of Mencius who spoke of the latter with contempt ("a gutter philosopher" was the phrase used). For the rest, a shocking proportion of the *Liki* is devoted to discourses on funeral ceremonies, while the "Great Tai" collection is devoid of these discussions. A good number of chapters are devoted to the philosophic meaning and actual ceremonial robes and vessels of public worship. There are also chapters on the rules and customs pertaining to all kinds of festivities—marriage, archery contests, dance, village, festivals, drinking and games (Chapter XL for instance, describes a game in detail similar to those we see in shooting galleries). An important chapter, Chapter V, is the basis of the "modern script" school on the ancient system of administration, as the *Chouli* is the basis for the "ancient script" school. There are other chapters dealing with the conduct of women and children and ordinary points of etiquette. The very first chapter, for instance, besides giving the philosophic justification for ritualism, also covers advice such as the following:

"Do not roll rice into a ball, do not leave rice on the table, do not let your soup run out of your mouth. Do not smack your lips, do not leave a bone dry, do not turn over the fish, do not throw bones to the dog, and do not persist in trying to get a particular piece of meat. Do not turn rice about to let it cool off, and do not take porridge with chop sticks. Do not gulp the soup up, do not stir the soup about, do not pick your teeth, and do not add sauce to your soup. . . . bite off boiled meat with your teeth, but do not bite off cured meet with your teeth."

This reads like Deuteronomy, and it is important that it be understood that the "religion of *Li*," like Judaism, embraces both religious worship and daily life, down to the matter of eating and drinking.

The present plan of the book is therefore as follows: Chapter II gives for the first time in English a translation of *The Life of Confucius*, the earliest and in fact the only biographical sketch of Confucius, written by the great historian Szema Ch'ien. Chapter III on "Central Harmony" gives a complete and adequate philosophic basis to the whole Confucian sytem, while Chapter IV on "Ethics and Politics" develops a coherent argument, whether sound or not for the connection between ethics and politics, between personal life, home life, national life and world order. Chapter V then gives the "aphorisms" of Confucius, selected and re-grouped from the *Analects*, on the whole the most witty chapter of the whole book. Chapters VI, VII, VIII form what I call the "Three Confucian Discourses" on the social order, which should sufficiently explain the true meaning of *li*, erroneously represented as mere ritualism. Chapter VIII in particular contains a short but important statement of Confucius' vision for world peace and his highest ideal of a moral order. Chapters IX and X then give us the Confucian ideas on education and music, singularly modern in point of view. The chapter on music is one of the longest in *Liki* and is actually compiled from a dozen chapters from the lost book on music. After all this, the reader is given a selection from Mencius, which represents a most important and influential development of Confucian philosophy. All the chapters except VIII and X are translated in full, the two exceptions being entirely too long.

I have done the translation of all the following texts myself, with the exception of the chapter on "Central Harmony." Ku Hung Ming's translation of that chapter is so brilliant and at the same time so correct and illuminating that I am sorry he did not translate more of the Confucian texts. It makes that chapter intelligible to the modern man. I have, however, considered it advisable to leave out his own comments bringing Goethe and Matthew Arnold and the *Proverbs* from the Christian Bible to elucidate the meaning of Confucianism; readers who are interested should go to Ku Hung Ming's own book (*The Conduct of Life*—John Murray, London). I have found it necessary also to make a number of corrections where Ku departs slightly from the Chinese text; besides, I do not accept Ku's rearrangement of the chapter, and have made my own. I have generally refrained from making comments, and have confined myself to making sectional divisions and providing sectional headings which will help the reader to follow the argument or the development of ideas more readily. But comments are implied throughout in the work of translation, and I regard a translation of this kind as commenting itself, for there is no really intelligent translation without the translator's interpretation of the text to be translated. This is especially true of translation from an ancient Chinese text into modern English. In the first place, the words used are necessarily so different in their general connotation, and in the second place, the ancient texts are unusually terse and concise, almost oracular in character at places, and one has to supply the necessary connectives and other words made necessary by the English syntax. Furthermore, Chinese interpretations of the same text vary a great deal, and the translator has to choose from one of them, or make a new one himself if he is convinced that he has new light on the subject. I therefore withhold myself from adding comments in the Ku Hung Ming manner, except where such comments are strictly necessary for guiding the reader with regard to the development of ideas, or for explaining certain terms.

Finally, I have found it necessary in Chapters III and IV to rearrange or re-edit the ancient texts. I realize fully such a responsibility. On the other hand, it is generally admitted that the texts of Chapters III and IV contain possible mistakes in arrangement, due to the fact that the separate paragraphs were inscribed on different pieces of bamboo and tied together in bundles. There are signs of reshuffling when these bamboo inscriptions were transcribed on silk in the Han Dynasty. Anyway, everyone admits that succeeding paragraphs in "Central Harmony" do not follow one another logically, although the main theme is always there. Chu Hsi took the bold step to re-edit the chapter on "Ethics and Politics," resulting in the transference of a whole section to an earlier part of the essay and making the development of thought much easier to follow. He even went as far as to write a paragraph of his own, declaring that he did so in order to supply a missing paragraph, but in the process enabling him to put a bit of Sung philosophy into the sacred text about meditation of the universe. However, if one confines himself to a mere reshuffling of already existing texts, with a view to establishing a more connected development of thought, without personal additions to the text itself, I believe it is justifiable on the ground of making a clearer presentation of ideas its sole aim. Naturally, I have not undertaken such reshuffling without the most careful consideration and understanding of the reason why such derangements of the original text took place.

IV. ON THE METHOD OF TRANSLATION

A little more must be said about the present method of translation. I consider a translation in this case as indistinguishable from paraphrase, and believe that is the best and most satisfying method.

The situation is as follows: The ancient texts were extremely sparing in the use of words, owing of course to the method of inscribing on bamboo sticks. Most of the important ideas and characterizations that covered a whole class of qualities were expressed by monosyllabic words, and in accordance with the general nature of Chinese grammar, the meaning was indicated by syntax or word order rather than by the usual English connectives. Here are two extreme instances in the Chinese form: "Confucius completely-cut-off four—no idea—no must—no *ku*—no I" ;"Language expressive only." It is clear that unless connectives are supplied by the translator, the translation would be practically unreadable. The extent to which connectives and amplifying phrases are allowable has by necessity to be left to the discretion of the translator, and for this the translator has no other guide than his own insight into the wisdom of Confucius, assisted, of course, by the commentators.

The first job is of course to determine the scope and connotation of a term in the general classical usage and secondly its particular meaning and shade of meaning in a given sentence. In the above instance of the word *ku,* this word meant several things: "strong," "stubborn," "persistence," "narrow-mindedness," "vulgarity," "limited in knowledge," and "sometimes also." From these different possible meanings, the translator has to make his choice. That is the terrible responsibility and the lati-

tude given to the translator of ancient Chinese texts, and
it is clear that a choice of a different word would alter
the sense of the line completely. In this particular instance, I have translated the passage as follows: "Confucius denounced (or tried completely to avoid) four
things: arbitrariness of opinion, dogmatism, narrow-
mindedness and egotism." It is of course, open to question whether the phrase "no must" should be translated
as "don't insist upon a particular course," "don't be persistent," "don't be insistent," or "don't assume that you
must be right (or don't be dogmatic)." Any of these
translations involves as much prarphrasing as the others.
In translating the phrase "no idea," I have paraphrased it
as meaning "don't start out with preconceived notions,"
or "don't be arbitrary." That is a sense or shade of meaning won from a knowledge of the general meaning of
the word "idea" in the Chinese language, and from an
insight into the whole character of Confucius' conduct.
But the mere use of the phrase "preconceived notion" or
"arbitrariness of opinion" necessarily expresses what at
best was only implied in the Chinese word "idea."

In the more fundamental concepts, like *li, jen, hsin,
chung,* etc., I have adopted a method of provisionally
translating these words in my mind by a certain English
concept and going over the body of the texts containing
these words to see which one would cover the field of
meaning most adequately in the majority of cases, allowing, of course, several meanings for one word. Thus I
have come to the conclusion that *li* usually translated as
"ritual" or "ceremony" must be translated as "the prin-

ciple of social order" in the general social philosophy of Confucius, and as "moral discipline" in certain passages dealing with personal conduct. I have also come to the conclusion that the translation of the word *jen* as "kindness," "charity," or "benevolence" is completely inadequate, but represents Confucius' ideal of the "true man," or the "great man" or the "most complete man." Likewise, *hsin* cannot be translated as "honesty" or "keeping one's promise," which latter quality Confucius rather despised and actually didn't care in his own conduct. Sometimes *hsin* means a condition of "mutual confidence in the state," and sometimes it means "faithfulness."

In the actual act of translation, the translator is faced with two jobs after he has grasped the meaning of the sentence. First he is faced with the choice of one of a number of synonyms, and failure to get at the exact word would completely fail to render the meaning of the remark clear to the reader. I found it impossible, for instance, almost to translate the word *teh* as "virtue" or "character," or the meaning would be hopelessly lost for the reader. Thus, Confucius said, "Thoroughbred, don't praise its strength praise its *character.*" The meaning becomes clear only when we translate it as follows: "In discussing a thoroughbred, you don't admire his strength, but admire his *temper.*" Now comes this same word for "character" in another passage: "Confucius said, 'One having virtue must have words; one having words not always has virtue.'" The meaning becomes clear only when we translate the word for "character" or "virtue" here by the word "soul" in the English language, as follows: "Confucius said, 'A man who has a beautiful soul always has some beautiful things to say, but a man who says beautiful things does not necessarily have a beautiful soul.'" Then again occurs the same word elsewhere in the phrase *tech yin;* to translate this as "virtuous sounds" may give the impression of scholarly fidelity, but merely hides the lack of understanding on the part of the scholarly translator that it means *"sacred* music." Again Confucius said, "Extravagant than not humble; frugal than *ku* (vulgar or stubborn, etc.). Rather than not humble, be *ku."* The connection between extravagance and lack of humility must be quite vague, and becomes clear only when we realize that people who live extravagantly are liable to be *conceited*. A fully clear and adequate translation must therefore involve a sure choice of words. I believe it should be translated as follows: "Confucius said, 'The people who live extravagantly are apt to be snobbish (or conceited), and the people who live simply are apt to be vulgar. I prefer vulgarity to snobbery (or I prefer the vulgar people to the snobs)."

In the second place, the translator cannot avoid putting the thought in the more precise concepts of a modern language. The translator does not only have to supply the connectives, but has also to supply a finer definition of ideas, or the English will be extremely bald. Thus in the example given above, "Language expressive only," the modern translator is forced to translate it as follows: "Expressiveness is the only *principle* of language," or "expressiveness is the sole *concern,* or *aim,* or *principle,* of rhetoric." It is clear that there are at least a dozen ways of translating this line in any case. But it is inevitable that the translator would have to slip in a word like "principle" or "aim" or "concern" or "standard." It simply cannot be helped, if the translation is not to become unreadable.

The use of parentheses—In the resulting text of the translation, I have to resort to the use of parentheses after dodging the above difficulties. The parentheses are used for two purposes. First, for giving an alternate translation, usually indicated by ("or . . . . .)." The situation is often such that no one can be sure that a particular interpretation is the only correct one. Secondly, the parentheses are used exclusively for explanatory matter necessary to a clear understanding of the rext without reference to footnotes. Without this device, such explanatory references would be endless. In this case, the parentheses are used with the sole purpose of supplying the minimum explanations to enable the reader to read a passage smoothly and understand its meaning without difficulty. The footnotes are then reserved for my comments and other reference material.

Chapter II

THE LIFE OF CONFUCIUS

(*K'ungtse Shihchia—Shiki,* Book XLVII)

THE following is a translation of the life of Confucius in the *Shiki* by Szema Ch'ien who lived about three hundred years after Confucius (145–85? B.C.). The translation of this document is important for two reasons. First, it is the earliest and in fact the only connected biographical sketch of Confucius, and it exists in that great standard book of Chinese history, written by a man who is acknowledged to be the father of Chinese historians and a prose master. The authority of the *Shiki* is unquestioned, and Szema Ch'ien himself travelled extensively and visited the birthplace of Confucius and talked with old people who kept alive the ancient tradition about Confucius. It is therefore as accurate a picture of Confucius' life as we can get. In the second place, Szema Ch'ien was thoroughly open-minded and unbiased; he was strictly an historian and not an advocate of Confucianism, taking sides in questions. While he expressed his intense admiration for Confucius, he was not himself a strict adherent of the narrow Confucian school. The

54

result was, he gave us a picture of Confucius the man, rather than Confucius the saint, and many Confucian critics have tried to distort the meaning of several passages in this life by far-fetched interpretations, and sometimes even to deny outright the correctness of the story. At any rate, we can take it as a very fair picture of Confucius as conceived in the mind of the most learned scholar of his times, living about three centuries after Confucius.

I. ANCESTRY, CHILDHOOD AND YOUTH (551–523 B.C.)

Confucius was born in the town of Tsou, in the county of Ch'angping, in the country of Lu. His early ancestor was K'ung Fangshu (who was a ninth-generation descendant of a king of Sung and the fourth-generation ancestor of Confucius). Fangshu was the father of Pohsia, and Pohsia was the father of Shuliang Ho. Ho was the father of Confucius by extra-marital union with a girl of the Yen family.* She prayed at the hill Nich'iu and begat Confucius in answer to her prayer, in the twenty-second year of Duke Hsiang of Lu (551 B.C.). There was a noticeable convolution on his head at his

---

* Confucius' mother's name was Yen Chentsai. The original words for "extra-marital" union are "wild union," or "wilds union," probably meaning union in the wilds. Some interpreters try to explain this by saying that the word "wild" simply means that the marriage was not in accordance with normal customs, his father marrying the girl after the age of sixty-four, after having married another wife and produced nine daughters, but no son. The explanation seems to me far-fetched.

birth, and that was why he was called "Ch'iu" (meaning a "hill"). His literary name was Chungni, and his surname was K'ung. ("Confucius" means "K'ung the Master").

Soon after Confucius was born, his father died, and was buried at Fangshan, which was in Eastern Lu (in Shantung). Therefore Confucius was in doubt as to the place of his father's tomb, because his mother had concealed the truth from him. When he was a child, he used to play at making sacrificial offerings and performing the ceremonies. When Confucius' mother died, he buried her temporarily, for caution's sake, in the Street of the Five Fathers, and it was not until an old woman, the mother of Wanfu of Tsou, informed him of the whereabouts of his father's grave, that he buried his parents together at Fangshan. Once, a Baron of Lu, Chi, was giving a banquet to the scholars of the town, and Confucius went while still in mourning. Yang Ho, a corrupt official, berated Confucius, saying, "The Baron is giving a banquet to the scholars and is not contemplating the pleasure of inviting you." So Confucius left.

When Confucius was seventeen years old, Baron Li Meng fell sick. On his deathbed he gave his son, Baron Yi Meng the following advice: "K'ung Ch'iu (that is, Confucius) is a descendant of great noblemen. The house of the K'ungs was destroyed in the country of Sung (Confucius' ancestors were persecuted out of the country by their rivals and migrated to the country of Lu). His great ancestor, Fufu Ho, was the oldest son of the Duke of Sung, but gave up the throne in favor of his brother, who became Duke Li. In a later generation, Chengk'aofu assisted the Dukes Tai, Wu and Hsuan of Sung in the government. His humility increased with his three successive promotions. Hence the tripod of the K'ung house bore the inscription: 'With the first promotion, I bend my head; with the second promotion, I bend my neck; and with the third promotion, I bend my back. I walk along the wall, and no one dares insult me. Herein I have my rice; and herein I have my porridge, to feed my mouth.' Such was his humility. I have heard that philosophers must come from the houses of great men, although they may not be in power. Now K'ung Ch'iu is young and a great lover of historic learning. Perhaps he is going to be a philosopher. When I die, you must go and follow him." On his death, his son Baron Yi went to study under Confucius, together with Nankung Chingshu (most probably his younger brother). That year Baron Chi of Lu died and his son Tai succeeded him.

Confucius was born of a poor and common family, but when he grew up, he was put in charge of the granary of the house of Baron Chi, and he was noted for the fairness of his measures. He also was made to take charge of the cattle and sheep and the cattle and sheep quickly multiplied. He was then promoted to be a minister of public works. But soon he left his home country Lu, was unceremoniously sent away from the country of Ch'i, driven out of Sung and Wei, and landed in difficulties and bodily danger in the suburbs between Ch'en and Ts'ai. After all these wanderings he returned to Lu.

Confucius was nine feet six inches tall (the ancient

unit of measure was very much shorter, for King Wen was reputed to be ten feet tall), and people all marvelled at his height and called him "a tall person." The government of Lu had always been courteous to him, and therefore he later returned to Lu. His disciple Nankung Chingshu asked permission from the ruler of Lu to go on a trip to the Emperor's capital, Chou. The Duke of Lu gave them a carriage with two horses and a page, and they both went to Chou to study the ancient rites and ceremonies and saw Laotse there. When Confucius was taking his departure, Laotse sent him off with the following advice: "I have heard that rich people present people with money and kind persons present people with advice, and I am going to present you with a piece of advice: A man who is brilliant and thoughtful is often in danger of his life because he likes to criticize people. A man who is learned and well read and clever at arguments often endangers himself because he likes to reveal people's foibles. Do not think of yourself only as a son or a minister at court.

II. BETWEEN THIRTY AND FIFTY (522–503 B.C.)

Confucius then returned from Chou to his own country, Lu, and more and more disciples came to study under him. At this time, Duke P'ing of Chin was a profligate. His six ministers took the power in their hands and indulged in invasions of the country to the east. King Ling of Ch'u (whose country was to the southwest of Lu) had a powerful army which dominated China. Ch'i was a big country lying right next to Lu (on the north). Lu was a small and weak country; if it allied itself with Ch'u, Chin was angry, and if it allied itself with Chin, then Ch'u would come and invade the country; and if it failed to cement its friendship with Ch'i, Ch'i too would invade the country. In the twentieth year of Duke Chao of Lu (522 B.C.), when Confucius was already thirty years old (or twenty-nine in the English reckoning), Duke Ching of Ch'i came to visit Lu, together with his minister Yen Ying. The Duke of Ch'i asked Confucius, "How is it that Duke Mu of Ch'in was able to dominate the other countries, although his country was then small and situated at a far-away corner of the empire?" "Although Ch'in was small," replied Confucius, "its ambition was great, and although it was situated at a far-away corner, their conduct of affairs was in accordance with the main moral principles. The Duke took Poli Hsi from prison and raised him to the rank of a noble. After talking with him for three days, he put him in charge of the government. That was how the Duke came into power. He might even have become a 'king,' and not merely a 'dictator' dominating the other states as he did." The Duke of Ch'i was pleased at Confucius' remark.

When Confucius was thirty-five years old (517 B.C.), Baron P'ing of Chi displeased Duke Chao of Lu because of a quarrel with Count Chao of Hou over a cock fight. Duke Chao led his troops to attack Baron P'ing, and Baron P'ing, together with the other two barons of Lu, Baron Meng and Baron Shusun, fought the Duke. The Duke lost the battle and ran away to Ch'i, where he was given a township at Kanhou. Soon after this, the country of Lu was plunged into disorder, and Confucius went to Ch'i, where he served as the secretary to Baron Chao Kao, in the hope of establishing a connection with the Duke of Ch'i. He also discussed music with the Master of Music in Ch'i. There he heard the music of *Hsiao* (symbolic dance music ascribed to an ancient Emperor Shun, 2255–2204 B.C.) and tried to learn it. For three months he forgot the taste of meat. The people of Ch'i were greatly impressed. One day the Duke asked Confucius about government, and Confucius replied, "The king should be like a king, the minister like ministers, the fathers like fathers and sons like sons." "Good!" replied the Duke. "If the king is not like a king, the ministers not like ministers, fathers not like fathers, and sons not like sons, how can I have anything to eat even if there is plenty of grain in the country?" On another day, he again asked about good government from Confucius, and Confucius replied, "Good government consists in limiting state expenditures." The Duke was pleased and was going to give the land at Nich'i to Confucius. Then minister Yen Ying spoke to the Duke, "The *Ju* (later identified with Confucianists) are bad models to follow because of their garrulousness, and they make bad subjects because of their pride and egotism. Their doctrines should hardly be applied to the people because of their emphasis on funerals and their habit of letting a family go bankrupt in order to provide an expensive burial. They also make bad rulers because they go about preaching and begging and borrowing. Since the great men have died and the imperial dynasty of Chou is in decline, our rituals and music today have degenerated or been partly forgotten. Now comes Confucius with his insistence on ceremonial robes and the details of ceremonial processions and court etiquette. One can spend a lifetime and not be able to master these studies, or spend entire years without being able to master the details of ceremonies. I rather question whether it is advisable for you to put him in power and change the customs of the country, bearing in mind the importance of considering the common people." Thereafter the Duke always received Confucius politely, but did not ask him questions regarding the historic rites and ceremonies. Another day, the Duke said to Confucius with the desire of keeping him in the country, "I'm not able to offer you the position of Baron Chi, but I will give you a position somewhere between the Barons Chi and Meng." The nobles of Chi were plotting against Confucius, which came to Confucius' ears. The Duke said to him, "I'm sorry I'm too old now to be able to put your doctrines into practice." Confucius then left and returned to Lu.

When Confucius was forty-two (511 B..C), Duke Chao of Lu died an exile at Kanhou. Duke Ting succeeded him, and in the summer of the fifth year of Duke Ting's reign, Baron P'ing of Chi died, and his son Baron Huan succeeded him. (Here follow two brief anecdotes. Confucius was consulted as a learned historian about certain finds which had been unearthed. One was about the discovery of animal bones during the razing of a city wall. One of the bones was said to be as long as an entire carriage, apparently the remains of some dinosaur, and a king sent a messenger all the way from a distant place to ask Confucius what bones these were, and Confucius was ready with an answer from early history.)

Baron Huan had a favorite secretary by the name of Chungliang Huai who had a favorite secretary by the name of Chungliang Huai who had a private quarrel with Yang Hu (also referred to in the *Analects* as Yang Ho), and the latter wanted to drive him away from the city, but stopped on the intervention of Kungshan Puniu. Yang finally arrested him and Baron Huan angrily protested, upon which Yang put the Baron in prison and made him sign a pledge before releasing him. Henceforth Yang behaved all the more arrogantly toward the Baron, but on his part Baron Huan Chi had also usurped the authority of the Duke, so that the government of Lu fell into the hands of the Barons. The country was therefore plunged into a state of moral chaos, from the lords down to the people, and Confucius decided not to go into the government, but retired to study, or edit the books of poetry and history and ritual and music. The number of his disciples rapidly grew, and there were many who came from distant parts of the land.

III. THE PERIOD OF GREAT POWER (502–496 B.C.)

In the eighth year of Duke Ting of Lu (502 B.C.), Kungshan Puniu did not get along with Baron Huan Chi and allied himself with Yang Hu to stir up a rebel-

lion, displace the eldest son of the Baron and make the
children of their concubines, who were friendly to Yang,
their heirs. They therefore arrested Baron Huan Chi, but
the latter escaped by a ruse, and in the following year,
Yang was defeated and escaped to the country of Ch'i.

At this time, Confucius was fifty years old. Kungshan
Puniu started a rebellion against Baron Huan in the city
of Pi, and Baron Huan sent a messenger to ask Confucius to see him. Confucius had then, for a long time,
devoted himself to the pursuit of learning; he was mild
and mellow and did not know exactly where to begin to
apply his teachings to the practice of government. He
said, "The Kings Wen and Wu rose to power from the
small cities of Feng and K'ao and finally established the
empire of Chou. Pi, I know, is a small place, but perhaps
I may try." So Confucius was about to go, but his disciple, Tselu (a kind of St. Peter), was displeased and
tried to stop him. "Since the Baron asks to see me,"
replied Confucius, "he must have a plan in his mind, and
if he would put me in power, we might achieve something resembling the work of Emperor P'ing" (who restored the power of the Chou Dynasty, beginning the so-
called East Chou Period). But after all he did not go.

Later on Duke Ting made Confucius the magistrate
of Chungtu. After a year the town became a model city
for all its neighbors. From the magistracy of Chungtu,
he was promoted to the office of the Secretary of Public
Works (or Labor) and finally became the Grand Secretary of Justice. In the spring of the tenth year of Duke
Ting (500 B.C.), Lu signed a treaty of friendship with

Ch'i and in the summer a Ch'i minister, by the name of Li Chu said to the Duke of Ch'i, "This is getting dangerous for us with Confucius in office at Lu." They then arranged for a good-will conference at Chiaku between the two countries. Duke Ting of Lu was going to attend the good-will conference in his carriage, but Confucius in his capacity as an acting Chief Minister, said, "I have heard it said that in attending civil conferences, one must send along a military delegation, and in attending military conferences, one must send along a civil delegation. The rulers of ancient times always provided themselves with a military escort when they visited a foreign country. I recommend that we bring along the Right and Left Secretaries of War." To this the Duke gave his consent and they started out toward Chiaku with the Secretaries of War. The formal meeting place where the oath was to be taken was provided with an altar surrounded by three successive earthen terraces. The two delegations met with the usual ceremonies. They bowed to each other and went up the terrace, and after drinking the ceremonial cup of wine, an official of Ch'i came forward and requested permission for the playing of an orchestra from different lands. The Duke of Ch'i gave his approval, and then the entertainers came forward and started a big noise, the civil dancers with their banners and pennants of ox-tail and pheasant feathers, the military dancers with their spears, forks, swords and shields. Confucius then came forward up the steps, and advanced just below the first terrace; he lifted his broad sleeves and said, "Why the presence of these barbarian musicians, when the rulers are celebrating a good-will conference? I request that they be dismissed." The Ch'i official tried to send them away, but the musicians refused to go. Everybody turned his eyes toward the Duke of Ch'i and his Minister Yen Ying. The Duke was greatly embarrassed and then waved his hand for the entertainers to leave the place. After a while, the Master of Ceremonies of Ch'i came forward and requested permission for the performing of palace music, and the Duke gave his consent. The actors and dwarfs in costume then began to play, and again Confucius went forward up the steps and advancing to the first terrace, he said, "Common people who try to corrupt the rulers should be killed. I request an order from the Master of Ceremonies." The Master of Ceremonies had these actors executed and their limbs were separated from their bodies.

The Duke of Ch'i was greatly ashamed and impressed and thought that he had better return to his country. Speaking in a tone of great concern, he said to his ministers at court, "The people of Lu have helped their ruler to act like a gentleman, while you people have taught me to behave like a barbarian. And now I have committed an offense in the eyes of the Ruler of Lu. What shall I do?" An official replied, "When a gentleman repents of his mistake, he makes amends by acts, and when a common man repents of his mistakes, he makes amends by words. If you are sorry for what you have done, then I suggest that you make amends by real acts." Therefore the Duke of Ch'i returned the lands of Yun, Wenyang and Kueit'ien which they had taken away from Lu, as a token of apology. In the summer of the thirteenth year of Duke Ting (497 B.C.), Confucius said to the Duke, "A subject ought not to keep a private armour, and a lord ought not to have a town with over a hundred parapets (each parapet repressing thirty feet)." The Duke then made Tselu, Confucius' disciple, Secretary of the Barony Chi, and ordered the razing of the cities of the three great Barons. First, Baron Shusun's city of Hou was razed. Baron Chi was going to raze his city Pi, but Kungshan Puniu and Sun Cheh led the people of Lu to attack the Duchy of Lu. The Duke and the three Barons went to the palace of Baron Chi and went up the Terrace of Baron Wu. The people of Pi attacked them there, but could not capture the place. The battle then raged around the Duke, and Confucius ordered the lords Shen Kouhsu and Yo Ch'i to go down and meet the attackers. The rebels were defeated and the soldiers of Lu chased them and defeated them at Kumi. The two Barons Shusun and Chi then fled to the country of Ch'i, and the city of Chi was razed down to the ground. The city of Ch'eng, the stronghold of Baron Meng, then came next in order to be razed, and the magistrate of Ch'eng said to Baron Meng, "When this city is razed, the people of Ch'i will have an open way to attack Lu from the north. Besides, Ch'eng is the stronghold of the Meng house. Without Ch'eng, there will be no Mengs. I refuse to have it razed." In December, the Duke laid seige to the city, but did not capture it.

In the fourteenth year of Duke Ting (496 B.C.), Confucius was fifty-six years old. From the position of the Grand Secretary of Justice, he was promoted to that of the Chief Minister. Confucius showed signs of evident pleasure at the news, and his disciples said, "I hear that a gentleman is not afraid at the sight of disaster and not delighted at success." "Is that so?" remarked Confucius. "Is it not said that one is happy because he rises to a position above the common people?" He then executed Shaochengmao, a minister who had plunged the government into disorder. After three months of his premiership, the mutton and pork butchers did not adulterate their meat, and men and women followed different lanes in the streets. Things lost on the streets were not stolen, and foreigners visiting the country did not have to go to the police, but all came to Lu like a country of their own.

When the people of Ch'i heard this, they were greatly worried and said, "If Confucius remains in power in Lu, Lu is certain to dominate the other states, and when it becomes a dominating power, we being the nearest neighbors would be the first to succumb. Why not cement friendship with them by presenting them with a bit of land?" The minister Li Chu said, "Let us try first to block him, and then if we fail, it won't be too late to give them some land." They then selected eighty of the prettiest girls of the country who were dressed in embroidery and could dance the *k'ang* dance. These maidens were presented together with a hundred and twenty fine horses to the Ruler of Lu, and they made a display of the girl entertainers and fine horses outside the South High Gate of Lu. Three times Baron Huan Chi went in plain clothes to see the show and thought he was going to receive this present, and told the Duke to go and see them by a circuitous route. So then the Duke and the Baron hung about the place for whole days and neglected their governmental duties. "I think it's time for us to quit," said Tselu. "Wait a minute," said Confucius, "it is near the time for the Sacrifice to Heaven now, and if the Duke should remember to send the burnt offerings to the ministers after the public worship, I will yet choose to stay." Baron Huan finally received the gift of girl entertainers of Ch'i, and for three days did not attend to his duties, nor did he remember to send the burnt offerings to the ministers. Confucius then left. While stopping over at the city of Tun, Shihchi said to Confucius on parting, "Master, I know you are not to blame for leaving Lu." Confucius replied, "May I sing a song?" Then he sang:

> "Beware of a woman's tongue,
>   Sooner or later you'll get stung.
>   Beware of a woman's visit
>   Sooner or later you'll get it.
>   Heigh ho! Heigh ho!
>   I'm going to run away."

Shihchi returned and Baron Huan asked him, "What did Confucius say?" Shihchi told him the truth, and Baron Huan heaved a sigh and said, "The Master is displeased with me on account of those wenches."

IV. FIVE YEARS OF WANDERINGS (496–492 B.C.)

Confucius then went to the country of Wei (to the west of Lu) and stopped at the home of Yen Tutsou, who was the brother of Tselu's wife. Duke Ling of Wei asked what salary Confucius had received in Lu and he was told that he had a salary of sixty thousand bushels of rice, and the state of Wei also gave him a salary of sixty thousand bushels. After staying in Wei for a time, someone spoke evil of Confucius to the Duke, and the Duke asked a man, Kungsun Yuchia, who was dressed in full military uniform, to pass in and out of the room occupied by Confucius. Confucius took this as a gentle hint and left Wei after having been there for ten months.

He then went to the country of Ch'en (further west) and had to pass through the city of K'uang. Yenk'eh was acting as the driver. He pointed with his whip to a crack in the city wall and remarked, "You know, I went into the city through that crack the last time." This remark was overheard by the natives who then thought it was Yang Hu of Lu coming to the city. Now Yang Hu had once been very cruel to the natives of K'uang and the natives therefore surrounded Confucius. Confucius looked like Yang and was arrested for five days. Yen Yuen (or Yen Huei, his favorite disciple) turned up later, and Confucius said to him, "I thought you were killed." "How dare I be killed, so long as you live!" replied Yen.

The situation became more threatening, and the disciples were afraid, but Confucius said, "Since King Wen died, is not the tradition of King Wen (the moral tradition of King Wen, who embodied the ideal system of government according to Confucius) in my keeping or possession? If it be Heaven's will that this moral tradition should be lost, posterity shall never again share in the knowledge of this tradition. But if it be Heaven's will that this tradition should not be lost, what can the people of K'uang do to me?" Confucius then was allowed to go away by asking one of his followers, Baron Wu Ning, to go and serve in the government of Wei.

After this, he passed through P'u where he stayed for over a month and then returned to Wei. He stopped at the home of Chu Poyu (a cultured old gentleman whom Confucius respected). The Queen Nancia of Wei sent a message to Confucius, saying, "The gentlemen of foreign countries who do us the honor of visiting our country and wish to be friends of our King always see me. May I have the pleasure of your company?" Confucius tried to decline, but could not get out of it. The Queen saw Confucius from behind a curtain of linen. Confucius entered and kowtowed facing north, and the Queen made a double curtsy from behind the curtain, and her jade hangings jingled. After the interview, Confucius said, "I did not intend to see her, but during the interview, we saw each other with perfect decorum." Tselu was greatly displeased (for Nancia was notoriously loose in her morals), and Confucius swore an oath, saying, "If I had done anything wrong, may Heaven strike me! May Heaven strike me!"

Confucius stayed for over a month at Wei. One day the Duke was riding in a carriage with the Queen, the eunuch Yung Chu acting as the driver and Confucius following behind in a second carriage (or occupying the second driver's seat). Thus they paraded through the streets, attracting the people's attention, and Confucius remarked, "I have never yet seen people attracted by virtuous scholars as they are by beautiful women." Confucius regarded this as a disgrace and left Wei for Ts'ao. That year (495 B.C.) Duke Ting of Lu died.

After leaving Ts'ao, Confucius went to Sung and studied the practice of ceremony with his disciples under a big tree. A military officer of Sung, Huan Tuei, wanted to kill Confucius and uprooted the big tree. Confucius decided to leave Sung and his disciples said, "We had better hurry." Confucius said, "Heaven has endowed me with a moral destiny (or mission). What can Huan Tuei do to me?"

Confucius went on to Cheng (in modern North Honan) and the Master and disciples lost track of each other. While Confucius stood alone at the East Gate of the outer city the natives reported to Tsekung, "There is a man at the East Gate whose forehead is like that of Emperor Yao, whose neck resembles that of an ancient minister Kaoyao, and whose shoulders resemble those of Tsech'an; but from the waist down, he is smaller than Emperor Yu by three inches. He looks crest-fallen like a homeless, wandering dog." Tsekung told Confucius this story (when they met) and Confucius smiled and said,

"I don't know about the descriptions of my figure, but as for resembling a homeless, wandering dog, he is quite right, he is quite right!"

Confucius then went on to Ch'en (Ch'en, Cheng, Ts'ai, and Sung were all quite close together) where he stayed for over a year at the home of the magistrate of the city Tsengtse. The King of Wu (a big country to the southeast in modern Kiangsu) invaded Ch'en and captured three of its towns. Chao Yang invaded Chuko (494 B.C.); the army of Ch'u laid siege to Ts'ai and the people of Ts'ai migrated to Wu. Wu defeated King Kouchien of Yueh (farther down southeast in modern Chekiang) Kueich'i. A hawk, with an arrow piercing its body, descended at the court of Ch'en (where Confucius was staying) and died. The arrow was made of *k'u* wood and was provided with a flint arrowhead, a foot and an inch long. The Duke of Ch'en sent a messenger to ask Confucius about this arrow, and Confucius replied, "This hawk must have come from very far away. This is an arrow used by the barbarians of Shushen. When Emperor Wu conquered Shang and built roads across to the 'Nine *Yi*' and 'Hundred Man' barbarians, he ordered tribute from the different lands as a sign of their perpetual homage. The barbarians of Shushen then sent in tributes of arrows with *k'u* wood and flint arrowheads, a foot and an inch long. The Emperor gave these arrows to his eldest princess as a sign of his love. She was married to a Duke Yuhu, who became the first Duke of Ch'en. It was the custom to present gifts of jade to the Emperor's relatives of the same surname as a symbol of affection, and to bring tributes from distant lands to the Emperor's relatives of a different surname, that they might not forget their allegiance to the Imperial House. That was how the Shushen arrows came to Ch'en. You may look in the old archives and may be able to find some yet." Actually, they did find similar arrows in the archives, as Confucius had told them.

Confucius stayed in Ch'en for three years. It happened that the countries Chin (modern Shensi) and Ch'u (modern Hupei) were fighting for power and often invaded Ch'en. When the country Wu invaded Ch'en and Ch'en Ch'ang was attacked, Confucius said, "Ah, let us go home! The young men of our country are either brilliant and erratic, or simple and retiring. But they have not lost their original simplicity of character." Confucius therefore left Ch'en and was passing through the city of P'u.

It happened that a certain Kungshu was starting a rebellion at P'u and the people of P'u surrounded Confucius. He had, however, a disciple by the name of Kungliang Ju who was following Confucius with five carriages. Kungliang Ju was tall, able, and distinguished for his bravery. He said, "Isn't this fate? the last time I was accompanying you at K'uang, we ran into trouble, and now we run into trouble again. I would rather fight and die this time." There was then a furious battle and the natives of P'u were afraid and said they would be willing to release Confucius if he promised not to go to Wei, and Confucius pledged an oath that he would not go there. He then left by the East Gate, but went straight to Wei. "Why, can one break an oath like that?" asked Tsekung. "Yes," replied Confucius, "it was an oath under duress which is disregarded by the gods."

The Duke of Wei was delighted to hear that Confucius was coming back and went to the suburb to welcome him. "Do you think I could attack the city of P'u?" asked the Duke. "Certainly," replied Confucius. "But my ministers think it inadvisable," said the Duke, "for P'u serves as a buffer state to protect us against Chin and Ch'u. Isn't it inadvisable for us to attack it?" Confucius replied, "The men of P'u are ready to defend their country to the last man, and their women, too, are ready to defend their homes. What we want to punish, however, are only four or five of the rebel leaders." "Good," said the Duke. But actually he did not attack P'u.

The Duke was then old and did not attend to his duties and was unwilling to put Confucius in power. Confucius sighed and said, "If some one will put me in power, I shall need only one month (to lay the foundation for a new order), and in three years time, I shall accomplish great results."

Confucius then left Wei. A certain Pi Hsi was acting as the magistrate of Chungmou (in the country of Chin), and Baron Chien Chao was fighting with Fan Chunghsing and attacked his city. Pi Hsi then rebelled and sent a messenger to ask Confucius to come and help him. Confucius was thinking of going, but Tselu protested, saying, "Master, I have heard from you that a gentleman does not enter the country of a ruler who leads a bad personal life. How is it now that you are going to help this rebel Pi Hsi at Chungmou?" "Yes, I did say so," replied Confucius. "But as the saying goes, a truly hard substance is not afraid of grinding, and a truly white substance is not afraid of dyes. Am I a dried up gourd that can stand hanging on the wall and go without food (for days)?"

Confucius was playing on a musical stone, the *ch'ing,* and a man carrying a wicker basket was passing his door and said, "How can a man have the heart to enjoy playing idly on the musical stone like that? Such a stodgy person doesn't seem to know himself. What can I say about such a person?"

Confucius was once learning to play on *ch'in* (a string instrument) from the music master Hsiangtse, and did not seem to make much progress for ten days. The music master said to him, "You may well learn something else now," and Confucius replied, "I have already learned the melody, but have not learned the beat and rhythm yet." After some time, the music master said, "You have now learned the beat and rhythm, you must take the next step." "I have not yet learned the expression," said Confucius. After a while, the music master again said, "Now you have learned the expression, you must take the next step." And Confucius replied, "I have not yet got an image in my mind of the personality of the composer." After some time the music master said, "There's a man behind this music, who is occupied in deep reflection and who sometimes happily lifts up his head and looks far away, fixing his mind upon the eternal." "I've got it now," said Confucius. "He is a tall, dark man and his mind seems to be that of an empire builder. Can it be any other person than King Wen himself (the founder of the Chou Dynasty)?" The music master rose from his seat and bowed twice to Confucius and said, "It *is* the composition of King Wen."

Confucius felt that he could not do anything in Wei and therefore was going west to Chin to see Baron Chien Chao. On reaching the bank of the Yellow River, he heard the news of the death of Tu Mingtu and Shun Hua. He stood on the bank and sighed, "How beautiful is the water! Eternally it flows! Fate has decreed that I should not cross this river." "What do you mean?" asked Tsekung coming forward. And Confucius replied, "Tu Mingtu and Shun Hua are good ministers of Chin. Before Baron Chien Chao got into power, he said that he would insist on taking these two men, should he get into power, and now that he is in power, he has killed them. I have heard that when people disembowel embryos or kill the young, the unicorn refuses to appear in the countryside, and that when people dry up a pond in order to catch fish, the dragon refuses to bring the *yin* and *yang* principles into harmony (resulting in famine or flood), and that when people snatch birds' nests and break birds' eggs, the phoenix refuses to come. Why? Because a gentleman avoids those who kill their own kind. If even the birds and beasts avoid the unrighteous, how much more should I do the same?* He therefore returned to

* This is of course in manifest contradiction to what he said in the paragraph above the preceding one, when he desired to go to Chungmou. Human nature is full of such contradictions, but Confucian critics

the village of Tsou and composed a piece of music for a string instrument called "Tsou Ts'ao" in commemoration of the two good ministers.

Confucius then returned to Wei again and stopped at the home of Chu Poyu. One day, the Duke of Wei asked him about military tactics and Confucius replied, "I know something about the ceremonial sacrifices, but as for the science of warfare, I know nothing about it whatsoever." The next day when Confucius was talking with the Duke, the latter merely turned up his head and looked at the flying wild geese in the sky and did not seem to pay any attention to Confucius. And so Confucius left for Ch'en again.

In the summer of that year (493 B.C.), the Duke died and was succeeded by his grandson Cheh, who was known as Duke Ch'u of Wei. In June, Chao Yang gave the eldest son, Kuei Huei, refuge at Ch'i.† Yang Hu then sent eight men dressed in mourning to welcome Kuei Huei, pretending that they were accompanying him directly from his own Duchy, Wei, in recognition of his rights. The welcoming delegation wailed in the usual fashion of a funeral procession, and Kuei Huei henceforth remained at Ch'i.

---

would not allow for contradictions in Confucius' life. Anyway, Confucius' remark about his being unable to "go without food" "like a dried up gourd" in the above incident, must be taken as a humorous remark. Efforts to harmonize Confucius' different attitudes in the two incidents would be futile.

† The eldest son was deprived of his rightful succession to the Duchy because of the intrigues of the notorious queen Nancia who had her protégé succeed the deceased Duke.

In the winter, the state of Ts'ai removed its capital to Choulai. This was in the third year of Duke Ai of Lu (492 B.C.), when Confucius was sixty years old. The state of Ch'i then sent an army to help Wei besiege the city of Ch'i* where the exiled prince Kuei Huei was staying. In the summer, the ancestral temple of Huanli in Lu was burnt down and Nankung Chingshu led the people to fight the fire. Confucius was in Ch'en at this moment, but when he heard of the fire, he said that it must have been the ancestral temple of Huanli that was burnt (because the worship at Huanli was against the rules of the ancient feudal order). Later they found that Confucius' guess was right.

In the summer Baron Huan Chi was ill and he drove over to the city of Lu. Upon seeing the city wall, he sighed and said, "This Lu once had a chance of becoming a strong state, but unfortunately it lost that opportunity because I had offended Confucius." Then he turned around and spoke to his heir Baron K'ang Chi and said, "I know that when I die you will become the Chief Minister of Lu, and when you do, you must call Confucius back into power." Baron Huan died a few days afterwards and Baron K'ang succeeded him. After the burial ceremony, he was going to send for Confucius, when his brother Yu said, "Our deceased father once appointed Confucius to a position of power and then failed to go through with it, thus making himself a laughing stock of the other Dukes. Now, if you try to

* This city of Ch'i was not in the state of Ch'i, the two names being written differently in Chinese.

appoint him again and then change your mind, you will again make yourself the laughing stock of the other states." "Whom then would you suggest?" asked Baron K'ang. "Send for Jan Ch'iu" (a disciple of Confucius), was the reply. A messenger was therefore sent to ask for Jan Ch'iu. When Jan Ch'iu was about to depart, Confucius said, "When the people of Lu send for Ch'iu, they are going to give him real authority, and not merely a small position." That day Confucius said, "Let us go home! Let us go home! The young men of our country are either brilliant and erratic or too simple and retiring. They make good material, and I must try to cut them into shape." Tsekung knew that Confucius was thinking of going home and on parting he spoke to Jan Ch'iu, "When you are in power, you must send for Confucius."

V. IN EXTREMITIES IN CH'EN AND TS'AI (491–489 B.C.)

After Jan Ch'iu had left, Confucius proceeded in the following year (491 B.C.) from Ch'en to Ts'ai. The Duke Chao of Ts'ai was going to Wu in obedience to a summons from the King of Wu. Now Duke Chao had previously deceived his subjects when he moved his capital to Choulai, and when he was going to Wu, his ministers were afraid that he was going to move his capital once more, and Kungsun P'ien shot the Duke and killed him.

The next year (490 B.C.), Confucius went from Ts'ai to Yeh (another small state), and the Duke of Yeh asked Confucius about good government, and Confucius replied, "Good government consists in winning the loyalty of the people nearby and attracting the people far away." Another day, the Duke asked about Confucius from his disciple Tselu, and Tselu did not reply. When Confucius heard this, he said, "Ah Yu (familiar name of Tselu), why didn't you tell him that I am a man who pursues the truth untiringly, and teaches people unceasingly, and who forgets to eat when he is enthusiastic about something, and forgets all his worries when happy or elated, and who is not aware that old age is coming on?"

After leaving Yeh, Confucius returned to Ts'ai. Ch'angchu and Chiehni were plowing the field together. Confucius thought they were retired philosophers and sent Tselu to inquire the way of them. "Who is that fellow driving the carriage?" asked Ch'angchu. "That's Confucius," was Tselu's reply. "Is he K'ung Ch'iu of Lu?" And Tselu replied, "Yes." "Oh, then he ought to know the way." And Chiehni asked Tselu, "Who are you?" "I am Chung Yu." "Are you a disciple of K'ung Ch'iu?" Tselu replied in the affirmative, and Chiehni said, "Oh, the world is full of those people wandering about, but who is ever going to change the present state of affairs? Furthermore, rather than follow one who avoids certain types of people, why not follow one who avoids society altogether?" Tselu told this to Confucius and Confucius sighed and said, "Birds and beasts (or those who try to imitate them) are not right company for us. If there were a moral order in the present world, why should I bother to change it?"

Another day Tselu was walking on the road and he met an old man who carried a wicker basket and asked the latter, "Have you seen the Master?" The old man replied, "Who is the 'Master'?—a man who doesn't work with his arms and legs and who doesn't know how to distinguish between the different kinds of grains!" And the old man planted his stick on the ground and began to weed the field. Tselu told this story to Confucius, and Confucius said, "He must be a retired philosopher." Tselu went again to find him, but he had disappeared.

Confucius wandered in Ts'ai for three years. The state of Wu was attacking Ch'en, and Ch'u came to the rescue of Ch'en (this was in 489 B.C.). The army of Ch'u was encamping at Ch'engfu, and when they heard that Confucius was somewhere between Ch'en and Ts'ai, they sent somebody to ask for Confucius. Confucius was going to pay his respects. Then the ministers of Ch'en and Ts'ai plotted together, saying, "Confucius is a very able man. He has pointed out the weaknesses of the rulers of the different states. Now he has remained for a long time around here and he doesn't seem to like what we are doing. Now Ch'u is a powerful state and is thinking of using Confucius, and if Confucius should ever get into power in Ch'u, our countries would be in trouble and we ourselves the ministers would be in danger." They therefore sent soldiers to surround Confucius in the countryside. Confucius' party could not get away and they were short of food supplies. Many of those in the party fell sick and were confined to bed, but Confucius kept on reading and singing and accompanying himself with a string instrument without stop. Tselu came to Confucius with evident anger in his face and said, "Does a gentleman sometimes also find himself in adversity?" "Yes," replied Confucius, "a gentleman also sometimes finds himself in adversity, but when a common man finds himself in adversity, he forgets himself and does all sorts of foolish things." Tsekung was evidently impressed with the aptness of the remark and Confucius said to him, "Ah Sze, do you think that I have merely tried to learn as much as possible and store it away in memory?" "I think so. Isn't it true?" "No," said Confucius, "I have a central thread which runs through all my knowledge."*

Confucius knew then that his disciples were angry or disappointed at heart, and so he asked Tselu to come in and questioned him. "It is said in the *Book of Songs,* 'Neither buffalos, nor tigers, they wander in the desert.' (A comparison to themselves.) Do you think that my teachings are wrong? How is it that I find myself now in this situation?" Tselu replied, "Perhaps we are not great enough and have not been able to win people's confidence in us. Perhaps we are not wise enough and people are not willing to follow our teachings." "Is that so?" said Confucius. "Ah Yu, if the great could always gain the confidence of the people, why did Poyi and Shuch'i have to go and die of starvation in the mountains? If the wise men could always have their teach-

* This is elsewhere explained in the *Analects* to be the Golden Rule or the Doctrine of Reciprocity.

ings followed by others, why did Prince Pikan have to commit suicide?"

Tselu came out and Tsekung went in, and Confucius said, "Ah Sze, it is said in the *Book of Songs,* 'Neither buffalos, nor tigers, they wander in the desert.' Are my teachings wrong? How is it that I find myself now in this situation?" Tsekung replied, "The Master's teachings are too great for the people, and that is why the world cannot accept them. Why don't you come down a little from your heights?" Confucius replied, "Ah Sze, a good farmer plants the field but cannot guarantee the harvest, and a good artisan can do a skillful job, but he cannot guarantee to please his customers. Now you are not interested in cultivating yourselves, but are only interested in being accepted by the people. I am afraid you are not setting the highest standard for yourself."

Tsekung came out and Yen Huei went in, and Confucius said, "Ah Huei, it is said in the *Book of Songs,* 'Neither buffalos, nor tigers, they wander in the desert.' Are my teachings wrong? How is it that I find myself now in this situation?" And Yen Huei replied, "The Master's teachings are so great. That is why the world cannot accept them. However, you should just do your best to spread the ideas. What do you care if they are not accepted? The very fact that your teachings are not accepted shows that you are a true gentleman. If the truth is not cultivated, the shame is ours; but if we have already strenuously cultivated the teachings of a moral order and they are not accepted by the people, it is the shame of those in power. What do you care if you are not accepted? The very fact that you are not accepted shows that you are a true gentleman." And Confucius was pleased and said smilingly, "Is that so? Oh, son of Yen, if you were a rich man, I would be your butler!"

Confucius then sent Tsekung to Ch'u, and King Chao of Ch'u sent an army to welcome Confucius, which got him out of his difficulty. The king was going to give Confucius land of seven hundred *li* (or settlements of twenty-five families each). A minister of Ch'u by the name of Tsehsi said, "Does your majesty have a diplomat as able as Tsekung?" "No," was the King's reply. "Does your majesty have a chief minister as good as Yen Huei?" "No," said the King again. "Does your majesty have a general as good as Tselu?" "No," said the King. "Does your majesty have an administrator as good as Tsai Yu?" "No," said the King. "Besides," continued the minister, "the ancestor of the rulers of Ch'u was appointed to this country with the rank of a Baron, and its original territory was only fifty *li* (*li*, about one third of a mile). Now comes Confucius, who is talking all the time about the ancient systems of the Three Great Kings and the moral tradition of Duke Chou and Duke Shao. How do you expect our country to go on ruling thousands of square miles from generation to generation if Confucius is able to put into practice his ideal social order? King Wen rose from the city of Feng and his son King Wu rose from the city of K'ao, starting only with a territory of a hundred *li*, but they finally succeeded in establishing an empire over the whole of China. I hardly think that it is for the good of our country to put Confucius in possession of a territory, with such able disciples assisting him." This completely changed the King's mind.

In the autumn of that year (489 B.C.), King Chao died at Ch'engfu. There was a madman of Ch'u by the name of Chiehyu who sang as he passed Confucius in the following manner,

"O phoenix! O phoenix!
  What has happened to thy character.*
  Let by-gones be by-gones,
  But make amends for what still lies ahead.
  Alack-a-day! A thousand pities for the rulers of today!"

Confucius got down from his carriage in order to talk with him, but the latter ran away, and Confucius failed to have an interview with him. Therefore Confucius returned from Ch'u to Wei. That was the fifth year of Duke Ai of Lu (still 489 B.C.), when Confucius was sixty-three years old.

VI. FURTHER YEARS OF WANDERINGS (488–484 B.C.)

The next year (488 B.C.), Wu and Lu were having a conference and a hundred sacrificial cows were offered on the altar (this being a presumptuous number and against the forms of Confucian feudal order). The Wu minister P'i asked Baron K'ang Chi to represent Lu, and, Baron K'ang being unwilling to go, got away by sending

---

* The phoenix is a mythical bird resembling the bird of paradise and a symbol of perfect virtue.

Tsekung in his place. Now Confucius had said Lu and Wei were cousins (the first ancestors of the two ruling houses were brothers), and at this time the successor to the Wei Duchy was staying abroad, unable to have himself established in his country, and the rulers of the different states were constantly considering possible future developments.

Confucius then had many disciples who were already in the government of Wei, and the ruler of Wei wanted to secure the services of Confucius. Tselu asked, "If the ruler of Wei should put you in power, how would you begin?" "I would begin with establishing a correct usage of terminology" (of ranks and titles), Confucius answered. "Do you really mean it?" asked Tselu. "How odd and impractical you are! What do you want to establish a correct terminology for?" "Ah Yu, you are simple-minded indeed!" Confucius replied. "If the terminology is not correct, then the whole style of one's speech falls out of form; if one's speech is not in form, then orders cannot be carried out; if orders are not carried out, then the proper forms of worship and social intercourse (in ritual and music) cannot be restored; if the proper forms of worship and social intercourse are not restored, then legal justice in the country will fail;*

* This passage here illustrates fully the philosophic significance Confucius attached to "ritual and music" and shows the inadequacy of translating the Chinese phrase *li* and *yo* merely as "ritual and music." The logical connection between ritual and music, as we ordinarily interpret these terms, and the administration of legal justice cannot be made, unless we amplify their meaning as representing principles of social order ("forms of public worship and social intercourse"), as will

when legal justice fails, then the people are at a loss to know what to do or what not to do. When a gentleman institutes something, he is sure by what terminology it should be called, and when he gives an order, he knows that the order can be carried out without question. A gentleman never uses his terminology indiscriminately."

The following year (484 B.C.)* Jan Ch'iu, who was then assisting in the administration of the government of Lu, led the army of Baron K'ang Chi against Ch'i and defeated the latter at the battle of Lang. And Baron K'ang asked Jan Ch'iu, "How did you come to know the science of warfare? Did you learn it by study or by nature?" Jan Ch'iu replied, "I learned it from Confucius." "What kind of a person is Confucius?" asked Baron K'ang. And Jan Ch'iu replied, "If you should put him in power, his reputation would spread immediately. You could apply his teachings to the people and lay them before the gods, and even the gods will find no fault with them. What he is seeking is to put a country into a condition of perfect moral order. Even if you should give him the rule over 25,000 families, he would not abuse the power for his own selfish ends." "May I then summon him?" asked Baron K'ang. "No," replied Jan Ch'iu, "you should not *summon* him—that would be

be made clear in Chapters VI to VIII. The philosophic meaning here is that if the basic moral and social order is not restored and the people's proper habits of mind are not established, it is superficial folly to hope for the establishment of peace and order by relying on punishing the law breakers.

* There is some confusion in the chronology here, but evidence shows it was in 484 B.C.

impolite, treating him like a common man; you should *entreat* him to come." It happened then that K'ung Wentse of Wei was going to attack T'aishu. He asked Confucius' advice about tactics, and Confucius declined politely, by saying that he didn't know about tactics. After the interview, Confucius ordered his carriage for departure, saying, "A bird can choose a tree for its habitation, but a tree cannot choose the bird." K'ung Wentse still tried to make him stay. Then Baron K'ang Chi drove away Kung Hua, Kung Pin and Kung Lin, and sent presents to Confucius to welcome him. Then Confucius returned to his own country Lu. So Confucius had left Lu and been broad for fourteen years before he returned to Lu (in 484 B.C.).*

VII. SCHOLARLY LABORS AND PERSONAL HABITS OF CONFUCIUS
(484–481 B.C.)

Duke Ai of Lu asked Confucius about government, and Confucius replied, "The secret of government lies in selecting the right ministers." Baron K'ang Chi asked Confucius concerning government, and Confucius replied, "Raise the righteous men into power and let them serve as the measure for the unrighteous, and the unrighteous will return to righteousness."† Baron Kang was

* Really 13 years, counting from his leaving Lu in 496 B.C. The chronological charts compiled by Szema Ch'ien himself give the year of departure as 498 B.C., which contradicts his own text.

† An example of the important Confucian theory of imitation, in the form of the doctrine of government by example (see Chapter V, Sec. 9).

worried about bandits or thieves in the country, and Confucius said, "If you yourself do not love money, even though you should present the thieves with money, they won't take it."

But after all, the government of Lu did not see its way clear to putting Confucius in power, nor did Confucius desire or seek office. In the time of Confucius, the power of the Chou Emperors had declined, the forms of worship and social intercourse ("ritual and music") had degenerated, and learning and scholarship had fallen into decay. Confucius studied the religious or ceremonial order and historical records of the three dynasties (Hsia, Shang and Chou), and he traced the events from the times of the Emperors Yao and Shun down to the times of Duke Mu of Ch'in and arranged them in chronological order. And he once said, "I should be able to talk about the feudal order (*li* or "rituals") of Hsia, but there are not enough surviving customs in the city of Chi (ruled by the descendants of the Hsia rulers). I should be able to discuss the feudal order of the Shang Dynasty (noted for the rule of the priestcraft), but there are not enough surviving customs in the city of Sung (ruled by the descendants of the Shang Emperors). If there were enough surviving customs, I should be able to reconstruct them with evidence." And he surveyed the changes of customs between the Hsia and Shang Dynasties, and after noting how these customs ran on into the Chou period with modifications, he said, "I can even predict how the future historical development will be for a hundred generations." He noted how one dynasty

(Shang) represented a culture with a wealth of ceremonial forms, and how the other dynasty (Hsia) represented a culture of the simple life, and how the Chou Dynasty had combined and merged the two previous cultures into a perfect, beautiful pattern, and he therefore decided that he would choose the Chou culture as the ideal.* Therefore, Confucius handed down a tradition of historic records (for instance, the present *Book of History*) and various records of ancient customs and ethnology.

In discussing music with the Grand Music Master of Lu, he said, "The principles of music may be known. A performance should begin peacefully, then it develops into full harmony and clarity, and closes with a continuation or repetition of the theme." He once also said, "After my return to Lu from Wei, I have been able to restore the musical tradition and classify the music of *sung* (ceremonial anthems) and *ya* (classical music of

* Confucius therefore had worked out a concrete ideal system of social order and rites and ceremonies and music, in the main following the Chou (1122–222 B.C.) pattern, which was a mean between the simpler system of Hsia (2205–1784 B.C.) and the more elaborate system of Shang (or Yin, 1783–1123 B.C.). This system was embodied in the book *Chouli*, which purported to have been devised by Duke Chou at the founding of the Chou Dynasty, according to the "ancient script" school. The "modern script" school regards the present text of *Chouli* as a fake, and maintains, moreover, that Confucius was the greatest forger, trying to give historic authority to his own ideal conceptions, by ascribing it to Duke Chou, a name to conjure with. The basis of this "modern script" school is *"The King's Order,"* Chapter X of *Liki*, in which a complete governmental system is outlined.

Chou) and restore the songs to their respective original music.* In the ancient times, there were over three thousand songs, but Confucius took out the duplicates and selected those that were suited to good form.† The collection began with the songs of Ch'i and Houchi (mythological ancestors of the Chou Emperors), covered the great period of the Shang and Chou kings and carried it down to the times of the tyrants Yu and Li. It begins with a song of marital love, and therefore it is said "the song *Kuanch'ih* heads the collection of *Feng*; *Luming* heads the collection of the 'Little *Ya'*; *Wenwang* heads the collection of 'The Great *Ya*,' and *Ch'ingmiao* heads the collection of the *Sung*." Confucius personally sang all the three hundred and five songs and played the music on a string instrument to make sure that it fitted in with the score of *hsiao, wu, ya* and *sung*. Through his efforts, the tradition of ancient rites and music was therefore rescued from oblivion and handed down to posterity, that they might help in the carrying out of this ideal of a king's government and in the teaching of "the six arts" (the six branches of study in the

* The *Book of Songs*, edited by Confucius, shows at present a classification into four musical categories: (1) the *sung*, (2) the great *ya*, (3) the little *ya*, and (4) the *feng*, or popular folk music of his day grouped according to the countries. Apart from the music, almost no trace of difference can be found in the different categories so far as the text is concerned.

† Confucius did include an amazing number of love songs, of secret meetings of lovers and elopements, which were in themselves marvelous poetry, but which have always frightened the Confucian ciritcs a little.

schools of Confucius' days: ceremonies, music, archery, carriage-driving, reading and mathematics; also taken as synonymous with the "six classics").

In his old age, Confucius developed a love for the study of *Yiking*, or the *Book of Changes*, its *Preface*, *T'uan*, *Hsi*, *Hsiang*, *Shuokua* and *Wenyuan*. He read the *Yiking* so thoroughly that the leather strap (holding the bundle of bamboo inscriptions) was worn out and replaced three times, and he said, "Give me a few more years to study the *Yiking*, and I should be pretty good at the philosophy of the mutation of human events."

Confucius taught poetry, history, ceremonies and music to 3,000 pupils of whom 72, like Yen Tutsou, had mastered "the Six Arts" (probably referring to the Six Classics). There were a great number of people who came to study under him.

Confucius taught concerning four things: literature, human conduct, being one's true self and honesty in social relationships. He denounced (or tried to avoid completely) four things: arbitrariness of opinions, dogmatism, narrow-mindedness and egotism. He showed concern and care in three circumstances: ceremonial bath (in preparation for worship), war and sickness. He seldom talked about profit, heaven's will or destiny or fate, and the true man.* If a man was not deeply concerned

---

* This last statement is literally incorrect because Confucius was talking all the time about the true man; only when it came to pointing out living examples of "true man," he constantly held back, as explained in my introduction. Evidently terms like "gentleman" and "a true man"

or determined to find out the truth, he would not try to explain and stimulate his thinking, and if Confucius told him one-fourth of what he wanted to say, and the man did not go back and reflect and think out the implications in the remaining three-fourths for himself, he would not teach him again.

In his private life,* in his native village or with his own people, he was gentle and refined, like one who could not talk much, but at the places of public worship and at the courts, he was eloquent, yet very careful in his choice of words. At court, he was eloquent, yet very careful in his choice of words. At courts, he would talk very serenely and respectfully with his superiors, and quite affably with his inferiors. On entering a public hall, he would bow and hasten forward respectfully. When a king's messenger came, he would at once assume a serious demeanor, and when a king summoned him, he would go without waiting for the carriage. When fish or meat were not fresh, or when they were not cut neatly, he would not eat them. When the mat was not laid out properly, he would not sit down. When

---

and "a real man" can become quite current concepts or expressions, without anyone being able to define them. Who can define what is "true manhood"? Socrates talked about "knowing thyself," but philosophers as well as common men will never be able to come to an agreement as to what is our true selves.

* The material here, as well as many quotations in this "Life," is evidently taken from the *Analects*. Most of the quotations are easily recognizable, although not always verbally identical with lines in the *Analects*.

he ate in the company of people in mourning, he would not eat his fill, and if he should cry (at a funeral ceremony), he would not sing that day. When he saw people in mourning or passed by blind people, he would change his countenance, even though they were children. (He said) "I never take a walk in the company of three persons, without finding that one of them has something to teach me." "What concern or worry me are the following: that I have forgotten to cultivate my character, that I have neglected my studies, that I have not been able to follow the right course when I see it, and that I have not been able to correct my mistakes." When he heard a man sing and liked it, he would ask for an *encore,* and then join in the refrain. He refused to discuss the mythological, exploits of physical prowess, unruly people, and the spirits.*

Tsekung said of Confucius, "The Master taught us literature and scholarship; this we can learn from him. What we cannot learn from him or what he did not teach us was what he thought about Nature and the ways

* Confucius had a deep religious sense and feeling of awe before the gods, whom he frankly declared that he could not know. He was, in any case, deeply concerned over the ceremonies or religious worship, and he also prayed, not in words, but apparently by a silent attitude. For when he was seriously ill and one of his disciples asked him to pray by going to the temple, he replied by saying that he had been praying for a long time. Also, he did not believe in answers to prayers in the usual sense of the church-goers, for he said, "A man who has committed sins against Heaven has nowhere or no God to pray to." The evident implication was that he did believe in prayer under other circumstances, and the efficacy of such a spiritual communion lay in putting the man's own heart or conduct in harmony with God's laws.

of Nature (or Heaven)." Yenyuan (or Yen Huei) sighed and said, "You look up to it and it seems so high. You try to drill through it, and it seems so hard. You seem to see it in front of you, and all of a sudden it appears behind you. The Master is very good at gently leading a man along and teaching him. He taught me to broaden myself by the reading of literature and then to control myself by the observance of proper conduct. I just felt carried along, but after I have done my very best, or developed what was in me, there still remains something austerely standing apart, uncatchable. Do what I could to reach his position, I can't find the way." A young man of Tahsiang said, "Great is Confucius! He knows about everything and is an expert at nothing," and when Confucius heard this he said, "Now what am I going to specialize in? Shall I specialize in archery, or in driving a carriage?" Tselo said, "Confucius said of himself that he didn't go into the government, and that was why he had plenty of time to study the different arts and literature."

In the spring of the fourteenth year of Duke Ai of Lu (481 B.C.), there was a hunt in the country and Baron Shusun's driver, by the name of Chushang, caught a strange animal which was regarded as bad luck. Confucius looked at it and declared it was a unicorn, and then the people brought the animal home.* Confucius then said, "Alas, no tortoise bearing magic anagrams has appeared in the Yellow River, and no sacred writings have

* Confucius' own annals, *Spring and Autumn,* ended with this year, and it is usually said that this book ended with the appearance of a unicorn, a sign of the appearance of a sage.

come out of the River Lo. I have given up."* When Yen Huei died, Confucius said, "I see Heaven is going to take away my mission from me." And when he saw the unicorn during the hunt in the Western countryside, he said, "This is the end of it all." And he heaved a sigh, saying, "There's no one in this world who understands me." And Tsekung said, "Why do you say that there is no one who understands you?" And Confucius said, "I don't blame Heaven, and I don't blame mankind. All I try to do is, my best to acquire knowledge, and to aim at a higher ideal. Perhaps Heaven is the only one who understand me!" He said of Poyi and Shuch'i that they did not compromise their principles, and were not disgraced (these persons and the following were famous scholars living as recluses); he said of Liuhsia Huei and Shaolien that they compromised their principles and were disgraced; he said of Yuchang and Yiyi that they lived in seclusion and indulged in high talks of philosophy, but that these people were at least not materialistic and that they adjusted themselves to their circumstances according to the principle of expedience. "But I'm different from all of them. I decide according to the circumstances of the time, and act accordingly" (literally "no *may,* no *may not*").

Confucius said, "This won't do! This won't do! A gentleman is ashamed to die without having accomplished something. I realize that I cannot get into a position of power to put into effect my governmental ideal.

* According to tradition, the appearance of these things would be considered an omen of the appearance of philosopher-king.

How am I going to account for myself in the eyes of posterity?" He therefore wrote the *Spring and Autumn* (Chronicles) on the basis of the existing histories, beginning from Duke Yin (722 B.C.) and coming down to the fourteenth year of Duke Ai (481 B..C), thus covering the period of twelve Dukes (of Lu). He wrote from the point of view of Lu, but tried to show proper respect to the Chou Emperors, harking back to the Shang Dynasty and showing the changes in the systems of the Three Dynasties. He adopted a most concise style, but injected into it a profound meaning. That was why, although the rulers of Wu and Ch'u usurped the title of "kings," the *Spring and Autumn* degraded their ranks and simply called them "Barons." At a certain conference, the Emperor was actually summoned by the Dukes to appear, but the *Spring and Autumn,* in an effort to whitewash the matter, wrote, "The celestial emperor came to hunt at Hoyang." In this manner, he used different words implying approval or condemnation in criticism of the practices of his times, in the hope that should a great king appear in the future and open that book and adopt the principles implied therein, the unruly princes and robbers of power would be ashamed and restrain themselves. When Confucius was an official, he would go over the cases of lawsuits and official documents with his colleagues and seek their opinions, and not make his own decisions, but in writing the *Spring and Autumn,* he wrote down and deleted exactly as he thought fit, and the disciples like Tsehsia were not able to put in a word. When Confucius taught the *Spring and Autumn* to his disciples, he said, "The future generations shall understand me through the *Spring and Autumn* and shall also judge me on the basis of the *Spring and Autumn*."

VIII. HIS DEATH (479 B.C.) AND POSTERITY

Next year (480 B.C.) Tselu died in Wei. Confucius himself also fell ill, and Tsekung came to visit him. Confucius was just then walking slowly around the door, supported by a walking stick, and said to him, "Ah Sze, why do you turn up so late?" Confucius then sighed and sang a song:

"Ah! the T'aishan (Mountain) is crumbling down!
The pillar is falling down!
The philosopher is passing out!"

He then shed tears and spoke to Tsekung. "For a long time the world has been living in moral chaos, and no ruler has been able to follow me. The people of Hsia Dynasty kept their coffins before burial, above the eastern steps (of the Chinese courtyard), the people of Chou Dynasty kept their coffins above the western steps, and the people of Shang Dynasty kept them (in the main hall) between two pillars. Last night I dreamt I was sitting and receiving (or making) a libation between the two pillars. Perhaps it was because I am a descendant of the Shangs." Seven days afterwards he died, aged seventy-three (or seventy-two according to English reckoning). This was on the day *chich'ou* of April, in the sixteenth year of Duke Ai (479 B.C.).

Duke Ai sent a prayer to the funeral of Confucius, which said, "Alas! Heaven has no mercy on me, and has not spared me the Grand Old Man. He has left me, the poor self, alone and helpless at the head of the state, and I am a sick person now. Alas! Father Ni (or Chung Ni, Confucius' name)! Great is my sorrow! Do not forget me (literally 'do not mind yourself')!" Tsekung said, "Did not Confucius die within the country of Lu? (It was the Duke's fault that Confucius was not put in power.) The Master said, 'When the ceremonies are improper, things become disorderly, and when the terminology used is incorrect, then things are out of place. Disorderliness means that a man who has lost his moral principles, and out of place means that a man does not get what he deserves (or is not placed in the right position).' When the Master was living, he could not use him, and waited till he is dead to send a prayer to his funeral, which is improper. In calling himself 'a poor self,' he also uses a wrong terminology."

Confucius was buried in Lu, on the River Sze in the north of the city. His disciples all observed the regular mourning of three years, and after the three years of mourning were over, they said good-bye to each other and left, weeping again at the grave before they departed. Some stayed on, but only Tsekung remained in a hut near the tomb for six years before he left. Over a hundred families, consisting of Confucius' disciples, and natives of Lu, went to live near the tomb ground, and there grew up a village known as K'ungli, or "K'ung's Village." For generations sacrifices were offered at the

Temple of Confucius at proper times, and the Confucianists also held academic discussions and village festivals and archery contests at the tomb. The tomb ground contained a hundred *mow*,* and therefore could accommodate the disciples in its halls. The personal belongings of Confucius, his caps, gowns, string instruments, carriages and books, were preserved in the Confucian Temple by succeeding generations. This was kept up for over two hundred years down to the time of the First Emperor of the Han Dynasty (from 206 B.C.), who worshipped Confucius with grand offerings (of cows, sheep and pigs, a great honor). Whenever princes and high ministers arrived at the place, they first paid their respects at the Confucian Temple before assuming office.

Confucius begat Li, alias Poyu, who died before Confucius at the age of 50; Poyu begat Ch'i, alias Tsesze, who died at 62, who was once arrested in Sung and who wrote the *Central Harmony;* Tseze begat Po, alias Tseshang, who died at 47; Tseshang begat Ch'iu, alias Tsechia, who died at 45; Tsechia begat Ch'i, alias Tseching, who died at 46; Tseching begat Ch'uan, alias Tsekao, who died at 51: Tsekao begat Tseshen, who died at 57, who once became the minister of Wei; Tseshen begat Fu, who died at 57, who was once *poshih* (scholar or master of particular Classics) under King Ch'en Sheh and died at Ch'en; Fu's younger brother, Tsehsiang, who died at 57, once served as *poshih* under Emperor Hsiaohuei (of Han) and again as magistrate of Ch'ang-

* A *mow* is about one-sixth of an acre.

sha and was nine feet six inches tall; Tsehsiang begat
Chung, who died at 57; Chung begat Wu; Wu begat
Yen-nien and Ankuo; Ankuo was *poshih* under the
present Emperor and was once magistrate of Linhuai
and died young; Ankuo begat Ang and Ang begat
Huan.

The Master Historian says:* "The *Book of Songs* says,
High is the mountain I look up to, and bright is his
example for our emulation! Although I cannot reach the
top, my heart leaps up to it." As I read the books of
Confucius, I thought to myself how he must have
looked. When visiting Lu, I saw the carriages, robes and
sacred vessels displayed at the Temple, and watched how
the Confucian students studied the historical systems at
his home, and hung around, unable to tear myself away
from the place. There have been many kings, emperors
and great men in history, who enjoyed fame and honor
while they lived and came to nothing at their death,
while Confucius, who was but a common scholar clad in
a cotton gown, became the acknowledged Master of
scholars for over ten generations. All people in China
who discuss the six arts, from the emperors, kings and
princes down, regard the Master as the final authority.

* Szema Ch'ien was official historian for the Han Court, coming from
a family which held that position. "T'ai-shih-kung," or "Master Historian," is his official title. At the end of every biography in his *Shiki,*
he usually gives a terse comment, appreciation or criticism of the man's
character.

Chapter III

CENTRAL HARMONY

(*Chungyung:* originally *Liki*, Ch. XXXI)

THIS is the book of *Chungyung,* usually translated as "The Doctrine of the Mean," or "The Golden Mean." It constitutes the second of the "Four Books," the following chapter (IV) being the first. Its importance in the Confucian philosophy will be readily seen from the text itself. I have put it here at the beginning of the Confucian text because it gives the best approach to Confucian philosophy. In itself it forms a fairly adequate and complete basis for the philosophy of Confucianism. The book, according to early authorities, was written by Tsesze, grandson of Confucius, disciple of Tsengtse and teacher of Mencius. Besides this chapter, Tsesze is traditionally said to have been responsible for Chapters XXX, XXXII and XXXIII of *Liki* also. The identity in style and thought between Mencius and this essay, especially Sections 1, 7, 8, is unmistakable, and part of Section 7 is actually repeated in *Mencius.* But if Tsesze was responsible for this work, he was a worthy teacher of Mencius, for we find here certain germinal ideas which mature and ripen into the full eloquence of Mencius. Careful students will see a deep connection between this chapter and the philosophy of Mencius (Chapter XI).

This is the only chapter in which I have not made my own translation, the one used being by the late Ku Hungming. Ku's translation has merits which are sufficiently apparent to make any justification for its use here superfluous. It is interesting to note that Ku translates *jen* as "the moral sense," *yi* as "the sense of justice," *li* as "moral and religious institutions (of the Three Dynasties)," and elsewhere as "the laws and usages of social life," *tao* as "the moral law," *chuntse* as "the moral man," *hsiaojen* as "the vulgar man," and *chungyung* as the "universal moral order" and in another place as "to find the central clue in our moral being which unites us to the universal order." These renderings are essentially correct; some are even brilliant. I have, however, found it necessary to add, delete and substitute phrases or lines, bringing about, I believe, a closer adherence to the original, and have naturally changed certain spellings of Chinese names to make them uniform with the rest of the book.

Ku has made a rearrangement of the sections, which I have not followed. It is admitted in general that the different sections or "chapters" as they are called in Chinese, are put together without a pretense at a proper order, the most evident cases being the "Chapters" 6, 14, and 16 (numbers in the original, not indicated below). "Chapter 28" is a very bad chapter, with a clearly later interpolation, which I have deleted; the rest I have incorporated into "Chapter 29" in Section 7 here. It is not possible to go into detailed explanations here without taking up a great deal of space to discuss the internal evidences. For the convenience of students who have access to the Chinese text, I give below the numbers of the Chinese "chapters" and their present sequence as re-arranged now under the different sections:

Section One: 1. *Section Two:* 2, 3, 4, 5, 6, 7, 8, 9, 10, 11,. *Section Three:* 12, 16. *Section Four:* 13, 15, 14. *Section Five:* 6, 17, 18, 19. *Section Six:* the greater part of 20, except the end. *Section Seven:* the end of 20, 21. *Section Eight:* 22, 23, 24, 25, 26. *Section Nine:* 27, 28 (partly deleted and partly combined with 29), 29, 30, 31, 32. *Section Ten:* 33.

I. THE CENTRAL HARMONY

What is God-given is what we call human nature. To fulfil the law of our human nature is what we call the moral law. The cultivation of the moral law is what we call culture.

The moral law is a law from whose operation we cannot for one instant in our existence escape. A law from which we may escape is not the moral law. Wherefore it is that the moral man (or the superior man) watches diligently over what his eyes cannot see and is in fear and awe of what his ears cannot hear.

There is nothing more evident than that which cannot be seen by the eyes and nothing more palpable than that which cannot be perceived by the senses. Wherefore the moral man watches diligently over his secret thoughts.

When the passions, such as joy, anger, grief, and pleasure, have not awakened, that is our *central* self, or moral being (*chung*). When these passions awaken and each and all attain due measure and degree, that is *harmony,* or the moral order (*ho*). Our central self or moral being is the great basis of existence, and *harmony* or moral order is the universal law in the world.

When our true central self and harmony are realised, the universe then becomes a cosmos and all things attain their full growth and development.

II. THE GOLDEN MEAN

Confucius remarked: "The life of the moral man is an exemplification of the universal moral order (*chung-yung,* usually translated as "the Mean").* The life of the vulgar person, on the other hand, is a contradiction of the universal moral order.

The moral man's life is an exemplification of the universal order, because he is a moral person who unceasingly cultivates his true self or moral being. The vulgar

* *Chung* means "central," and *yung* means "constant." The whole idea expresses the conception of a norm. It is possible that Sections 2, 3, 4, 5, 6 originally formed a separate book, later amalgamated with the other Sections (1, 7, 8, 9, 10). The styles of the two parts are quite different. This accounts for the abrupt change from *chungho* (central harmony) in the first section to *chungyung* (Golden Mean) in the second section.

person's life is a contradiction of the universal order, because he is a vulgar person who in his heart has no regard for, or fear of, the moral law.

Confucius remarked: "To find the central clue to our moral being which unites us to the universal order, that indeed is the highest human attainment. For a long time, people have seldom been capable of it."

Confucius remarked: "I know now why the moral life is not practiced. The wise mistake moral law for something higher than what it really is; and the foolish do not know enough what moral law really is. I know now why the moral law is not understood. The noble natures want to live too high, high above their moral ordinary self; and ignoble natures do not live high enough, i.e., not up to their moral ordinary true self. There is no one who does not eat and drink. But few there are who really know flavor."

Confucius remarked: "There is in the world now really no moral social order at all."

Confucius remarked: "Men all say 'I am wise'; but when driven forward and taken in a net, a trap, or a pitfall, there is not one who knows how to find a way of escape. Men all say, 'I am wise'; but in finding the true central clue and balance in their moral being (i.e., their normal, ordinary, true self), they are not able to keep it for a round month."

Confucius remarked of his favorite disciple, Yen Huei: "Huei was a man who all his life sought the central clue in his moral being, and when he got hold of one thing that was good, he embraced it with all his might and never lost it again."*

Confucius remarked: "A man may be able to put a country in order, be able to spurn the honors and emoluments of office, be able to trample upon bare, naked weapons: with all that he is still not able to find the central clue in his moral being."

Tselu asked what constituted strength of character.

Confucius said: "Do you mean strength of character of the people of the southern countries or force of character of the people of the northern countries; or do you mean strength of character of your type? To be patient and gentle, ready to teach, returning not evil for evil: that is the strength of character of the people of the southern countries. It is the ideal place for the moral man. To lie under arms and meet death without regret; that is the strength of character of the people of the northern countries. It is the ideal of brave men of your type. Wherefore the man with the true strength of moral character is one who is gentle, yet firm. How unflinching is his strength! When there is moral social order in the country, if he enters public life he does not change from what he was when in retirement. When there is no moral social order in the country, he is content unto death. How unflinching is his strength!"

* *Note by Ku Hungming:* As the Emperor Shun in the text above is the type of the intellectual nature, true representative of what Mr. Matthew Arnold calls Hellenism, so Yen Huei here is the type of the moral, emotional, or religious nature, true representative of what Mr. Arnold calls Hebraism.

Confucius remarked: "There are men who seek for the abstruse and strange and live a singular life in order that they may leave a name to posterity. This is what I never would do. There are again good men who try to live in conformity with the moral law, but who, when they have gone half way, throw it up. I never could give it up. Lastly, there are truly moral men who unconsciously live a life in entire harmony with the universal moral order and who live unknown to the world and unnoticed of men without any concern. It is only men of holy, divine natures who are capable of this."*

III. MORAL LAW EVERYWHERE

The moral law is to be found everywhere, and yet it is a secret.

The simple intelligence of ordinary men and women of the people may understand something of the moral law; but in its utmost reaches there is something which even the wisest and holiest of men cannot understand. The ignoble natures of ordinary men and women of the people may be able to carry out the moral law; but in its utmost reaches even the wisest and holiest of men cannot live up to it.

Great as the Universe is, man is yet not always satisfied with it. For there is nothing so great but the mind of

* For fuller and clearer expositions of the Golden Mean, see Chapter V, Sections 6, 7, 8, particularly Section 8 (the types of persons Confucius hated).

the moral man can conceive of something still greater which nothing in the world can hold. There is nothing so small but the mind of the moral man can conceive of something still smaller which nothing in the world can split.

The *Book of Songs* says: "The hawk soars to the heavens above and fishes dive to the depths below." That is to say, there is no place in the highest heavens above nor in the deepest waters below where the moral law is not to be found. The moral man finds the moral law beginning in the relation between man and woman; but ending in the vast reaches of the universe.

Confucius remarked: "The power of spiritual forces in the Universe—how active it is everywhere! Invisible to the eyes, and impalpable to the senses, it is inherent in all things, and nothing can escape its operation."

It is the fact that there are these forces which makes men in all countries fast and purify themselves, and with solemnity of dress institute services of sacrifice and religious worship. Like the rush of mighty waters, the presence of unseen Powers is felt; sometimes above us, sometimes around us.

In the *Book of Songs* it is said:

> "The presence of the Spirit:
> It cannot be surmised,
> How may it be ignored!

Such is the evidence of things invisible that it is impossible to doubt the spiritual nature of man.

IV. THE HUMANISTIC STANDARD

Confucius said: "Truth does not depart from human nature. If what is regarded as truth departs from human nature, it may not be regarded as truth. The *Book of Songs* says: 'In hewing an axe handle, the pattern is not far off.' Thus, when we take an axe handle in our hand to hew another axe handle and glance from one to the other, some still think the pattern is far off. Wherefore the moral man in dealing with men appeals to the common human nature and changes the manner of their lives and nothing more.

"When a man carries out the principles of conscientiousness and reciprocity he is not far from the moral law. What you do not wish others should do unto you, do not do unto them.

"There are four things in the moral life of a man, not one of which I have been able to carry out in my life. To serve my father as I would expect my son to serve me: that I have not been able to do. To serve my sovereign as I would expect a minister under me to serve me: that I have not been able to do. To act towards my elder brothers as I would expect my younger brother to act towards me: that I have not been able to do. To be the first to behave towards friends as I would expect them to behave towards me: that I have not been able to do.

"In the discharge of the ordinary duties of life and in the exercise of care in ordinary conversation, whenever there is shortcoming, never fail to strive for improvement, and when there is much to be said, always say less than what is necessary; words having respect to actions and actions having respect to words. Is it not just this thorough genuineness and absence of pretense which characterizes the moral man?"*

The moral life of man may be likened to traveling to a distant place: one must start from the nearest stage. It may also be likened to ascending a height: one must begin from the lowest step. The *Book of Songs* says:

"When wives and children and their sires are one,
 'Tis like the harp and lute in unison.
 When brothers live in concord and at peace
 The strain of harmony shall never cease.
 The lamp of happy dnion lights the home,
 And bright days follow when the children come."

Confucius, commenting on the above, remarked: "In such a state of things what more satisfaction can parents have?"

The moral man conforms himself to his life circumstances; he does not desire anything outside of his position. Finding himself in a position of wealth and honor, he lives as becomes one living in a position of wealth and honor. Finding himself in a position of poverty and humble circumstances, he lives as becomes one living in a position of poverty and humble circumstances. Finding himself in uncivilized countries, he lives as becomes one living in uncivilized countries. Finding himself in circumstances of danger and difficulty, he acts according to

* For further elucidations of the humanistic standard of "measuring man by man," see quotations from the *Analects*, Chapter V, Section 6.

what is required of a man under such circumstances. In one word, the moral man can find himself in no situation in life in which he is not master of himself.

In a high position he does not domineer over his subordinates. In a subordinate position he does not court the favors of his superiors. He puts in order his own personal conduct and seeks nothing from others; hence he has no complaint to make. He complains not against God, nor rails against men.

Thus it is that the moral man lives out the even tenor of his life, calmly waiting for the appointment of God, whereas the vulgar person takes to dangerous courses, expecting the uncertain chances of luck.

Confucius remarked: "In the practice of archery we have something resembling the principle in a moral man's life. When the archer misses the center of the target, he turns round and seeks for the cause of his failure within himself."

V. CERTAIN MODELS

Confucius remarked: "There was the Emperor Shun. He was perhaps what may be considered a truly great intellect. Shun had a natural curiosity of mind and he loved to inquire into ordinary conversation. He ignored the bad (words?) and broadcast the good. Taking two extreme counsels, he took the mean between them and applied them in dealings with his people. This was the characteristic of Shun's great intellect."

Confucius remarked: "The Emperor Shun might perhaps be considered in the highest sense of the word a pious man. In moral qualities he was a saint. In dignity of office he was the ruler of the empire. In wealth all that the wide world contained belonged to him. After his death his spirit was sacrificed to in the ancestral temple, and his children and grandchildren preserved the sacrifice for long generations.

"Thus it is that he who possesses great moral qualities will certainly attain to corresponding high position, to corresponding great prosperity, to corresponding great name, to corresponding great age.

"For God in giving life to all created things is surely bountiful to them according to their qualities. Hence the tree that is full of life. He fosters and sustains, while that which is ready to fall He cuts off and destroys.*

The *Book of Songs* says:

> That great and noble Prince displayed
> The sense of right in all he wrought;
> The spirit of his wisdom swayed
> Peasant and peer; the crowd, the court.
> So Heav'n, that crowned his sires, restored
> The countless honors they had known;
> For Heav'n aye keepeth watch and ward,
> The Mandate gave to mount the throne.

It is therefore true that he who possesses exceedingly great moral qualities will certainly receive the divine mandate to the Imperial throne."

* I cannot refrain from paying tribute to Ku Hungming for rendering this passage with such beauty. The surprising thing is that it is almost verbally faithful to the original.

Confucius remarked: "The man perhaps who enjoyed the most perfect happiness was the Emperor Wen. For father he had a remarkable man, the Emperor Chi, and for son also a remarkable man, the Emperor Wu. His father laid the foundation of his House and his son carried it on. The Emperor Wu, continuing the great work begun by his ancestor, the great Emperor, his grandfather Chi and his father the Emperor Wen, had only to buckle on his armor and the Empire at once came to his possession. In dignity of office he was the ruler of the Empire; in wealth all that the wide world contained belonged to him. After his death his spirit was sacrificed to in the ancestral temple, and his children and grandchildren preserved the sacrifice for long generations.

"The Emperor Wu received Heaven's mandate to rule in his old age. His brother, Duke Chou, ascribed the achievement of founding the Imperial House equally to the moral qualities of the Emperors Wen and Wu. He carried the Imperial title up to the Great Emperor (Wen's grandfather) and the Emperor Chi (Wen's father). He sacrificed to all the past reigning Dukes of the House with imperial honors.

("This rule is now universally observed from the reigning princes and nobles to the gentlemen and common people. In the case where the father is a noble and the son is a simple gentleman, the father, when he dies, is buried with the honors of a noble, but sacrificed to as a simple gentleman. In the case where the father is a simple gentleman and the son a noble, the father, when he dies, is buried as a simple gentleman, but sacrificed to with honors of a nobleman. The rule for one year of mourning for relatives is binding up to the rank of a noble, but the rule for three years of mourning for parents is binding for all up to the Emperor. In mourning for parents there is only one rule, and no distinction is made between noble and plebeian.")*

Confucius remarked: "The Emperor Wu and his brother, Duke Chou, were indeed eminently pious men. Now, true filial piety consists in successfully carrying out the unfinished work of our forefathers and transmitting their achievements to posterity.

"In spring and autumn they repaired and put in order the ancestral temple, arranged the sacrificial vessels, exhibited the regalia and heirlooms of the family, and presented the appropriate offerings of the season.

"The principle in the order of precedence in the ceremonies of worship in the ancestral temple is, in the first place, to arrange the members of the family according to descent. Ranks are next considered, in order to give recognition to the principle of social distinction. Services rendered are next considered as a recognition of distinction in moral worth. In the general banquet those below take precedence of those above in pledging the company, in order to show that consideration is shown to the meanest. In conclusion, a separate feast is given to the elders, in order to recognize the principle of seniority according to age.

"To gather in the same places where our fathers before us have gathered; to perform the same ceremonies which

* The foregoing paragraph is part of the original Confucian text.

they before us have performed; to play the same music which they before us have played; to pay respect to those whom they honored; to love those who were dear to them—in fact, to serve those now dead as if they were living, and now departed as if they were still with us: this is the highest achievement of true filial piety.

"The performance of sacrifices to Heaven and Earth is meant for the service of God. The performance of ceremonies in the ancestral temple is meant for the worship of ancestors. If one only understood the meaning of the sacrifices to Heaven and Earth, and the significance of the services in ancestral worship in summer and autumn, it would be as easy to govern a nation as to point a finger at the palm."

VI. ETHICS AND POLITICS*

Duke Ai (ruler of Lu, Confucius' native state) asked what constituted good government.

Confucius replied: "The principles of good government of the Emperors Wen and Wu are abundantly illustrated in the records preserved. When the men are there, good government will flourish, but when the men are gone, good government decays and becomes extinct. With the right men, the growth of good government is as rapid as the growth of vegetation is in the right soil.

* This section must have been placed here from other "ancient records." Confucius had a number of interviews with Duke Ai, some in the "Great Tai" collection; see for comparison Chapter VII of the present book.

Indeed, good government is like a fast-growing plant. The conduct of government, therefore, depends upon the men. The right men are obtained by the ruler's personal character. To cultivate his personal character, the ruler must use the moral law (*tao*). To cultivate the moral law, the ruler must use the moral sense (*jen,* or principles of true manhood).

"The moral sense is the characteristic attribute of man. To fell natural affection for those nearly related to us is the highest expression of the moral sense. The sense of justice (*yi* or propriety) is the recognition of what is right and proper. To honor those who are worthier than ourselves is the highest expression of the sense of justice. The relative degrees of natural affection we ought to feel for those who are nearly related to us and the relative grades of honor we ought to show to those worthier than ourselves: these give rise to the forms and distinctions in social life (*li,* or principles of social order). For unless social inequalities have a true and moral basis (or unless those being ruled feel their proper place with respect to their rulers), government of the people is an impossibility.

"Therefore it is necessary for a man of the governing class to set about regulating his personal conduct and character. In considering how to regulate his personal conduct and character, it is necessary for him to do his duties toward those nearly related to him. In considering how to do his duties toward those necessary related to him, it is necessary for him to understand the nature and organization of human society. In considering the nature and organization of human society it is necessary for him to understand the laws of God.

"The duties of universal obligation are five, and the moral qualities by which they are carried out are three. The duties are those between ruler and subject, between father and son, between husband and wife, between elder brother and younger, and those in the intercourse between friends. These are the five duties of universal obligation. Wisdom, compassion and courage*—these are the three universally recognized moral qualities of man. It matters not in what way men caome to the exercise of these moral qualities, the result is one and the same.

"Some men are born with the knowledge of these moral qualities; some acquire it as the result of education; some acquire it as the result of hard experience. But when the knowledge is acquired, it comes to one and the same thing. Some exercise these moral qualities naturally and easily; some because they find it advantageous to do so; some with effort and difficulty. But when the achievement is made it comes to one and the same thing."

Confucius went on to say: "Love of knowledge is akin to wisdom. Strenuous attention to conduct is akin to compassion. Sensitiveness to shame is akin to courage.

"When a man understands the nature and use of these three moral qualities, he will then understand how to put in order his personal conduct and character. When a man understands how to put in order his personal conduct and character, he will understand how to govern

* Ku translates them as "intelligence, moral character and courage."

men. When a man understands how to govern men, he will then understand how to govern nations and empires.

"For every one called to the government of nations and empires there are nine cardinal directions to be attended to:

1. Cultivating his personal conduct.
2. Honoring worthy men.
3. Cherishing affection for, and doing his duty toward, his kindred.
4. Showing respect to the high ministers of state.
5. Identifying himself with the interests and welfare of the whole body of public officers.
6. Showing himself as a father to the common people.
7. Encouraging the introduction of all useful arts.
8. Showing tenderness to strangers from far countries.
9. Taking interest in the welfare of the princes of the Empire.

"When the ruler pays attention to the cultivation of his personal conduct, there will be respect for the moral law. When the ruler honors worthy men, he will not be deceived (by the crafty officials). When the ruler cherishes affection for his kindred, there will be no disaffection among the members of his family. When the ruler shows respect to the high ministers of state, he will not make mistakes. When the ruler identifies himself with the interests and welfare of the body of public officers, there will be a strong spirit of loyalty among the gentle-men of the country. When the ruler becomes a father to the common people, the mass of the people will exert themselves for the good of the state. When the ruler encourages the introduction of all useful arts, there will be sufficiency of wealth and revenue in the country. When the ruler shows kindness to the strangers from far countries, people from all quarters of the world will flock to the country. When the ruler takes interest in the condition and welfare of the princes of the empire, he will inspire awe and respect for his authority throughout the whole world.

"By attending to the cleanliness and purity of his person and to the propriety and dignity of his dress, and in every word and act permitting nothing which is contrary to good taste and decency; that is how the ruler culti-vates his personal conduct. By banishing all flatterers and keeping away from the society of women, holding in low estimation possession of worldly goods, but valuing moral qualities in men—that is how the ruler gives encouragement to worthy men. By raising them to high places of honor and bestowing ample emoluments for their maintenance; sharing and sympathizing with their tastes and opinions—that is how the ruler inspires love for his person among the members of his family. By extending the powers of their functions and allowing them discretion in the employment of their subordi-nates—that is how the ruler gives encouragement to the high ministers of state. By dealing loyally and punctually with them in all engagements which he makes with them and allowing a liberal scale of pay—that is how the ruler gives encouragement to men in the public service. By strictly limiting the time of their service and making all imposts as light as possible—that is how the ruler gives encouragement to the mass of the people. By ordering daily inspection and monthly examination and rewarding each according to the degree of his workmanship—that is how the ruler encourages the artisan class. By welcoming them when they come and giving them protection when they go, commending what is good in them and making allowance for their ignorance—that is how the ruler shows kindness to strangers from far countries. By restoring lines of broken succession and reviving subjugated states, putting down anarchy and disorder wherever they are found, and giving support to the weak against the strong, fixing stated times for their attendance and the attendance of their envoys at court, loading them with presents when they leave, while exacting little from them in the way of contribution when they come—that is how the ruler takes interest in the welfare of the princes of the empire.

"For every one who is called to the government of nations and empire, these are the nine cardinal directions to be attended to; and there is only one way by which they can be carried out.

"In all matters success depends on preparation; without preparation there will always be failure. When what is to be said is previously determined, there will be no difficulty in carrying it out. When a line of conduct is previously determined, there will be no occasion for vexation. When general principles are previously determined, there will be no perplexity to know what to do."

VII. BEING ONE'S TRUE SELF

"If the people in inferior positions do not have confidence in those above them, government of the people is an impossibility. There is only one way to gain confidence for one's authority: if a man is not trusted by his friends, he will not have confidence in those above him. There is only one way to be trusted by one's friends: if a man is not affectionate toward his parents, he will not be trusted by his friends. There is only one way to be affectionate toward one's parents: if a man, looking into his own heart, is not true to himself, he will not be affectionate towards his parents. There is only one way for a man to be true to himself. There is only one way for a man to be true to himself. If he does not know what is good, a man cannot be true to himself.

"Being true to oneself is the law of God. To try to be true to oneself is the law of man.*

"He who is naturally true to himself is one who, without effort, hits upon what is right, and without thinking understands what he wants to know, whose life is easily and naturally in harmony with the moral law. Such a

* This part from the beginning of the section is found in the *Book of Mencius,* Book IV, Part I. The complete interview is found also in "Confucius' Family Records" (*K'ungtse Chiayu*), without the section that follows immediately.

one is what we call a saint or a man of divine nature. He who learns to be his true self is one who finds out what is good and holds fast to it.

"In order to learn to be one's true self, it is necessary to obtain a wide and extensive knowledge of what has been said and done in the world; critically to inquire into it; carefully to ponder over it; clearly to sift it; and earnestly to carry it out.

"It matters not what you learn; but when you once learn a thing, you must never give it up until you have mastered it. It matters not what you inquire into, but when you inquire into a thing, you must never give it up until you have thoroughly understood it. It matters not what you try to think out, but when you once try to think out a thing you must never give it up until you have got what you want. It matters not what you try to sift out, but when you once try to sift out a thing, you must never give it up until you have sifted it out clearly and distinctly. It matters not what you try to carry out, but when you once try to carry out a thing you must never give it up until you have done it thoroughly and well. If another man succeed by one effort, you will use a hundred efforts. If another man succeed by ten efforts, you will use a thousand efforts.

"Let a man really proceed in this manner, and, though dull, he will surely become intelligent; though weak, he will surely become strong."

To arrive at understanding from being one's true self is called nature, and to arrive at being one's true self from understanding is called culture. He who is his true self has thereby understanding, and he who has understanding finds thereby his true self.*

VIII. THOSE WHO ARE ABSOLUTE TRUE SELVES

Only those who are their absolute true selves in the world can fulfil their own nature; only those who fulfil their own nature can fulfil the nature of others; only those who fulfil the nature of others can fulfil the nature of things; those who fulfil the nature of things are worthy to help Mother Nature is growing and sustaining life; and those who are worthy to help Mother Nature in growing and sustaining life are the equals of heaven and earth.

The next in order are those who are able to attain to the apprehension of a particular branch of study. By such studies, they are also able to apprehend the truth. Realization of the true self compels expression; expression becomes evidence; evidence becomes clarity or luminosity of knowledge; clarity or luminosity of knowledge activates; active knowledge becomes power and power becomes a pervading influence. Only those who are absolutely their true selves in this world can have pervading influence.

It is an attribute of the possession of the absolute true self to be able to foreknow. When a nation or family is

* This paragraph constitutes a "chapter" by itself in the Chinese text. The translation of this paragraph and the following two paragraphs is entirely mine, differing from Ku's.

about to flourish, there are sure to be lucky omens. When a nation or family is about to perish, there are sure to be signs and prodigies. These things manifest themselves in the instruments of divination and in the agitation of the human body. When happiness or calamity is about to come, it can be known beforehand. When it is good, it can be known beforehand. When it is evil, it can also be known beforehand. Therefore he who has realized his true self is like a celestial spirit.

Truth means the fulfilment of our self; and moral law means following the law of our being. Truth is the beginning and end (the substance) of material existence. Without truth there is no material existence. It is for this reason that the moral man values truth.

Truth is not only the fulfilment of our own being; it is that by which things outside of us have an existence. The fulfilment of our being is moral sense. The fulfilment of the nature of things outside of us is intellect. These, moral sense and intellect, are the powers or faculties of our being. They combine the inner or subjective and outer or objective use of the power of the mind. Therefore, with truth, everything done is right.

Thus absolute truth is indestructible. Being indestructible, it is eternal. Being eternal, it is self-existent. Being self-existent, it is infinite. Being infinite, it is vast and deep. Being vast and deep, it is transcendental and intelligent. It is because it is vast and deep that it contains all existence. It is because it is transcendental and intelligent that it embraces all existence. It is because it is infinite and eternal that it fulfils or perfects all existence.

In vastness and depth it is like the Earth. In transcendental intelligence it is like Heaven. Infinite and eternal, it is the Infinite itself.

Such being the nature of absolute truth, it manifests itself without being seen; it produces effects without motion; it accomplishes its ends without action.

The principle in the course and operation of nature may be summed up in one word: because it obeys only its own immutable law, the way in which it produces the variety of things is unfathomable.

Nature is vast, deep, high, intelligent, infinite and eternal. The heaven appearing before us is only this bright, shining mass; but in its immeasurable extent, the sun, the moon, stars and constellations are suspended in it, and all things are embraced under it. The earth, appearing before us, is but a handful of soil; but in all its breadth and depth, it sustains mighty mountains without feeling their weight; rivers and seas dash against it without causing it to leak. The mountain appearing before us is only a mass of rock; but in all the vastness of its size, grass and vegetation grow upon it, birds and beasts dwell on it, and treasures of precious minerals are found in it. The water appearing before us is but a ladleful of liquid; but in all its unfathomable depths, the largest crustaceans, dragons, fishes, and turtles are produced in them, and all useful products abound in them.

In the *Book of Songs* it is said:

> "The ordinance of God,
> How inscrutable it is and goes on for ever."

That is to say, this is the essence of God. It is again said:

> "How excellent it is,
> The moral perfection of King Wen."

That is to say, this is the essence of the noble character of the Emperor Wen. Moral perfection also never dies.

IX. EULOGY ON CONFUCIUS

Oh, how great is the divine moral law of the Sage. Overflowing and illimitable, it gives birth and life to all created things and towers high up to the very heavens. How magnificent it is! How imposing the three hundred principles and three thousand rules of conduct!* They await the man who can put the system into practice. Hence it is said: Unless there be the highest moral character, the highest moral law cannot be realized.

Wherefore the moral man, while honoring the greatness and power of his moral nature, yet does not neglect inquiry and pursuit of knowledge. While broadening the scope of his knowledge, he yet seeks to exhaust the mystery of the small things. While seeking to attain the highest understanding he yet orders his conduct according to the middle course (literally *"chungyung."*). Going over what he has already learned, he gains some new knowledge. Earnest and simple, he respects and obeys the laws and usages of social life (*li*).

Therefore, when in a position of authority, he is not

* Think of *Deuteronomy*.

proud; in a subordinate position, he is not insubordinate. When there is moral social order in the country, what he speaks will bring prosperity to the nation; and when there is no moral social order in the country, his silence will ensure forbearance for himself.*

In the *Book of Songs* it is said:

> "With wisdom and good sense,
> He guards his life from harm."

That is the description of the moral man.

To attain to the sovereignty of the world, there are three important things necessary, which would make it perfect.†

Although a man may occupy a position of authority, yet, unless he possesses the moral character fitting him for his task, he may not take upon himself to make changes in the established religious and artistic institutions (literally "ritual and music"). Although one may possess the moral character fitting him for his task, yet, unless he occupies the position of authority, he may not take upon himself to make changes in the established religious and artistic institutions.

Confucius remarked: "I have tried to understand the moral and religious institutions (*li*) of the Hsia Dynasty, but what remains of those institutions in the present

---

* Here we see the connection between the realization of the true self and harmony with the outside world, between "neutrality" and "harmony."

† The following two paragraphs are incorporated here from "Chapter 28." The "three important things" (position, character and appeal to history) become otherwise unintelligible.

state of Ch'i does not furnish sufficient evidence. I have studied the moral and religious institutions of the Shang (Yin) Dynasty; the remains of them are still preserved in the present state of Sung. I have studied the moral and religious institutions of the present Chou Dynasty, which being now in use, I follow in practice."

Coming from those in power, a system may be lacking in historical authority ("historic evidences"), however excellent it may be; what is lacking in historical authority cannot command credence; and what cannot command credence the people will never obey. Coming from those not in authority, a system may not command respect, however excellent it may be; what does not command respect cannot command credence; and what cannot command credence the people will obey.

Therefore every system of moral laws must be based upon the man's own consciousness, verified by the common experience of mankind, tested by due sanction of historical experience and found without error, applied to the operations and processes of nature in the physical universe and found to be without contradiction, laid before the gods without question or fear, and able to wait a hundred generations and have it confirmed without a doubt by a Sage of posterity. The fact that he is able to confront the spiritual powers of the universe without any fear shows that he understands the laws of God. The fact that he is prepared to wait a hundred generations for confirmation from the Sage of posterity without any misgiving shows that he understands the laws of man.

Wherefore it is that it is true of the really great moral

man that every move he makes becomes an example for generations; every act he does becomes a model for generations and every word he utters becomes a guide for generations. Those who are far away look up to him, while those who are near do not decrease their respect for him. In the *Book of Songs* it is said:

> "There they found no fault of him,
> Here they never tire of him;
> Thus from day to day and night to night
> They will perpetuate his praise!"

There never was a moral man who did not answer this description and who yet could obtain timely recognition throughout the world.

Confucius taught the truth originally handed down by the ancient Emperors Yao and Shun, and he adopted and perfected the system of social and religious laws established by the Emperors Wen and Wu. He shows that they harmonize with the divine order which governs the revolutions of the seasons in the Heaven above and that they fit in with the moral design which is to be seen in physical nature upon the Earth below.

These moral laws form one system with the laws by which Heaven and Earth support and contain, overshadow and canopy all things. These moral laws form the same system with the laws by which the seasons succeed each other and the sun and moon appear with the alternations of day and night. It is this same system of laws by which all created things are produced and develop themselves each in its order and system without injuring one another, and by which the operations of Nature take their course without conflict or confusion; the lesser forces flowing everywhere like river currents, while the great forces of Creation go silently and steadily on. It is this (one system running through all) that makes the Universe so impressively great.

It is only the man with the most perfect divine moral nature who is able to combine in himself quickness of apprehension, intelligence, insight and understanding—qualities necessary for the exercise of command, magnanimity, generosity, benignity and gentleness—qualities necessary for the exercise of patience; originality, energy, strength of character and determination—qualities necessary for the exercise of endurance, piety, noble seriousness, order and regularity—qualities necessary for the exercise of dignity, grace, method, subtlety and penetration—qaulities necessary for the exercise of critical judgment.

Thus all-embracing and vast is the nature of such a man. Profound it is and inexhaustible, like a living spring of water, ever running out with life and vitality. All-embracing and vast, it is like Heaven. Profound and inexhaustible, it is like the abyss.

As soon as such a man shall make his appearance in the world, all people will reverence him. Whatever he says, all people will believe it. Whatever he does, all people will be pleased with it. Thus his fame and name will spread and fill all the civilized world (literally "China"), extending even to savage countries, wherever ships and carriages reach, wherever the labor and enter-

prise of man penetrate, wherever the heavens overshadow and the earth sustain, wherever the sun and
moon shine, wherever frost and dew fall. All who have
life and breath will honor and love him. Therefore we
may say: "He is the equal of God."

It is only he in this world who has realized his absolute self that can order and adjust the great relations of
human society, fix the fundamental principles of morality, and understand the laws of growth and reproduction
of the Universe.

Now, where does such a man derive his power and
knowledge, except from himself? How simple and self-
contained his true manhood!* How unfathomable the
depth of his mind! How infinitely grand and vast the
moral height of his nature! Who can understand such a
nature except he who is gifted with the most perfect
intelligence and endowed with the highest divine qualities of character, and who has reached in his moral
development the level of the gods?

X. EPILOGUE

In the *Book of Songs* it is said:

> "Over her brocaded robe,
>   She wore a plain and simple dress,"

in that way showing her dislike of the loudness of its
color and magnificence. Thus the ways of the moral man

* Ch'en Li regards this phrase as the best description of *jen*, or "true
manhood."

are unobtrusive and yet they grow more and more in power and evidence; whereas the ways of the vulgar person are ostentatious, but lose more and more in influence until they perish and disappear.

The life of the moral man is plain, and yet not unattractive; it is simple and yet full of grace; it is easy, and yet methodical. He knows that accomplishment of great things consists in doing little things well. He knows that great effects are produced by small causes. He knows the evidence and reality of what cannot be perceived by the senses. Thus he is enabled to enter into the world of ideas and morals.

In the *Book of Songs* it is said:

> "How deep the fish may dive below,
> And yet it is quite clearly seen."

Therefore the moral man must examine into his own heart and see that he has no cause for self-reproach, that he has no evil thought in his mind. Wherein the moral man is superior to other men consists even in those things that people do not notice.

In the *Book of Songs* it is said:

> "In your secret chamber even you are judged;
> See you do nothing to blush for,
> Though but the ceiling looks down upon you."

Therefore the moral man, even when he is not doing anything, is serious; and, even when he does not speak, is truthful.

In the *Book of Songs* it is said:

> "All through the solemn rite not a word was spoken,
> And yet all strife was banished from their hearts."

Hence the moral man, without the inducement of rewards, is able to make the people good; and without the show of anger, to awe them into fear more than if he had used the most dreadful instruments of punishment.

In the *Book of Songs* it is said:

> "He makes no show of his moral worth,
> Yet all the princes follow in his steps."

Hence the moral man, by living a life of simple truth and earnestness, alone can help to bring peace and order in the world.

In the *Book of Songs* it is said:

> "I keep in mind the fine moral qualities
> Which make no great noise or show."

Confucius remarked: "Among the means for the regeneration of mankind, those made with noise and show are of the least importance."

In another place in the *Book of Songs,* it is said:

> "His virtue is light as hair."

Still a hair is something material. "The workings of Almighty God has neither sound nor smell." That is the highest development of our moral nature.

Chapter IV

ETHICS AND POLITICS

(*Tahsueh, Liki,* Chapter XLII)

THIS essay, originally Chapter XLII of *Liki,* is now ranked among the *Four Books,* and as it stands first among these, all Chinese school children used to begin their first studies with this essay. The philosophy behind this essay and "Central Harmony," which used to come next, was of course entirely beyond the mental range of children of seven or eight. Nevertheless, they were studiously conned over and committed to memory so that the lines in these essays stuck in their minds for life, and served them usefully afterwards. Regarding the basic importance of this essay, the Sung Confucianist, Ch'eng Yich'uan, said, "This *Tahsueh* is a book in the surviving tradition of the Confucian school and constitutes the gateway through which beginners enter into the path of virtue. The fact that we can see now the order and sequence in which the ancients proceeded in their education, depends entirely on the existence of this essay, with the *Analects* and *The Book of Mencius* coming next. All students should begin their studies with this essay; then it may be hoped that they will not go far wrong."

The original title of this essay is *Tahsueh,* translated by James Legge as "The Great Learning," but more accurately translated by Ku Hungming as "The Higher Education." According to the school age defined for this "higher education," it seemed to correspond to the American junior college. This is made clear in another chapter of *Liki,* which I have translated here as Chapter IX, where the educational system for the princes and sons of aristocrats is more concretely described. (Chapters VIII and XII of *Liki,* not translated here, throw further light on the educational system.) The whole Confucian point of view regarding education seemed to be influenced by the basic assumption of an intellectual upper class, who were to be the rulers or who were to assist the rulers in the art of government; hence the always implicit assumption of preparing to govern a country in discussions on education. This essay seems to have been written expressly for the education of the princes (see especially Section 8), and this explains, I believe, its title *Tahsueh,* or "The College," where the princes were educated. The use of the word *chuntse* (literally "prince") must have been general at the College, and later became a more general term for "the gentlemen." In content, this essay actually deals with the connection between the cultivation of personal life and a general world order, or between ethics and politics.

The usual version of this essay has been re-edited by the Sung commentator Chu Hsi, resulting in the transposition of an entire section to an earlier part of the essay and in a much clearer arrangement of ideas. The disarrangement was said to be due to the mixing up of the strips of inscribed bamboo, which were perforated and tied together in bundles by leather straps. While I regard Chu Hsi's transposition as admirable and have adopted it, he did not seem to see why the original disarrangement took place. The result was, there was an awkward transition at the end of his transposed section, resulting in two identical lines coming together—"This is knowing the root, This is knowing the root. This is the perfection of knowledge." What Chu Hsi did was to regard the second of the identical lines and the third line as the conclusion of a separate "missing paragraph," and he proceeded to supply the "missing paragraph" himself, giving him an opportunity to put in a bit of Sung philosophy regarding meditation and the arrival at true knowledge. This entirely changed the picture of the object and method of investigation of knowledge, which has caused unending dispute and no end of speculation. I have (by comparing the original version of the text of Cheng Hsuan, prior to the editing of Chu Hsi) come to the conclusion that the mistake was due to the existence of two identical lines originally apart in the same essay, and as these were learned by rote by old scholars who had survived the massacre of Ch'in Shih-huang, a wrong connection leading off from an identical line was perfectly natural—similar to what often happens in the composing room. The result of this perception of the original error, existing in Cheng Hsuan's text, leads me to believe that there was no "missing paragraph," but merely a wrong transposition, and that the object of investigation of knowledge discussed in that section was just human nature and the human heart, and not the physical universe. This will be quite plain in the following text, re-edited by myself. I have kept to Chu Hsi's transposition of an entire section, but have merely restored the original connecting identical lines to what I regard to be where they belong.

I. GENERAL IDEA OF THIS ESSAY

The principles of the higher education consist in preserving man's clear character, in giving new life to the people, and in dwelling (or resting) in perfection, or the ultimate good. Only after knowing the goal of perfection where one should dwell, can one have a definite purpose in life. Only after having a definite purpose in life can one achieve calmness of mind. Only after having achieved calmness of mind, can one have peaceful repose. Only after having peaceful repose can one begin to think. Only after one has learned to think, can one achieve knowledge. There are a foundation and a superstructure in the constitution of things, and a beginning and an end in the course of events. Therefore to know the proper sequence or relative order of things is the beginning of wisdom.

The ancients who wished to preserve the fresh or clear character of the people of the world, would first set about ordering their national life. Those who wished to order their national life, would first set about regulating their family life. Those who wished to regulate their family life would set about cultivating their personal life. Those who wished to cultivate their personal lives, would first set about setting their hearts rights. Those who wished to set their hearts right would first set about making their wills sincere. Those who wished to make their wills sincere would first set about achieving true knowledge. The achieving of true knowledge depended upon the investigation of things. When things are investigated, then true knowledge is achieved; when true knowledge is achieved, then the will becomes sincere; when the will is sincere, then the heart is set right (or then the mind sees right); when the heart is set right, then the personal life is cultivated; when the personal life is cultivated, then the family life is regulated; when the family life is regulated, then the national life is orderly; and when the national life is orderly, then there is peace in this world. From the emperor down to the common men, all must regard the cultivation of the personal life as the root or foundation. There is never an orderly upshoot or superstructure when the root or foundation is disorderly. There is never yet a tree whose trunk is slim and slender and whose top branches are thick and heavy. This is called "to know the root or foundation of things."*

* The original text (Cheng Hsuan's), before the re-editing of Chu Hsi, ends with two lines: "This is called 'to know the root of things.' This is called 'achieving true knowledge.' " The second line then leads off to what are here Sections 4 and 5, which causes an abrupt break in the

II. ON THE MEANING OF CERTAIN EXPRESSIONS USED IN THE
ABOVE SECTION

What is meant by "making clear man's character" is this: In the *Announcement to K'ang* (a document in the *Book of History*), it is said, "He was able to make his character clean." In *T'aichia* (another document in the same book), it said, "He contemplated the *clear* mandates of Heaven." In the *Canon of Yao* (another document), it is said, "He was able to make *clear* his great character." These all show that the ancient kings started by making their own characters *clear*.

What is meant by "giving new life to the people" is this: The inscription on the bath-tub of Emperor T'ang read, "If you make yourself fresh (or "renew yourself"), then daily make yourself fresh, and again make yourself every day fresh.* The *Announcement to K'ang* said,

---

discussion. Actually, I believe these two lines belong to Section 3, where Confucius said that he was as good a judge as anyone, but that he would make it so that people who had committed crimes would be ashamed to defend themselves, and the people would be in awe of the great wise judge—as an illustration of achieving true knowledge or wisdom. I believe that this paragraph in the uncorrupted text before Cheng merely ended with the line "This is called 'to know the root or foundation of things.' " Chu Hsi, on the other hand, took the two lines at the end of this paragraph in the text he was trying to re-edit and transposed them to a latter part, considering them the last lines of a missing paragraph. See note to Section 3.

* Actually this was already a mis-reading in Confucius' own day of the bronze inscription. The sentiment is fine, but the philosophy was deplorable. Actually, the inscription read, "My elder brother was called Hsin; my grandfather was called Hsin, and my father was called Hsin,"

"Become a *new* nation." The *Book of Songs* said, "Although the state of Chou is an old country, the mandates it has received from Heaven are forever *new*." Therefore the gentleman tries at all times to do his utmost.*

What is meant by "resting, or dwelling, in perfection" is this: The *Book of Songs* says, "The Imperial domain of a thousand *li* is where the people *dwell*." It is again said in the *Book of Songs,* "The twittering yellow bird *rests* or alights on a little mound." And Confucius remarked, "When the bird *rests,* it knows where to *rest*. Should a human being be inferior to a bird in knowing where to *rest* (or in knowing what to *dwell in*)?" The *Book of Songs* again says, "How dignified and inspiring was King Wen! How bright was his virtue! He was careful in choosing that which he would *dwell in*."† As a ruler, he dwelled in benevolence. As a minister, he dwelled in respectfulness. As a son, he dwelled in filial piety; as a father, he dwelled in kindness; and in his dealings with the people of the country, he dwelled in honesty.

The *Book of Songs* says, "Look at that curve in the River of Ch'i. How luxurious and green are the bamboo trees there! Here is our elegant and accomplished prince. He looks like a piece of jade, cut and filed and chiseled

---

Hsin being one of the commonest names in the Shang Dynasty, and a term in the duodecimal cycle.

* This last sentence does not make any sense in this connection, and seems to belong logically in the section about achieving true knowledge.
† This is also probably a misinterpretation of the original text by the early Confucianists.

and polished. How grave and dignified in figure and majestic and distinguished! It is impossible to forget our elegant and accomplished prince!" The expression "cut and filed" refers to polishing his scholarship. The expression "chiseled and polished" refers to the cultivation of his character. The expression "grave and dignified" refers to his fear and caution, and the expression "majestic and distinguished" refers to his inspiring appearance. And the expression "it is impossible to forget our elegant and accomplished prince" means that the people could never forget his great character and his *perfection*.

The *Book of Songs* says, "Ah! the ancient kings are never forgotten by their people!" Future princes respected what they respected and loved what they loved, while the common people enjoyed what they enjoyed and benefited from their beneficial arrangements. That was why for generations the people could not forget them.*

III. ON ACHIEVING TRUE KNOWLEDGE

What is meant by "achieving true knowledge" is this: Confucius said, "In presiding over lawsuits, I am as good as anyone. The thing is we should make it our aim that there may be no lawsuits at all, so that people who have actually done wrong will be too ashamed of themselves to indulge in words of self-defense. Thus the people are

* Here I have mainly followed Legge. This paragraph has been transferred here from another place by Chu Hsi.

inspired with a great respect or fear (of the magistrate). This is called "to know the root (or bottom) of things." This is called "achieving true knowledge (or wisdom)."*

IV. ON MAKING THE WILL SINCERE

What is meant by "making the will sincere" is that one should not deceive oneself. This sincerity should be like the sincerity with which we hate a bad smell or love what is beautiful. This is called satisfying your own conscience. Therefore a superior man is watchful over himself when he is alone. The common man does wrong without any kind of self-restraint in his private life, and then when he sees the superior man, he is ashamed of himself and tries to hide the bad and show off the good in him. But what is the use? For people see into their very hearts when they look at them. That is what is meant when we say, "What is true in a man's heart will be shown in his outward appearance." Therefore the superior man (or the prince) must be watchful over himself when he is alone. Tsengtse said, "What ten eyes are beholding and what ten hands are pointing to—isn't it frightening?" Just as wealth beautifies a house, so character beautifies the body. A big-hearted man also has

* In Cheng's text, the very last line stands at the end of Section 1, from which place I have transferred it here. This is all the alteration I have made, besides following Chu Hsi's transposing of Section 2 to where it stands at present. I believe the existence of the last line at the end of Section 1 in Cheng's text caused the displacement or shifting of Section 4 and two other quotations to follow immediately Section 1.

big proportions. (Probably a proverb, like "A fat man is good-natured.") Therefore a superior man must make his will sincere.

V. ON SETTING THE HEART RIGHT AND PERSONAL CULTIVATION

What is meant by saying that "the cultivation of the personal life depends on setting one's heart right" is this: When one is upset by anger, then the heart is not in its right place; when one is disturbed by fear, then the heart is not in its right place; when one is blinded by love, then the heart is not in its right place; when one is involved in worries and anxieties, then the heart is not in its right place (or the mind has lost its balance). When the mind isn't there, we look but do not see, listen but do not hear and eat but do not know the flavor of the food. This is what is meant by saying that the cultivation of the personal life depends on setting the heart right.

VI. ON THE RELATIONSHIP BETWEEN PERSONAL AND FAMILY LIFE

What is meant by saying that "the regulation of the home life depends on the cultivation of one's personal life" is this: People usually lose their sense of judgment toward those whom they love, toward those whom they despise or dislike, toward those whom they fear, toward those whom they pity and toward those whom they pamper or are proud of. Therefore, there are few people in this world who can see the bad in those whom they like and see the good in those whom they dislike. Hence the saying that "People do not know their own children's faults, as they do not know the imperceptible growth of the rice plants in their fields." That is why it is said that those who do not cultivate their personal life cannot regulate their home life.

VII. ON THE RELATIONSHIP BETWEEN FAMILY AND NATIONAL LIFE

What is meant by the saying that "those who would order their national life must set about ordering their home life" is this: There is no one who fails in teaching the members of his own family and yet is capable of teaching others outside the family. Therefore the superior man spreads his culture to the entire nation by merely remaining at home. The teaching of filial piety is a preparation for serving the ruler of the state; the teaching of respect to one's elder brothers is a preparation for serving all the elders of the country; and the teaching of kindness in parents is a training for ruling over the people. In the *Announcement to K'ang,* it is said, "Act as if you were watching over an infant." No girl ever needs to learn about nursing a baby before she marries. If your instinct is correct (or sound or normal), you will not be far from the highest ideal, although you may not exactly achieve it. When the individual families have learned kindness, then the whole nation has learned kindness. When the individual families have learned courtesy, then the whole nation has learned courtesy.

When one man is greedy or avaricious, then the whole country is plunged into disorder. Such is the law of things. That is why it is said that "A single word may spoil an affair, and a single man can set the country in order." The Emperors Yao and Shun set an example of kindness to the world and the people followed them. The Emperors Chieh and Chou set an example of cruelty to the world, and the people also followed them. The people did not follow what they commanded, if their command was contradicted by what they themselves did. Therefore, the superior man searches himself first before he demands it of others, and makes sure first that he himself is not a transgressor before he forbids transgressions to others. There is never a man who does not apply the principle of reciprocity (or the Golden Rule) in laying the foundation for his own personal conduct, and yet is able to influence others to his way of thinking. Therefore, the ordering of the national life depends on the regulation of one's home life.

The *Book of Songs* says, "Look at that peach tree, so fresh and pretty! How green and thick are its leaves! The girl (a princess) is going to her husband's house, and she will live in harmony with the people of her husband's home." By living in harmony with the people in one's home, one is qualified then to be an example to the people of the nation. Again the *Book of Songs* says, "They (the rulers) live in harmony with their elder brothers and their younger brothers." By living in harmony with their elder and younger brothers, they are then qualified to serve as examples to the people of the nation. The *Book of Songs* also says, "The deportment of the prince is all correct, and he set a country in order." Because he himself served as a worthy example as a father, son, an elder brother and a younger brother, therefore the people took him for their model. That is why it is said the "Ordering of the national life depends upon regulating one's home life."

VIII. ON THE RELATIONSHIP BETWEEN NATIONAL LIFE AND WORLD PEACE

What is meant by saying that "the restoration of peace in the world depends on ordering the national life" is this: When those in authority are respectful toward the old people, then the common people learn to be good sons. When those in authority show respect to their superiors, then the common people learn respect and humility. When those in authority show kindness to the young and helpless, then the common people do not follow the opposite course. Therefore the superior man (or prince) has a principle with which, as with a measuring square, he may regulate his conduct.

What a man dislikes in his superiors, let him not display in his own dealings with his inferiors; what he dislikes in his inferiors, let him not display in his service to his superiors; what he dislikes in those in front of him, let him not display toward those behind; what he dislikes in those following behind, let him not display toward those in front; what he dislikes in those on his right, let him not display toward those on his left; and what he dislikes in those on his left, let him not display in those on his right. This is the principle of the measuring square (or footrule).

The *Book of Songs* says, "How the people are pleased with their ruler, who is like a parent to the people." The ruler loves what the common people love and hates what the common people hate. That is how to be a parent to the common people.

Again the *Book of Songs* says, "Oh, the magnificent Southern Mountains! How majestic are the rocks! How magnificent is the Grand Tutor Yin! The people look up to him." Thus those in a position of authority should never be careless; once they go wrong, the whole world will denounce them.

Again the *Book of Songs* says, "Before the sovereigns of the Shang Dynasty had lost the following of their people, they could appear before God in sacrifice. Take warning from the House of Shang. It is not easy to keep the Mandate of Heaven." This shows that those who have the people with them can keep their rule over a country, and those who have forfeited the following of their people thereby forfeit their rule over the country.

On this account, the superior man (or prince or ruler) will first be watchful over his own character. If he has character, then he has the people with him; if he has the people with him, then he has authority over a territory; if he has authority over a territory, then he has wealth; and having wealth, he then can get things done. Thus character is the foundation, while wealth is the result. If the ruler neglects the foundation and attends to the outward results, he will lead the people in mutual robbery or competition for profit. Therefore, when a ruler gains his personal wealth, he loses his people; and when he loses his personal wealth, he gains the following of his people. Therefore if a man is cunning or deceitful in his speech, he is answered by cunning or deceitful speech, and if his wealth comes in by crooked methods, it flows out again by crooked methods.

The *Announcement to K'ang* says, "The Mandate of Heaven is not fixed and unchangeable. The good rulers get it and the bad rulers forfeit it." The *History of Ch'u* says, "The state of Ch'u has no treasures; doing good is our only treasure." Tsefan (maternal uncle to a prince of Chin in exile) said, "Our exiled prince has no treasure; association with the kind people is his only treasure."

The *Oath of Duke Mu of Ch'in* (to his subjects) says, "Let me but have one minister, plain and sincere, not pretending to other abilities, but with a big simple heart, generous and tolerant toward others. When he sees another person has a certain kind of ability, he is pleased as if he had it himself; and when he sees another man who is handsome and wise, he likes him in his heart, as if he said so in so many words, thus showing that he can really tolerate them. Well may such a person be an asset to the nation, for he shall be able to protect my sons and grandsons and the black-haired people. But if a minister is jealous and hates a person, when he sees the latter has a certain ability, or tries to stand in the way of a handsome and wise man, when he sees one, such a person can really not tolerate others, and he cannot protect my sons and grandsons and the black-haired people. Such a person is a danger to the country." It is only the truly great man who can send away such a minister and banish him, driving him to live among the barbarians and not allowing him to share China with us. It is only the truly great man who knows how to love and how to hate. To see men of worth and not recommend them to office, or to fail to be the first to do so—that is being disrespectful or negligent of one's duty toward his ruler. To see bad men and not be able to remove them from office and to fail to remove them as far away as possible—that is weakness. To love what the people hate and to hate what the people love— that is to act contrary to human nature, and disaster will overtake such a person. Thus we see there is a basic principle for the sovereign: Through sincerity and faithfulness, he maintains his rule, and through pride and self-indulgent living he loses it.

There is a basic principle in the accumulation of wealth and it is this: If there are many producers of wealth and few spenders, and if people are quick at earning money and slow at spending it, then wealth will always be sufficient. The true man develops his personality by means of his wealth, and the unworthy man develops wealth at the expense of his personality. There has never been a case of a ruler who loved benevolence, with his subjects failing to love righteousness, and there has never been a case where the people have come to love righteousness and the affairs of the state cannot be accomplished successfully. And there has never been a case where in such a state the wealth collected in the national treasury did not continue in the possession of the ruler.

Baron Hsien Meng said, "The scholars who have just become officials and begun to keep a horse and carriage do not look after poultry and pigs. The higher officials who use ice in their sacrifices do not keep cattle and sheep. And the nobles who can keep a hundred carriages do not keep rapacious tax-gatherers under them. It would be better to keep a minister who robbed them of their own treasury, than to keep such rapacious tax-gatherers. That is what is meant by saying that "the material prosperity of a nation does not consist in its material prosperity, but in righteousness."

He who is at the head of a government and is bent upon gathering wealth is forced to use petty persons in office. He may want to do good, but the petty officials rule the country and bring disaster to the state, and all his good intentions are to no purpose. That is why it is said that "the material prosperity of a nation does not consist in its material prosperity, but in righteousness."*

* This idea was later fully developed by Mencius.

Chapter V

APHORISMS OF CONFUCIUS

(*The Analects*)

THE *Analects* is generally regarded as the Confucian Bible, being a miscellaneous, unclassified and unedited collection of the remarks of Confucius on various occasions, mostly without any suggestion as to the circumstances in which the remarks were made, and certainly torn from their context. Reading the *Analects* is like reading Bartlett's *Familiar Quotations,* an exciting taste of bits of choice sayings, giving the reader plenty of room for meditation, imagination and wonder as to what the variety of brilliant writers really mean. A comparison with chapters of the *Liki, Mencius,* and other sources shows that the most pithy and epigrammatic sayings have been cut off from longer discourses and preserved because they were so much admired. It is illuminating, for instance, to read in the *Analects* the remark by Confucius that "I have never seen people attracted by virtuous scholars as they are by beautiful women," and then to learn from Szema Ch'ien (see Chapter II) that he made this remark after he had paraded the streets of Wei in a carriage with a beautiful queen, and found the people looked at the queen but did not look at him. The text of the *Analects* itself does not mention the circumstance, and actually puts it in the form of a more abstract remark: "I haven't yet seen people who love virtue as they love beauty." The *Analects* is full of short sentences of four or five words, like the following: "The gentleman is not a vessel (has not only one particular ability)," or "The goody-goodies are the thieves of virtue." In the last instance, we are fortunate to have an amplification of this idea of the "goody-goodies" in the *Book of Mencius*. One cannot believe that Confucius talked in three or four syllables at a time. It is further impossible to believe that the full meaning of Confucius' replies to various questions can be understood without knowing more fully what the questioner asked. As Yuan Mei has pointed out, this was essentially a book of the sayings of Confucius, and therefore the questions of his disciples were cut as short as possible. Thus the only hint we get of the questions is mostly in one word: this man asked about "government," that man asked about "true manhood," and a third man asked about *"li,"* and Confucius came out with the most diverse and contradictory answers to the same questions put by different people. Actually the commentators were sometimes misled into an interpretation that is not justifiable. Thus, once Confucius said to Chung Kung, "Look at that beautiful calf, with such a light brown skin and such pretty little horns! Even if I wanted to spare it, do you think the (spirits of the) mountains and rivers would spare it (for sacrifices to them)?" This is interpreted to mean that Chung Kung had such a beautiful character, fit to become a moral ruler, but Yuan Mei suggests that this was merely a casual remark of Confucius as he and his disciple were looking out of the window and saw a beautiful calf passing by.

What then is the chief charm of the *Analects,* apart from Confucian wisdom contained therein? Its charm centers around the character of Confucius and the different remarks he made upon his contemporaries, the charm of a biography and sayings of Confucius, disorderly, suggestive and done by a few impressionistic strokes. It is essentially like the charm of Boswell's *Johnson,* and of the entire Johnsonian circle, here represented by the circle of Confucius' disciples and friends. It can be opened and read from any page, revealing to us the charm of a wise, terribly rude and withal an affable character. That is the fascination of the *Analects* for the Chinese. For dogmatism has its charm, and one is always impressed by the dogmatic judgments of Confucius and of Dr. Johnson because they both pronounced their judgments with so much force and self-assurance. The entire character of the *Analects* is therefore merely illustrative, and in itself gives us no well-rounded view of the Confucian system of thought, except by some very hard thinking on the part of the reader.

We also get a glimpse through the *Analects* of the Confucian circle. Sometimes we get a suggestion by a mere word that Confucius was "happy" when he was surrounded by two or three of his favorite disciples.

Mixed, of course, with the sayings of Confucius himself are also quite a few sayings by his greater disciples, like Tsengtse, Tsehsia, Yutse, Tsechang, etc., for the various chapters of the *Analects* are certainly of diverse origin, some being recorded by the disciples of the disciples. We have Yen Huei, a quiet, thoughtful person, the oldest of the disciples, whom Confucius admired and praised in superlative terms. On the other hand, we have Tselu, the Confucian St. Peter, who constantly questioned the Master's conduct. This man receives very rough handling in the *Analects,* because he was dead and there were no disciples to defend him at the time the *Analects* were recorded. There were also the garrulous, fluent Tsekung, the very much younger, but philosophic Tsengtse (who later became probably the most important interpreter of Confucius), the more literary-minded Tsehsia, and the practical politician Jan Ch'iu, whom Confucius finally disowned from his circle of disciples. Confucius was, therefore, broad enough to be a teacher of all types of persons, and it is said that each disciple was one "limb" of the "body of the Sage." Later on, the Tsengtse-Tsesze-Mencius tradition developed the idealistic-philosophic side of Confucianism, while the Tsehsia-Hsuntse tradition developed along the line of historic learning and scholarship. Just as St. John developed the idealistic side of Jesus' teachings and added a little of his own, so we see, for instance in the chapter on "Central Harmony," how Tsesze developed the philosophic significance of the Doctrine of the Golden Mean, of Humanism and of "the true self." Briefly, we may compare

Tsesze and Mencius to St. John and Hsuntse to St. James.

The abrupt, jumpy style of the *Analects* requires of course some hard thinking on the part of the reader. It isn't the kind of book that can be read with profit by a lazy reader who expects the author to talk on and on, while he assumes an entirely passive role. The full participation of the reader is necessary and the truths must be apprehended by personal insight; the reader must draw upon his own personal experience. Of course the ancient Chinese school system did not expect young school children to master the philosophic meaning of one of the most mature philosophies of the world. What was expected, however, was mainly a thorough conning over of the text so that the lines would stick forever in their memory, a fountain of wisdom to be drawn upon later on. But then the Confucianists also taught the proper way of reading the *Analects*. These were the methods advised by the Sung scholars. Ch'eng Yich'uan said, "Regard the questions by the disciples in the *Analects* as your own questions, and the answers of Confucius as answers to yourself, then you will get some real benefit." Chu Hsi said, "Read the *Analects* first. Just take one or two sections a day. Never mind whether the passage is difficult or easy to understand, or whether it is a profound passage or not. Just read on from the beginning of the section, and if you don't get the meaning by reading, then use some thinking, and if you don't get the meaning by thinking, then read again. Turn it back and forth and try to get its flavor. Thus after a long while, you will understand what is in it." In his letter to a friend, Chu Hsi said, "In reading be most careful not to read too much. Read a little and it will be easy to thoroughly master it. All real insight from studies is gained in this manner." Again in his *Yulei* or "Sayings," we read, "To understand the language of the text is one thing; to appreciate the beauty of its meaning is another. It is a great common weakness of readers to understand the superficial side without catching what is good in a book." Again, "The proper method of reading is to spend some real thought on it. At first, you will find that this understanding requires a lot of time or energy, but (after you have gained enough general insight and understanding yourself), it will require little time to run through a book. At first, a book requires a hundred per cent energy in reading; afterwards it may require only eighty or ninety per cent, and later on, sixty or seventy per cent, and at last only forty or fifty per cent." To regard reading and thought as two necessary complementary elements in the progress of knowledge is basic in the Confucian system of education, and Confucius himself had something to say about these two elements, as will be seen in the last section of this chapter.

It is amazing that no Chinese scholar has tried to revise or re-edit the *Analects,* in order to give the reader a better conception of the contents, although a few have written essays on the different ideas dealt with in the book (for instance, the *Lunyu T'ungshih* "Studies on the *Analects*" by Ch'iao Hsun, 1763–1820, and the splendid work on the "Meaning of Words in Mencius," *Mengtse*

Tseyi Shuncheng by Tai Chen, 1723–1777). No one, apart from Western scholars, has even compiled a collection of all Confucius' descriptions of "the superior man." This most important conception forms a composite picture of the qualities of this "superior man." In this chapter I have selected probably one-fourth of the contents of the *Analects* and regrouped them according to certain ideas. Unless otherwise indicated, the sayings are all by Confucius and are taken from the *Analects*. Where necessary, however (e.g., for a clearer statement of the humanistic position), I have drawn upon Chapters XXVIII, XXIX, XXX, XXXII and XXXIII of the *Liki* —about a dozen passages, all told. Chapters XXXII and XXXIII, in particular differ not in the slightest as regards contents and style from the *Analects,* and are extremely rich in records of Confucius' sayings.

I. DESCRIPTION OF CONFUCIUS BY HIMSELF AND OTHERS

Duke Yeh (of Ch'u) asked Tselu about Confucius, and Tselu did not make a reply. Confucius said, "Why didn't you tell him that I am a person who forgets to eat when he is enthusiastic about something, forgets all his worries when he is happy, and is not aware that old age is coming on?"

Tselu was stopping for the night at the Stone Gate and the gate-keeper asked him, "Where are you from?" "I'm from Confucius," replied Tselu. "Oh, is he the fellow who knows that a thing can't be done and still wants to do it?"

Weisheng Mou said to Confucius, "Why are you so self-important and constantly rushing about? Don't you talk a little bit too much?" "It isn't that I want to talk. It's because I hate (the present moral chaos)."

Confucius said, "At fifteen I began to be seriously interested in study. At thirty I had formed my character. At forty I had no more perplexities. At fifty I knew the will of heaven. At sixty nothing that I heard disturbed me.* At seventy I could let my thought wander without trespassing the moral law."

Yen Huei and Tselu were sitting together with Confucius, and Confucius said, "Why don't you each tell me your ambitions in life?" Tselu replied, "It is my ambition in life to go about with a horse and carriage and a light fur coat and share them with my good friends until they are all worn out without any regret." Yen Huei said, "It is my ambition never to show off and never to brag about myself." Then Tselu said, "May I hear what is your ambition?" And Confucius replied, "It is my ambition that the old people should be able to live in peace, all friends should be loyal and all young people should love their elders."

There were the famous recluses, Poyi, Shuch'i, Yuchung, Yiyi, Chuchang, Liuhsia Huei and Shaolien. Confucius said, "Not to compromise with their own ideals and not to be disgraced—these were Poyi and Shuch'i." He said of Liuhsia Huei and Shaolien that

* Here is an example of the great responsibility and room for conjecture on the part of a translator of ancient texts. The original text merely consists of two works "Ears accord."

they compromised with their ideals and were disgraced, but that they managed to be able to maintain a standard in their words and their conduct. He said of Yuchung and Yiyi that they escaped from society and were unconventional or untrammeled in their speech, and that they were able to live a clean private life and to adjust themselves according to the principle of expediency in times of chaos. "I am different from these people; I decide according to the circumstances of the time, and act accordingly."*

A great official asked Tsekung, "Is the Master a Sage? Why is it that he is so many-sided?" Tsekung replied, "Heaven has sent him to become a Sage, and he is many-sided, to boot." When Confucius heard this he said, "Perhaps this great official knows me well. I was a poor man's son and can therefore do many things that belong to a common man. Does a superior man have to learn all these things? No, he doesn't." Tsechang said, "Confucius said, 'I did not enter the government, that was how I had time for learning the arts.' "

Confucius said, "There is pleasure in lying pillowed against a bent arm after a meal of simple vegetables with a drink of water. On the other hand, to enjoy wealth and power without coming by it through the right means is to me like so many floating clouds."

* Literally, in five words, "No *may,* no *may not.*" Later Mencius fully commented upon this, saying that Confucius was a great flexible character, acting according to the requirements of the occasion. He could be an official if necessary, and he could refuse to be an official if necessary. In contrast with the other recluses mentioned, there was a positive urge in his character, as well as a philosophic resignation.

Confucius said, "There are three things about the superior man that I have not been able to attain. The true man has no worries; the wise man has no perplexities; and the brave man has no fear." Tsekung said, "But, Master, you are exactly describing yourself."

Confucius said, "In the study of literature, I am probably as good as anyone, but personally to live the life of the superior man, I don't think I have succeeded."

Confucius said, "As to being a sage and a true man, I am not so presumptuous. I will admit, however, that I have unceasingly tried to do my best and to teach other people."

Confucius said, "Do you think I know a great deal? I don't. There was an uneducated man who asked me about something, and I couldn't say a word in reply. I merely discussed the two sides of the question and was at my wit's end."

Confucius said, "In every hamlet of ten families, there are always some people as honest and faithful as myself, but none who is so devoted to study."

Confucius said, "I may perhaps compare myself to my old friend Laop'eng. I merely try to describe (or carry on) the ancient tradition, but not to create something new. I only want to get at the truth and am in love with ancient studies."

Confucius said, "To silently appreciate a truth, to learn continually and to teach other people unceasingly—that is just natural with me."

"The things that trouble or concern me are the following: lest I should neglect to improve my character, lest I should neglect my studies, and lest I should fail to move forward when I see the right course, or fail to correct myself when I see my mistake."

Confucius said, "I'm not born a wise man. I'm merely one in love with ancient studies and work very hard to learn them."

Confucius said, "Ah Sze, do you suppose that I merely learned a great deal and tried to remember it all?" "Yes, isn't that what you do?" "No," said Confucius, "I have a system or a central thread that runs through it all."

Confucius said, "There are some people who do not understand a subject, but go ahead and invent things out of their own head. I am not like those people. One can come to be a wise man by hearing a great deal and following the good, and by seeing a great deal and remembering it."

Confucius said, "Sometimes I have gone the whole day without food and a whole night without sleep, occupied in thinking and unable to arrive at any results. So I decided to study again."

Confucius said, "Whenever walking in a company of three, I can always find my teacher among them (or one who has something to teach me). I select a good person and follow his example, or I see a bad person and correct it in myself."

Confucius said, "I won't teach a man who is not anxious to learn, and will not explain to one who is not trying to make things clear to himself. And if I explain one-fourth and the man doesn't go back and reflect and think out the implications in the remaining three-fourths for himself, I won't bother to teach him again."

Confucius said, "There was never yet a person who came to me with the present of dried meat (equivalent of tuition) that I have refused to teach something."

The young men of a certain village Hu were given to mischief, and one day some young people from that village came to see Confucius, and the disciples were surprised that Confucius saw them. Confucius said, "Don't be too hard on people. What concerns me is how they come, and not what they do when they go away. When a man approaches me with pure intentions, I respect his pure intentions, although I cannot guarantee what he does afterwards."

Confucius was in difficulties at K'uang and he said, "Since King Wen died, is not the tradition of King Wen in my keeping or possession? If it be the will of Heaven that this moral tradition should be lost, posterity shall never again share in the knowledge of this tradition. But if it be the will of Heaven that this tradition shall not be lost, what can the people of K'uang do to me?"

Confucius said, "Heaven has endowed me with a moral destiny (or mission). What can Huan T'uei (a military officer who was driving him away) do to me?"*

Confucius said, "Give me a few more years to finish the study of the *Book of Changes,* then I hope I shall be able to be free from making serious mistakes (or errors of judgment)."

* See Chapter II, Section 4, for fuller details.

These were the things Confucius often talked about: Poetry, history, and the performance of ceremonies—all these were what he often talked about.

Confucius seldom talked about profit or destiny or true manhood.*

Confucius did not talk about monsters, physical exploits, unruly conduct and the heavenly spirits.

Confucius taught four things: Literature, personal conduct, being one's true self and honesty in social relationships.

Confucius fished with a fishing rod, but would not use a net. While shooting he would not shoot a bird at rest.†

Confucius denounced or tried to avoid completely four things: arbitrariness of opinion, dogmatism, narrow-mindedness and egotism.

Confucius was gentle but dignified, austere yet not harsh, polite and completely at ease.

Yen Huei heaved a sigh and said, "You look up to it and it seems so high. You try to drill through it and it seems so hard. You see to see it in front of you, and all of a sudden it appears behind you. The Master is very good at gently leading a man along and teaching him. He taught me to broaden myself by the reading of literature and then to control myself by the observance of proper

* There is no other topic which Confucius and his disciples more constantly talked about than "true manhood." See below Section 6. This is therefore a palpable falsehood, unless it means that Confucius refused to admit that many persons whom his disciples admired could be called "true men."
† Both being unfair.

conduct. I just felt being carried along, but after I have done my very best, or developed what was in me, there still remains something austerely standing apart, uncatchable. Do what I could to reach his position, I can't find the way."

Shusun Wushu said to the officials at court, "Tsekung is a better man than Confucius." Tsefu Chingpo told this to Tsekung, and Tsekung said, "It is like the matter of housewalls. My housewall comes up only to the shoulder, and the people outside are therefore able to see my beautiful house, whereas the wall of Confucius is twenty or thirty feet high, and unless you go right inside, you do not see the beauty of its halls and the grandeur of its furniture. But there are very few people who can penetrate inside that household. What Shusun says is therefore perfectly easy to understand."

Again Shusun Wushu tried to belittle the greatness of Confucius, and Tsekung said, "There is no use trying. Confucius cannot be belittled. Other great men are like mounds or hillocks which you can climb up, but Confucius is like the moon and the sun, which you can never reach. A man can shut his eyes to the sun and the moon, but what harm can it do to the sun and the moon? You are just trying to do the impossible."

II. THE EMOTIONAL AND ARTISTIC LIFE OF CONFUCIUS

When Yen Huei died, Confucius wept bitterly and his followers said, "You are all shaken up." Confucius said, "Am I all shaken up? But if I don't feel all shaken up at the death of this person, for whom else shall I ever feel shaken up?"

Confucius never ate his fill in the company of people in mourning. If he wept on that day, then he did not sing.

What Confucius took very serious were: The ceremonial bath before religious worship, war, and sickness.

Someone asked Confucius about the meaning of the Grand Sacrifice to the Imperial Ancestors, and Confucius said, "I don't know. One who knows the meaning of the Grand Sacrifice would be able to rule the world as easily as pointing a finger at the palm."

When Confucius offered sacrifice to his ancestors, he felt as if his ancestors were present bodily, and when he offered sacrifice to the other gods, he felt as if the gods were present bodily. Confucius said, "If I don't offer sacrifice by being personally present, it is as if I didn't sacrifice at all."

Wangsun Chia asked, "Why do people say that it is better to get on good terms with the kitchen god than with the god of the southwestern corner of the house?" Confucius replied, "Nonsense, if you have committed sins against Heaven, you haven't got a god to pray to."*

Tsekung wanted to do away with the ceremony of sacrificing the lamb in winter. Confucius said, "Ah Sze, you love the lamb, but I love the ritual."

Confucius said, "Respect the heavenly and earthly spirits and keep them at a distance."

* These gods in modern China are supposed to intercede for human beings before Heaven.

Confucius said, "My, how old I have grown! For a long time I have not dreamed of Duke Chou again."*

Confucius heard the music of Hsiao in Ch'i, and for three months he forgot the taste of meat, saying, "I never thought that music could be so beautiful." When Confucius was singing with some other men and liked the song, he always asked for an *encore* and then would join in the chorus.

Confucius said, "Wake yourself up with poetry, establish your character in *li* and complete your education in music."

Confucius said, "Since my return to Lu from Wei, I have been able to classify the different kinds of music, and the *ya* and the *sung* are restored to their proper place."

Yen Huei asked about running a government. Confucius replied, "Use the calendar of Hsia Dynasty (the Hsia year begins with "January," or about February in the solar calendar, while the Chou year begins with "November"), adopt the (heavy and strong and comparatively unadorned wooden) carriages of the Shang Dynasty, and use the imperial crown of the Chou Dynasty. For music, adopt the dance of *Hsiao*. Suppress the music of Cheng and keep away the petty flatterers. The music of Cheng is lascivious, and the petty flatterers are dangerous."

(Tselu was playing the *seh,* and) Confucius said,

* Duke Chou was the symbol of the moral ruler and founder of the governmental system of the Chou Dynasty which Confucius was trying to restore.

"How dare Ah Yu play such atrocious music in my house!" The disciples then began to look down upon Tselu and Confucius said, "Ah Yu has entered the hall, but he has not entered the inner room.*

Confucius would not use navy blue or scarlet for the binding and collar of his dress. He would not have red or purple pajamas. In summer he would wear underclothes beneath the thin (transparent) coarse or fine linen gown. He would match a lamb coat with a black material; match a coat of white fawn with white material, and match a fox coat with brown (or yellow) material. He always wore a nightgown longer than his body by half. At home he used to wear a long-haired fox coat. Except during mourning, he wore all sorts of pendants (on his girdle).

For him rice could never be white enough and mince meat could never be chopped fine enough. When the food was mushy or the flavor had deteriorated, or when the fish had become bad or the meat was tainted, he would not eat. When its color had changed, he would not eat. When the smell was bad, he would not eat. When it was not cooked right, he would not eat. When food was not in season, he would not eat. When the meat was not cut properly, he would not eat. When a food was not served with its proper sauce, he would not

* The orthodox interpretation is that Tselu had made some progress in learning the teachings of Confucius, but had not mastered them yet. I am inclined to think that Confucius meant that Tselu was playing only in the outside hall and not in the inner chamber, and that therefor it was not so unforgivable after all.

eat. Although there was a lot of meat on the table, he would not take it out of proportion with his rice; as for wine, he drank without any set limit, except not to get drunk. Wine or shredded meat bought from the shops he would not eat. A meal without ginger on the table, he would not eat. He did not overeat.

During thunderstorms, his face always changed color.

III. THE CONVERSATIONAL STYLE

Tselu, Tseng Hsi, Jan Ch'iu and Kunghsi Hua were sitting together one day and Confucius said, "Do not think that I am a little bit older than you and therefore am assuming airs. You often say among yourselves that people don't know you. Suppose someone should know you, I should like to know how you would appear to that person." Tselu immediately replied, "I like to rule over a country with a thousand carriages, situated between two powerful neighbors, involved in war and suffering from famine. I like to take charge of such a country and in three years, the nation will become strong and orderly." Confucius smiled at this remark and said, "How about you, Ah Ch'iu?" Jan Ch'iu replied, "Let me have a country sixty or seventy *li* square or perhaps only fifty or sixty *li* square. Put it in my charge, and in three years, the people will have enough to eat, but as for teaching them moral order and music, I shall leave it to the superior man." (Turning to Kunghsi Hua) Confucius said, "How about you, Ah Ch'ih?" Kunghsi Hua replied, "Not that I say I can do it, but I'm willing to learn this. At the ceremonies of religious worship and at the conference of the princes, I should like to wear the ceremonial cap and gown and be a minor official assisting at the ceremony." "How about you, Ah Tien?" The latter (Tseng Hsi) was just playing on the *seh,* and with a bang he left the instrument and arose to speak. "You know my ambition is different from theirs." "It doesn't matter," said Confucius, "we are just trying to find out what each would like to do." Then he replied, "In late spring, when the new spring dress is made, I would like to go with five or six grown-ups and six or seven children to bathe in the River Ch'i, and after the bath go to enjoy the breeze in the Wuyi woods, and then sing on our way home." Confucius heaved a deep sigh and said, "You are the man after my own heart."

Confucius said, "Do you think that I have hidden anything from the two or three of you? No, I have hidden nothing from you. There is nothing that I do that I don't share with the two or three of you. That is I."

Confucius went to the city of Wu (where his disciple Tseyu had been made the magistrate), and heard the people singing to the accompaniment of string instruments. Confucius grinned and said to Tseyu, "You are trying to kill a chicken with a big cleaver for killing a cow." "But I heard from you," replied Tseyu, "that when the superior man had learned culture, he became kind to people, and when the common people learned culture, they would become well-disciplined." Confucius (turned to the other disciples and) said, "You fellows, what he says is right. I was only pulling his leg."

Some people of Tahsiang said, "Great indeed is Confucius! He knows about everything and is an expert at nothing." When Confucius heard this, he said, "Now what am I going to specialize in? Shall I specialize in archery, or in driving a carriage?"

The Secretary of Justice of Ch'en asked Confucius if Duke Chao of Lu understood propriety (or *li*) and Confucius replied that he did. After Confucius had left, the Secretary asked Wuma Ch'i to come in and said to him, "Is a superior man partial to his own country? I heard that a superior man should not be partial. Duke Chao married a princess of Wu, who was of the same family name, and called her Mengtse of Wu. Now if that man understands propriety, who doesn't?" Later on Wuma Ch'i told this to Confucius, and Confucius said, "How lucky I am! Whenever I make a mistake, people are sure to discover it."

Tsekung said, "Here is a beautiful piece of jade, kept in a casket and waiting for a good price for sale." Confucius remarked, "For sale! For sale! I'm the one waiting for a good price for sale!"

Someone asked about Tsech'an (a good minister of Cheng) and Confucius said, "He is a kind man." The man then asked about Prince Tsehsi (of Ch'u), and Confucius said, "Oh, that fellow! oh, that fellow!"

Confucius asked Kungming Chia about Kungsun Wentse, "Is it true that your Master doesn't talk, doesn't smile and doesn't take goods from the people?" Kung-ming Chia replied, "That is an exaggerated story. My Master talks only when he should talk and people are not bored with his talk. He smiles only when he is happy, and people are not bored with his smiles. And he takes goods from the people only when it is right to do so, and people do not mind his taking their goods." Confucius said, "Really! Is that so?"

Tsekung loved to criticize people, and Confucius said, "Ah Sze, you're clever, aren't you? I have no time for such things."

Confucius said, "I greatly admire a fellow who goes about the whole day with a well-fed stomach and a vacuous mind. How can one ever do it? I would rather that he play chess, which would seem to me to be better.

"I have seen people who gather together the whole day and never talk of anything serious among themselves, and who love to play little tricks on people. Marvellous, how can they ever do it!"

Confucius said, "I am going to remain quiet!" Tsekung remarked, "If you remain quiet, how can we ever learn anything to teach to the others?" And Confucius said, "Does Heaven talk? The four seasons go their way in succession and the different things are produced. Does Heaven talk?"

Confucius said. "I have sometimes talked with Huei for a whole day, and he just sits still there like a fool. But then he goes into his own room and thinks about what I have said and is able to think out some ideas of his own. He is not a fool."

IV. THE JOHNSONIAN TOUCH

Confucius said, "By looking at a man's faults, you know the man's character."*

Tsekung asked Confucius, "What kind of a person do you think can be properly called a scholar?" Confucius replied, "A person who shows a sense of honor in his personal conduct and who can be relied upon to carry out a diplomatic mission in a foreign country with competence and dignity can be properly called a scholar." "What kind of a person would come next?" "One who is known to be a good son in his family and has a reputation for humility and respect in a village." "What kind of a person would come next after that?" "A person who is extremely careful of his conduct and speech and always keeps his word. That is a priggish, inferior type of person, but still he can rank below the above two types." "What do you think of the officials today?" "Oh!" said Confucius, "those rice-bags! They don't count at all."

---

* *Liki,* Chapter XXXII, gives a fuller quotation, as follows: "Confucius said, 'There are three kinds of true manhood. There are some who show the same behavior as the true man but proceed from different motives. So those who show the same behavior as the true man are not necessarily true men. Some have the same faults as the true men, and these you can be sure are the true men. The true men are happy and natural in their true manhood; the wise men choose the behavior of true manhood because it pays; and those who are afraid to get in jail take the course of true manhood much against their will. . . .'" This is also an example of the way in which certain excellent sayings of Confucius are incorporated in the *Analects* without their contexts. The above saying itself, so much like Sainte-Beuve's, seems to point the way to a truer conception of Confucius' character by examining Confucius' foibles.

Confucius was once seriously ill, and Tselu asked his disciples to serve as stewards (for his funeral to emulate the style of official families). When Confucius got a little better, he remarked, "The scoundrel! He has gone on preparing to do these things behind my back. I have no stewards in my house and he wants to pretend that I have stewards. Whom can I deceive? Can I deceive God?"

Confucius saw Queen Nancia and Tselu was displeased. Confucius swore an oath, "If I had said or done anything wrong during the interview, may Heaven strike me! May Heaven strike me!"

Tsai Yu slept in the daytime and Confucius remarked "There is no use trying to carve on a piece of rotten wood, or to whitewash a wall made of earth from a dunghill. Why should I bother to scole him?" Confucius said. "At first when I heard a man talk, I expected his conduct to come up to what he said. But now when I hear a man talk, I reserve my judgment until I see how he acts. I have learned this lesson from Tsai Yu."

(*Confucius hates a bad pun.*) Duke Ai asked about the customs of the worship of the Earth, and Tsai Yu replied, "The Hsias planted pine trees on the altar, the Shangs used cypresses, and the Chous used chestnuts, in order to make the people nuts." (Literally "give the people the creeps," a pun on the Chinese word *li.*) When Confucius heard this, he said, "Oh, better forget your history! Let what has come, come! Don't try to remedy the past!"

Ju Pei wanted to see Confucius and Confucius declined by saying that he was sick. When the man was just outside the door, Confucius took a string instrument, the *seh,* and sang, in order to let him hear it (and know that he was not sick after all).

Yang Ho wanted to see Confucius, and Confucius would not see him. Yang then presented Confucius with a leg of pork, and Confucius took care to find out when he would not be at home and then went to pay his return call, but met him on the way.* Yang Ho said to Confucius, "Come, I want to talk to you!" And he said, "Can you call a man kind who possesses the knowledge to put the country in order, but allows it to go to the dogs? "Of course not," said Confucius. "Can you call a man wise who loves to get into power, and yet lets an opportunity pass by when it comes?" "Of course not," said Confucius. "But the time is passing swiftly by," said Yang Ho. Confucius replied (sarcastically), "Yes, sir, I'm going to be an official." (Yang Ho was a powerful but corrupt official in Lu, and Confucius refused to serve under him.)

Baron Ch'eng Ch'en assassinated Duke Chien (in Ch'i), and Confucius took a ceremonial bath and went to see the Duke of Lu and said, "Ch'en Heng has assassinated the Duke, his superior. We must send a punitive expedition." "You speak to the three Barons (of Lu)." Confucius replied, "You know in my capacity as an official, I have to inform you formally of this matter." "You speak to the three Barons," said the Duke again. Confucius then went to speak to the three Barons who disap-

* This story is repeated in the *Book of Mencius.*

proved, and Confucius said to them, "You know in the capacity of an official I have to inform you formally of this matter."

Yuan Jan (who was reputed to sing at his mother's death) squatted in Confucius' presence and Confucius said, "As a child, you were impudent; after you are grown up, you have absolutely done nothing; and now in your old age you refuse to die! You're a thief!" And Confucius struck him in the shin with a cane.

Baron K'ang Chi was worried about thieves and burglars in the country and consulted Confucius about it. Confucius replied, "If you yourself don't love money you can give it to the thieves and they won't take it."

Baron K'ang Chi was richer than Duke Chou and Jan Ch'iu (Confucius' disciple who was his secretary) continued to tax the people in order to enrich the Baron. Confucius said (to his disciples), "He is not my disciple. You fellows may strike the drum and denounce him. You have my permission."

Baron K'ang Chi was going to attack Ch'uanyu and Jan Ch'iu and Tselu came to see Confucius and said, "The Baron is going to send an expedition against Ch'uanyu." Confucius said, "Ah Ch'iu, isn't this your fault? The town of Ch'uanyu was originally designated by the ancient emperors as a fief to maintain the worship of the Tungmeng Hill, and besides it is situated within the boundaries of Lu, and the ruler was directly appointed by the founder of the Dynasty. How can you ever think of sending an expedition to take it over (to enlarge the territory of the Baron)?" "The Baron wants it. We don't," replied Jan Ch'iu. "Ah Ch'iu," said Confucius, "the ancient historian Chou Jen said, 'Do your best according to your official capacity, and if you can't stop it, then you quit.' If a person is approaching danger and you do not assist him, or if a person is falling down and you do not support him, then what is the use of being an assistant or guide? What you have just said is wrong. When a tiger or a buffalo escapes from the fenced enclosure or when a piece of sacred jade is found broken in its casket, whose fault is it (but that of the keeper)?" "But this Ch'uanyu lies right next to Pi (city of the Baron)," said Jan Ch'iu, "and if we don't take it now, it will remain a constant threat to our defense in the future." Confucius replied, "Ah Ch'iu, a gentleman hates the person who is embarked upon a course for selfish gains and then tries to create all sorts of pretexts. I have heard that a man in charge of a state or a family doesn't worry about there being too few people in it, but about the unequal distribution of wealth, nor does he worry about poverty, but about general dissatisfaction. For when wealth is equally distributed, there is no poverty; when the people are united, you cannot call it a small nation, and when there is no dissatisfaction (or when people have a sense of security), the country is secure. Accordingly, if people in the neighboring cities do not pay homage to you, you attend to the civil development in your own country to attract them, and when they come, you make it so that they would like to settle down and live in peace. Now you two as secretaries assisting your chief, have not been able to induce people in the neighboring cities to pay homage and come to you. You see the country of Lu divided against itself without being able to do anything about it, and then you set about thinking of starting wars right inside the country. I'm afraid that what the Baron will have to worry about will not be the city of Ch'uanyu, but right within your own household."

V. WIT AND WISDOM

Confucius said, "To know what you know and know what you don't know is the characteristic of one who knows."

Confucius said, "A man who does not say to himself, 'What to do? What to do?'—indeed I do not know what to do with such a person!"

Confucius said, "A man who has committed a mistake and doesn't correct it is committing another mistake."

Confucius said, "A melon-cup that no longer resembles a melon-cup and people still say, 'A melon-cup! A melon-cup!'"

Confucius said: "It is said, 'It is difficult to be a king, but it is not easy to be a minister, either.'"

Baron Wen Chi said that he always thought three times before he acted. When Confucius heard this, he remarked, "To think twice is quite enough."

Confucius said, "I do not expect to find a saint today. But if I can find a gentleman, I shall be quite satisfied."

Confucius said, "A man who has a beautiful soul always has some beautiful things to say, but a man who says beautiful things does not necessarily have a beautiful soul. A true man (or truly great man) will always be found to have courage, but a courageous man will not always be found to have true manhood."

Confucius said, "A man who brags without shame will find great difficulty in living up to his bragging."

Confucius said, "The man who loves truth (or learning) is better than the man who knows it, and the man who finds happiness in it is better than the man who loves it."*

Confucius said, "In speaking to a sovereign, one must look out for three things: To talk before you are asked is called 'impulsiveness.' To fail to talk when you are asked is called 'lack of candor.' And to talk without noticing the sovereign's mood is called 'blindness.' "

Confucius said, "When you find a person worthy to talk to and fail to talk to him, you have lost your man. When you find a man unworthy to talk to and you talk to him, you have lost (i.e., wasted) your words. A wise man neither loses his man, nor loses his words."

Confucius said, "A gentleman does not praise a man (or put him in office) on the basis of what he says, nor does he deny the truth of what one says because he dislikes the person who says it (if it is good)."

Tsekung asked Confucius, "What would you say if all the people of the village like a person?" "That is not enough," replied Confucius. "What would you say if all the people of the village dislike a person?" "That is not

* There is no indication in the text as to whether the reference is to loving truth or loving learning. It uses only the word "it."

enough," said Confucius. "It is better when the good people of the village like him, and the bad people of the village dislike him." (When you are disliked by the bad persons, you are a good person.)

Confucius said, "The common man often gets in trouble because of his love for the water (literally "gets drowned" in it); the gentleman often gets into trouble because of his love for talking; and the great man often gets into trouble because of his love for the people. All of them get submerged in what they come close to or are familiar with. Water seems so familiar to the people, but easily drowns them because it is a thing that seems so easy to approach and yet is dangerous to get too near to. Talking easily leads one into trouble because when you talk, you use so many words, and it is easy to let them out of your mouth, but difficult to take them back. The people often get one into trouble because they are mean and not open-minded; you can respect them, but you must not insult or offend them. Therefore the gentleman must be very careful."

Confucius said, "The people who live extravagantly are apt to be snobbish (or conceited), and the people who live simply are apt to be vulgar. I prefer the vulgar people to the snobs."

Confucius said, "It is easy to be rich and not haughty; it is difficult to be poor and not grumble."

Confucius said, "When a country is in order, it is a shame to be a poor and common man. When a country is in chaos, it is a shame to be rich and an official."

Confucius said, "Can you ever imagine a petty soul serving as a minister of the state? Before he gets his post, he is anxious to get it, and after he has got it, he is anxious about losing it, and if he begins to be anxious about losing it, then there is nothing that he will not do."

Confucius said, "Do not worry about people not knowing your ability, but worry that you have not got it."

Confucius said, "A gentleman blames himself, while a common man blames others."

Confucius said, "If a man would be severe toward himself and generous toward others, he would never arouse resentment."

Confucius said, "A man who does not think and plan long ahead will find trouble right by his door."

Confucius said, "Polished speech often confuses our notion of who is good and who is bad. A man who cannot put up with small losses or disadvantages will often spoil a big plan."

Confucius said, "In talking about a thoroughbred, you do not admire his strength, but admire his temper."

Someone said, "What do you think of repaying evil with kindness?" Confucius replied, "Then what are you going to repay kindness with?" "Repay kindness with kindness, but repay evil with justice (or severity)."

Confucius said, "When you repay kindness with kindness, then the people are encouraged to do good. When you repay evil with evil, then people are warned from doing bad."

Confucius said. "To repay evil with kindness is the sign of a generous character. To repay kindness with evil is the sign of a criminal." (*Liki,* Chapter XXXII.)

Confucius said, "Men are born pretty much alike, but through their habits they gradually grow further and further apart from each other."

Confucius said, "Only the highest and the lowest characters don't change."

Confucius said, "I have seen rice plants that sprout, but don't blossom, and I have seen rice plants that blossom, but don't bear grains."

Confucius said, "Even though a man had the beautiful talent of Duke Chou, but if he were proud and egoistic, he would not be worth looking at."

Confucius said, "If the superior man is not deliberate in his appearance (or conduct), then he is not dignified. Learning prevents one from being narrow-minded. Try to be loyal and faithful as your main principle. Have no friends who are not as good as yourself. When you have mistakes, don't be afraid to correct them."

Confucius said, "When you see a good man, try to emulate his example, and when you see a bad man, search yourself for his faults."

Confucius said, "Well, well! I have never yet seen a person who knows his own faults and accuses himself before himself!"

Confucius said, "Don't criticize other people's faults, criticize your own."

Tsekung said, "What do you think of a person who is not snobbish (or subservient to the great) when he is poor, and not conceited when he is rich?" Confucius replied, "That's fairly good. It would be better if he were happy when he was poor, and had self-discipline when he was rich."

Confucius said, "You can kill the general of an army, but you cannot kill the ambition in a common man."

VI. HUMANISM AND TRUE MANHOOD

Humanism:

Confucius said, "It is man that makes truth great, and not truth that makes man great."

Confucius said, "Truth may not depart from human nature. If what is regarded as truth departs from human nature, it may not be regarded as truth."

Tselu asked about the worship of the celestial and earthly spirits. Confucius said, "We don't know yet how to serve men, how can we know about serving the spirits?" "What about death?" was the next question, and Confucius said, "We don't know yet about life, how can we know about death?"

A certain stable was burned down. On returning from the court, Confucius asked, "Was any man hurt?" And he did not ask about the horses.

*The measure of man is man:**

Confucius said, "To one who loves to live according to the principles of true manhood without external induce-

* Cf. Chapter III, Section 2.

ments and who hates all that is contrary to the principles of true manhood without external threats of punishments, all mankind seems but like one man only. Therefore the superior man discusses all questions of conduct on the basis of himself as the standard, and then set rules for the common people to follow." (*Liki,* Chapter XXXII.)

Confucius said, "True manhood requires a great capacity and the road thereto is difficult to reach. You cannot lift it by your hands and you cannot reach it by walking on foot. He who approaches it to a great degree than others may already be called 'a true man.' Now is it not a difficult thing for a man to try to reach this standard by sheer effort? Therefore, if the gentleman measures men by the standard of the absolute standard of righteousness, then it is difficult to be a real man. But if he measures men by the standard of man, then the better people will have some standard to go by." (*Liki,* Chapter XXXII.)

Confucius said, "To a man who feels down in his heart that he is happy and natural while acting according to the principles of true manhood, all mankind seems like but one man." (What is true of the feelings of one person will serve as the standard of feelings for all people.) (*Liki,* Chapter XXXII.)

Tsekung asked, "If there is a man here who is a benefactor of mankind and can help the masses, would you call him a true man?" "Why, such a person is not only a true man," said Confucius, "he is a Sage. Even the Em-

perors Yao and Hsun would fall short of such a standard. Now a true man, wishing to establish his own
character, also tries to establish the character of others,
and wishing to succeed himself, tries also to help others
to succeed. To know how to make the approach from
one's neighbors (or from the facts of common, everyday
life) is the method or formula for achieving true manhood."

Confucius said, "Is the standard of true manhood so
far away, after all? When I want true manhood, there it
is right by me."

The Golden Rule:

Chung Kung asked about true manhood, and Confucius replied, "When the true man appears abroad, he
feels as if he were receiving distinguished people, and
when ruling over the people, he feels as if he were worshipping God. What he does not want done unto himself, he does not do unto others. And so both in the state
and in the home, people are satisfied."

Tsekung said, "What I do not want others to do unto
me, I do not want to do unto them." Confucius said,
"Ah Sze, you cannot do it."

Confucius said, "Ah Ts'an, there is a central principle
that runs through all my teachings." "Yes," said Tsengtse. When Confucius left, the disciples asked Tsengtse
what he meant, and Tsengtse replied, "It is just the principle of reciprocity (or *shu*)."

Tsekung asked, "Is there one single word that can

serve as a principle of conduct for life?" Confucius replied, "Perhaps the word 'reciprocity' (*shu*) will do. Do not do unto others what you do not want others to do unto you."

True manhood:

Confucius said, "For a long time it has been difficult to see examples of true men. Everybody errs a little on the side of his weakness. Therefore it is easy to point out the shortcomings of the true man." (*Liki,* Chapter XXXII.)

Confucius said, "For a long time it has been difficult to find examples of true men. Only the superior man can reach that state. Therefore the superior man does not try to criticize people for what he himself fails in, and he does not put people to shame for what they fail in. . . ." (*Liki,* Chapter XXXII.)

Confucius said, "To find the central clue to our moral being which unites us to the universal order (or to attain central harmony), that indeed is the highest human attainment. For a long time people have seldom been capable of it."

Yen Huei asked about true manhood, and Confucius said, "True manhood consists in realizing your true self and restoring the moral order or discipline (or *li*). If a man can just for one day realize his true self, and restore complete moral discipline, the world will follow him. To be a true man depends on yourself. What has it got to do with others?"

Confucius said, "Humility is near to moral discipline (or *li*); simplicity of character is near to true manhood; and loyalty is near to sincerity of heart. If a man will carefully cultivate these things in his conduct, he may still err a little, but he won't be far from the standard of true manhood. For with humility or a pious attitude, a man seldom commits errors; with sincerity of heart, a man is generally reliable; and with simplicity of character, he is usually generous. You seldom make a mistake when you start off from these points." (*Liki,* Chapter XXXII.)

Confucius said, "Yen Huei's heart does not leave the condition of true manhood for as long as three months. The others are able to live on that level only for a month or for a few days."

Someone said, "Would you call a man who has succeeded in avoiding aggressiveness, pride, resentment and greed a true man?" Confucius said, "I would say that he is a very rare person, but I do not know whether he can be called a true man."

Tsechang asked Confucius: "Secretary Tsewen (of Ch'u) was three times made a secretary and didn't seem to show particular satisfaction at his appointment, and three times he was relieved of his office and did not seem to show any disappointment. And when he was handing over the affairs of his office to his successors, he explained everything to the latter. Now what would you say about such a person?" Confucius said, "I would call him a sincere, faithful person." "Would you say that he is a true man?" "I do not know," said Confucius. "How should I call him a true man?"*

Someone said that Chung Kung (a disciple of Confucius) was a true man and that he was not a glib talker. Confucius said, "What is the use of being a glib talker? The more you talk to defend yourself, the more the people hate you. I do not know about his being a true man. What is the use of being a glib talker?"

Count Wu Meng asked if Tselu was a true man, and Confucius said, "I do not know." On being asked again, Confucius said, "You can put Yu in charge of a country with a thousand carriages and let him take care of its finance. But I do not know about his being a true man." "How about Ch'iu?" Confucius said, "You can put Ch'iu in charge of a township of a thousand families or make him the steward of a household with a hundred carriages (that is, of a minister), but I do not know about his being a true man." "How about Ch'ih (Kung-hsi Hua)?" Confucius said, "You can let Ch'ih stand at court, dressed in his official gown and girdle and let him entertain the guests, but I do not know about his being a true man."

Further descriptions of the true man:

Confucius said, "One who is not a true man cannot long stand poverty, nor can he stand prosperity for long.

* An actual example like this shows how inadequate it is to translate the Chinese word *jen* as "kindness," "benevolence" or "a kind person," or "a benevolent person."

A true man is happy and natural in living according to the principles of true manhood, but a wise man thinks it is advantageous to do so."

Confucius said, "Only a true man knows how to love people and how to hate people."

Confucius said, "How can the superior man keep up his reputation when he departs from the level of the true man? The superior man never departs from the level of true manhood for the time of a single meal. In his most casual moments, he lives in it, and in the most compromising circumstances, he still lives in it."

Confucius said, "If a man is not a true man, what is the use of rituals? If a man is not a true man, what is the use of music?"

Confucius said, "The wise man has no perplexities, the true man has no sorrow, and the brave man has no fear."

Confucius said, "A true man is very slow to talk." Someone asked, "Can a man who is slow to talk then be called a true man?" Confucius said, "Because it is so difficulty for a man to do what he says, of course he would be very slow to talk."

VII. THE SUPERIOR MAN AND THE INFERIOR MAN

Confucius said, "The superior man understands what is right; the inferior man understands what will sell."

Confucius said, "The superior man loves his soul; the inferior man loves his property. The superior man always remembers how he was punished for his mistakes; the inferior man always remembers what presents he got."

Confucius said, "The superior man is liberal towards others' opinions, but does not completely agree with them; the inferior man completely agrees with others' opinions, but is not liberal toward them."

Confucius said, "The superior man is firm, but does not fight; he mixes easily with others, but does not form cliques."

Confucius said, "The superior man blames himself; the inferior man blames others."

Confucius said, "The superior man is easy to serve, but difficult to please, for he can be pleased by what is right, and he uses men according to their individual abilities. The inferior man is difficult to serve, but easy to please, for you can please him (by catering to his weaknesses) without necessarily being right, and when he comes to using men, he demands perfection."

Confucius said, "You can put a superior man in an important position with large discretionary powers, but you cannot give him a nice little job; you can give an inferior man a nice little job, but you cannot put him in an important position with great discretionary powers."

Confucius said, "The superior man is not one who is good for only one particular kind of position."

Confucius said, "The superior man is broad-minded toward all and not a partisan; the inferior man is a partisan, but not broad-minded toward all."

Confucius and his followers had to go for days without food in Ch'en, and some of his followers felt ill and were confined to bed. Tselu came to see Confucius in low spirits and asked, "Does the superior man also land in difficulties?" Confucius said, "Yes, the superior man also sometimes falls into difficulties, but when an inferior man falls into difficulties, he is likely to do anything."

Confucius said, "The superior man attends to the spritual things and not to his livelihood. You let him cultivate a farm, and he will be starved, but if you let him attend to his studies, he will find riches in it. The superior man does not worry about his poverty, but worries about the spiritual things."

Confucius said, "The superior man is always candid and at ease (with himself or others); the inferior man is always worried about something."

Confucius said, "The superior man develops upwards; the inferior man develops downwards."

Confucius said, "The superior man is dignified, but not proud; the inferior man is proud, but not dignified."

Confucius said, "The superior man keeps to the standard of right, but does not (necessarily) keep his promise."

Szema Niu asked Confucius about being a gentleman, and Confucius replied, "A gentleman has no worry and no fear." "Does having no worry and no fear then constitute a gentleman?" Confucius said, "If he looks within himself and is sure that he has done right, what does he have to fear or worry about?"

Confucius said, "The superior man goes through his

life without any one preconceived course of action or any taboo. He merely decides for the moment what is the right thing to do."

Confucius said, "The superior man doesn't insist on good food and good lodging. He is attentive to his duties and careful in his speech, and he finds a great man and follows him as his guide. Such a person may be called a lover of learning."

Confucius said, "A scholar who intends to follow the truth and is ashamed of his poor dress and poor food is not worth talking to."

Confucius said, "A scholar who is in love with living comforts is not worthy to be called a scholar."

Confucius said, "A man who serves his king and three times finds his advice rejected and still does not leave the country, is hanging on to his post for the sake of the salary. Even though he says that it is not the salary that attracts him, I won't believe him." (*Liki*, Chapter XXXII.)

Confucius said, "A gentleman is ashamed that his words are better than his deeds."

Confucius said, "A gentleman is careful about three things: In his youth, when his blood is strong, he is careful about sex. When he is grown up, and his blood is full, he is careful about getting into a fight (or struggle in general). When he is old and his blood is getting thinner, he is careful about money." (A young man loves women; a middle-aged man loves struggle; and an old man loves money.)

VIII. THE MEAN AS THE IDEAL CHARACTER AND TYPES
OF PERSONS THAT CONFUCIUS HATED

The people of the mean:

Confucius said, "Since I cannot find people who follow the Mean (or Golden Mean) to teach, I suppose I will have to work with those who are brilliant or erratic (*k'uang*) and those who are a little dull but careful (*chuan*). The brilliant but erratic persons are always ready to go forward (or are too active), and the dull but careful persons always hold themselves back (or are not active enough)."

Confucius said, "The goody-goodies are the thieves of virtue.*

* In the Confucian teachings, there are, therefore, four classes of persons, which were clearly recognized and more fully commented upon by Mencius. According to Mencius, the people who followed the Mean are the ideal human material. Secondly, according to Mencius, since this ideal material cannot be obtained, Confucius preferred to work with the brilliant but erratic; this is the class that Mencius described as "being of an idealistic and expansive nature, always saying, 'The ancient people! The ancient people!' and being free and easy in their ways without trying to conceal their fault." As examples of this class, Mencius quoted a few people who violated Confucian canons of conduct. (According to Chuangtse, they were reputed to sing at their friends' funerals.) Mencius then went on to say that "since Confucius could not get brilliant but erratic people, he would be content to work with those who were anxious to be correct, the *chuan,* who came after the *k'uang* as a class." In describing the last or fourth class, the thieves of virtue, Mencius said that Confucius said, "The kind of people whom I don't mind failing to come into my house or visiting me when passing my door, are the *hsiangyuan* (or goody-goodies). The *hsiangyuan* are

Confucius said (when he was wandering in Ch'en and decided to return to his country to devote himself to editing books and teaching), "Let us go home! The scholars of our country are brilliant but erratic, but they are anxious to go forward, and have not lost their original simplicity of character."

Tsekung asked whether Shih (Tsechang) or Shang (Tsehsia) was the better man. Confucius said, "Ah Shih

---

the thieves of virtue." Then in answer to a question about this class of people, Mencius described them as follows: "They say, 'Why be idealistic like those people? When their words do not tally with their conduct and their conduct does not tally with their words, they say, "The ancient people! The ancient people!" Why are they so supercilious toward the world and so cool and detached in their conduct? When a man lives in the present world and acts according to the standard of the present world, and succeeds, it is quite enough!' They are the class of people who are quite contented to secure the approval of society. These are the *hsiangyuan.*" *Hsiangyuan* literally means what the country folk call "good men," or "goody-goodies." The questioner then asked Mencius, "Since all the country folk call them 'good men,' and everywhere they go they are called 'good men' (or 'nice people' or 'respectable people'), why did Confucius call them 'thieves of virtue'?" Mencius then said, "You want to criticize them and they seem so perfect; you want to lampoon them, and they seem so correct; they fall in with the current conventions and thoroughly identify themselves with the ways of the times. In their living, they seem to be so honest and faithful, and in their conduct they seem to be so moral. Everybody likes them and they are quite pleased with themselves. But it is impossible to lead them into the ways of Emperors Yao and Hsun. Therefore Confucius said, 'The goody-goodies (or *hsiangyuan,* or the so-called "respectable people") are the thieves of virtue.'" Directly after this description, Mencius quoted what Confucius had said about the things that resemble the real things but are not the real things, and the types of persons that he hated. See below toward the end of this section.

goes a little too far (or is above the normal) and Ah Shang doesn't go far enough (or is a little below the normal)." "Then is Ah Shih a better person?" Confucius said, "To go a little too far is as bad as not going far enough."*

Confucius said to Tsehsia, "You must be a gentleman-scholar and not a petty scholar."

Confucius said, "When a man has more solid worth than polish, he appears uncouth, and when a man has more polish than solid worth, he appears urbane. The proper combination of solid worth and polish alone makes a gentleman."

Confucius said, "The earlier generations were primitive or uncouth people in the matter of ritual and music; the later generations are refined (literally "gentlemen") in the matter of ritual and music. But if I were to choose between the two, I would follow the people of the earlier generations."†

Types of persons that Confucius hated:

Confucius said, "The ancient people have three kinds of faults, and nowadays we haven't even got them. The

---

* Evidences seem to show that Tsechang was the more brilliant one and more interested in philosophic principles, while Tsehsia, who later became a great teacher specializing in the teaching of the *Book of Songs* after Confucius' death, was the type of a humdrum, conscientious professor.

† A choice between uncouth simplicity and decadent elaborateness and formalism—a very important point, considering the common charge of formalism against Confucianism. This common criticism was certainly justifiable when it was directed against the Confucianists in the centuries after him.

ancient people who were impulsive were just unconventional in their ways, but today the impulsive people indulge themselves. The ancient people who were correct and smug were at least austere and careful in their conduct, but today the smug people are always condemning other people and are bad-tempered. The ancient lower class were simple and honest souls, but today the lower class are a deceitful lot."

Tsekung asked, "Does the superior man also have certain things that he hates?" "Yes, there are things that the superior man hates," said Confucius. "He hates those who like to criticize people or reveal their weaknesses. He hates those who, in the position of inferiors, like to malign or spread rumors about those in authority. He hates those who are chivalrous and headstrong but are not restrained by propriety. He hates those who are sure of themselves and are narrow-minded." "But what do you hate?" asked Sze. "I hate those who like to spy on others and think they are very clever. I hate those who think they are brave when they are merely unruly. And I hate the wily persons who pretend to be honest gentlemen."

Confucius said, "A man who is impulsive and headstrong without having the virtue of simple honesty, who doesn't know a thing and has not enough wit to speak or behave cautiously, or who has no particular ability and withal has not the virtue of honesty or faithfulness—why, there is nothing to be done about such a person."

Confucius said, "I hate things that resemble the real things but are not the real things. I hate cockles because they get mixed up with the corn. I hate the ingratiating fellows, because they get mixed up with the good men. I hate the glib talkers because they confuse us with honest people. I hate the music of Cheng, because it brings confusion into classical music. I hate the purple color, because it confuses us with the red color. I hate the goody-goodies because they confuse us with the virtuous people." (Mencius.)

Confucius said, "A man who appears dignified and austere but is all hollow and weak inside seems to me to be like a little petty burglar who slips into the house through a hole at night."

Confucius said, "Women and the uneducated people are most difficult to deal with. When you are familiar with them, they become cheeky, and when you ignore them, they resent it."

Confucius said, "I hate the garrulous people."

Confucius said, "A glib talker with an ingratiating appearance is seldom a gentleman."

Confucius said, "The gentleman does not judge a person entirely by his words. Therefore in a cultured world, we have flowery conduct, and in an uncultured world, we have flowery speeches." (*Liki*, Chapter XXXII.)

IX. GOVERNMENT

The moral ideal of government:

Confucius said, "Guide the people with governmental measures and control or regulate them by the threat of punishment, and the people will try to keep out of jail, but will have no sense of honor or shame. Guide the people by virtue and control or regulate them by *li*, and the people will have a sense of honor and respect.

Confucius said, "When the kingdom of Ch'i moves a step forward, it will have reached the culture of the kingdom of Lu, and when the kingdom of Lu moves a step forward, it will have reached the stage of true civilization."

Confucius said, "In presiding over lawsuits, I'm as good as any man. The thing is to aim so that there should be no lawsuits."

Someone asked Confucius, "Why don't you go into the government?" Confucius replied, "Doesn't the *Book of History* speak about the good son? When the sovereign is a good son, and a good brother, and applies the same principles to the government of the nation, that is also what we call government. Why should I go into the government?"

Yutse said, "We seldom find a man who is a good son and a good brother that is disrespectful to authority, and we never find a man who is not disrespectful to authority wanting to start a rebellion."

Government by moral example:

Confucius said, "A sovereign who governs a nation by virtue is like the North Polar Star, which remains in its place and the other stars revolve around it."

Baron K'ang Ch'i asked Confucius concerning government, and Confucius replied, "Government is merely setting things right. When you yourself lead them by the right example, who dares to go astray?"

Baron K'ang Ch'i asked Confucius concerning government, saying, "If I kill off the bad citizens, and associate with the good citizens, what do you think?" Confucius replied, "What's the need of killing off people on the part of a ruler of a country? If you desire what is good, the people will become good also. The character of the ruler is like wind, and the character of the common people is like grass, and the grass bends in the direction of the wind."

Confucius said, "When the ruler himself does what is right, he will have influence over the people without giving commands, and when the ruler himself does not do what is right, all his commands will be of no avail."

Confucius said, "If a ruler rectifies his own conduct, government is an easy matter, and if he does not rectify his own conduct, how can he rectify others?"

Factors of government:

Tsekung asked about government, and Confucius replied: "People must have sufficient to eat; there must be a sufficient army; and there must be confidence of the people in the ruler." "If you are forced to give up one of these three objectives, what would you go without first?" asked Tsekung. Confucius said, "I would go without the army first." "And if you were forced to go without one of the two remaining factors, what would you rather go without?" asked Tsekung again. "I would rather go without sufficient food for the people. There have always been deaths in every generation since man lived, but a nation cannot exist without confidence in its ruler."

X. ON EDUCATION, RITUAL AND POETRY

Confucius said, "Education begins with poetry, is strengthened through proper conduct and consummated through music."

Confucius said, "The gentleman broadens himself by scholarship or learning, and then regulates himself by *li* (proper conduct or moral discipline). Then he will not fall away from the proper principles."

Yutse said, "Among the functions of *li,* the most valuable is that it establishes a sense of harmony. This is the most beautiful heritage of the ancient kings. It is a guiding principle for all things, big and small. If things do not go right, and you are bent only on having social harmony (or peace) without regulating the society by the pattern of *li* (or the principle of social order),* still things won't go right."

Confucius said, "We are saying all the time, '*Li! Li!*' Does *li* mean merely a collection of jades and silks (in ceremonial use)? We are saying all the time 'Music! Music!' Does music merely mean playing about with drums and bells?"

Tseshia asked (concerning a passage in the *Book of*

* See Chapters VI, VII, VIII, "Discourses on the Social Order."

Songs), "What is the meaning of the passage, 'She has a winning smile, and her eyes are so clear and bright. Her dress is of a colored design on a plain background'?" Confucius said, "In painting, we must have a plain background." "Does that mean that the ceremonial forms of *li* must be based on a background of simplicity of character?"* Confucius said, "Now you have contributed a fresh thought, Ah Shang! You are worthy to study the *Book of Songs.*"

Lin Fang asked concerning the foundation of *li,* and Confucius replied, "You are asking an important question! In this matter of rituals or ceremony, rather than be extravagant, be simple. In funeral ceremonies, rather than be perfunctory, it is more important to have the real sentiment of sorrow."

Confucius said, "If you have the wisdom to perceive a truth, but have not the manhood to keep to it, you will lose it again, though you have discovered it. If you have the wisdom to perceive a truth, and the true manhood to keep to it, and fail to preserve decorum in your public appearance, you will not gain the people's respect for authority. If you have the wisdom to perceive a truth, the manhood to keep to it, and have decorum of appearance, but fail to be imbued with the spirit of *li* (or social discipline) in your actions or conduct, it is also not satisfactory."

Confucius said, "Ah Sze is worthy to discuss the *Book*

* This is the orthodox interpretation, and probably correct. This sentence consists of merely three words in the original: *"Li*—behind—is-that-so?"

of Songs with me. I tell him something, and he comes up with a fresh suggestion."

Confucius said, "One phrase will characterize all the three hundred poems (actually three hundred and five), and that is: Keep the heart right."

Ch'en K'ang asked Poyu (or Li, the name of Confucius' only son, meaning "a carp"), "Is there anything special that you were taught by your father?" Poyu replied, "No. One day he was standing alone and I ran past the court, and he asked me, 'Have you learned poetry?' And I said, 'Not yet.' He said, 'If you don't study poetry, your language will not be polished.' So I went back and studied poetry. Another day he was standing alone, and I went past the court, and he said to me, 'Have you studied the ceremonies?' And I said, 'Not yet.' And he said, 'If you don't study the ceremonies, you have no guide for your conduct.' And I went back and studied the ceremonies. I was taught to study these two things." Ch'en K'ang came away quite pleased and said, "I asked him one question and learned three things. I learned what Confucius said about poetry. I learned what he said about ceremonies. And I learned that the Master taught his own son in exactly the same way as he taught his disciples (was not partial to his son)."

Confucius said, "Reading without thinking gives one a disorderly mind, and thinking without reading makes one flighty (or unbalanced)."

Confucius said, "Isn't it a great pleasure to learn and relearn again?"

Confucius said, "A man who goes over what he has

already learned and gains some new understanding from it is worthy to be a teacher."

Confucius said, "That type of scholarship which is bent on remembering things in order to answer people's questions does not qualify one to be a teacher."

Confucius said, "The ancient scholars studied for their own sake; today the scholars study for the sake of others (out of obligations to their teachers, their parents, etc.)."

Confucius said, "Ah Yu, have you heard of the six sayings about the six shortcomings?" "No," said Tselu. "Sit down, then, and I will tell you. If a man loves kindness, but doesn't love study, his shortcoming will be ignorance. If a man loves wisdom but does not love study, his shortcoming will be having fanciful or unsound ideas. If a man loves honesty and does not love study, his shortcoming will be a tendency to spoil or upset things. If a man loves simplicity but does not love study, his shortcoming will be sheer following of routine. If a man loves courage and does not love study, his shortcoming will be unruliness or violence. If a man loves decision of character and does not love study, his shortcoming will be self-will or headstrong belief in himself."

Confucius said, "Those who are born wise are the highest type of people; those who become wise through learning come next; those who learn by sheer diligence and industry, but with difficulty, come after that. Those who are slow to learn, but still won't learn, are the lowest type of people."

Confucius said, "The young people should be good

sons at home, polite and respectful in society; they should be careful in their conduct and faithful, love the people, and associate themselves with the kind of people. If after learning all this, they still have energy left, let them read books."

Chapter VI

FIRST DISCOURSE:
ON EDUCATION THROUGH
THE SIX CLASSICS

(Chingchieh, Liki, Chapter XXVI)

THE following three discourses constitute chapters XXVI, XXVII, and IX of *Liki*. There is a stylistic elaboration in these records, and in certain places it is impossible to decide whether the words were those of Confucius or those of the authors of the different chapters. Practically all three discourses deal with the philosophic significance of *li*. As has been partly explained in the introduction, this conception of *li*, which is again and again said in these discourses to be the essence, the *sine qua non,* the foundation, or the indispensable principle, of government, cannot merely mean the observance of ritual, but represents a philosophy of social order and social control. *Li* practically covers the entire social, moral and religious structure of ancient Chinese society, as shown and regulated by forms of religious worship and social intercourse, revealed by history and rationalized by

Confucius. Specifically, its aim was to restore the ancient feudal order, which a clear hierarchy of ranks, but this principle of social order was extended and broadened to cover the essential human relationships in the family and social and political life. It was therefore to establish a complete moral order in the nation by a clear and simple, but sharp, definition of social status and its specific obligations, thus providing the moral basis for political order. This philosophy of harmony of essential human relationships remains good today for modern China—in fact it is the foundation for the Chinese *ethos*—while the ancient feudal order which was Confucius' aim to restore is definitely out of date.

It must be noted, however, that the feudal system, as Confucius conceived it, was of a clearly religious character and was very much occupied with discussions of the philosophic meaning, as well as the actual rules and practices, of public worship. Whole chapters, for instance, in the *Liki* are devoted to the discussion of ceremonial robes, and to a description of sacrificial vessels, and seven or eight chapters cover the funeral rites alone (absent in the "Great Tai" collection). But then the curious aspect of it was, the conception of *li* dealt with the rites of religious worship at one end, and imperceptibly extended to the rites of village dance and hunting and drinking and archery and general social intercourse at the other end. Hence it is easy to see why the conception of *li* embodies at the same time a philosophy of social order and social control and a historical tradition of rites and ceremonies. Confucius himself warned his disciple

Tsechang that *li* did not consist in playing about with sacrificial vessels, just as music did not consist in the mere beating of bells and drums; but that both ritual and music emanated from, and created, a state of mind, a state of God-fearing piety in the performance of ritual and a state of happiness and harmony in the performance of music.

In fact, such was the Confucian preoccupation with the rituals of religious worship—worship of Heaven, of Earth, of Imperial ancestors, of the sun and moon, and mountains and rivers, the kitchen god, the god of the southwestern corner of the house, and all folk festivals— and such was its preoccupation with the religious state of mind that I have often been tempted to translate *li* as merely "religion," which I have not done. Such a translation would make it perfect in passages like the following: "Broaden your knowledge with learning, and then control your conduct with religion," and "Realize your true self and return to religion" (a formula for achieving true manhood given by Confucius). The religious character of *li* cannot be doubted, and the Chinese have actually called Confucianism "the religion of *li*," a current term even today. But the term "religion" must be avoided here, because it suggests a type of religion such as we see in Christianity, which draws a sharp distinction between religious and secular affairs. Such a distinction was not made in ancient China, and certainly not in the laws of Moses, where all laws of social, as well as religious conduct were regarded as of a religious character. Modern men no longer live in that age of theocracy or semitheocracy, and it is difficult for them to realize what the ceremonial selection, killing, and inspection of animals and ceremonial washing of hands before eating their meat had to do with "religion." We delegate the washing of hands before meals strictly to the sphere of "hygiene." But for Moses, hygiene was also religion, for religion was all-inclusive. Such was exactly the position of Confucianism. Were it not so difficult to bear in mind this interpretation of "religion," there would be no objection to simply rendering *li* as the "religion" of Confucianism as Confucius taught it. Psychologically, the religious condition of mind—the Hebrew "fear of God" and the Christian "piety"—was also the aim of the Confucian religion in man's personal life, but again this state of mind, expressed as *ching* and usually translated as "respect," included both the condition of religious piety at worship and the God-fearing attitude in common, everyday life, as seen in respect for social order and moral discipline. I have therefore often translated *ching* by the word "piety," for I have often found the term "respect" wholly inadequate.

Li, the central conception of Confucian teachings, therefore, means the following things: It means religion; it means the general principle of social order, religion included; it means the rationalized feudal order; it means the entire body of social, moral and religious practices, as taught and rationalized by Confucius. Consequently, it also means historical scholarship. It means the study of the ritualism of religious worship, state ceremonies, folk festivals, the marriage ceremony, funerals, "capping" and "coiffure" ceremonies for boys and girls reaching maturity (at the age of twenty for boys and fifteen for girls), army discipline, the educational system, conduct of the sexes and home life, eating and drinking and sports (especially archery, carriage driving, and the hunt), music and dance. It means a system of well-defined social relationships with definite attitudes towards one another, love in the parents, filial piety in the children, respect in the younger brothers, friendliness in the elder brothers, loyalty among friends, respect for authority among subjects and benevolence in the rulers. It means the mental state of piety. It means moral discipline in man's personal conduct. As a broad principle of personal conduct, it means "propriety" in everything, or doing the proper thing. As a broad social principle, it means "the order of things," or "everything in its right place." It means ritualism and the observance of forms. It means continuity with the past. Finally, it means courtesy and good manners.

I have the definite feeling that it was the teaching of *li* and this tremendous body of historic scholarship that was back of Confucius' great prestige in his times. In other words, he knew so many things that the average scholars of his day did not know about—the usual basis for "respect." The public always respect what they don't understand. The more you talk about what most people don't understand, the greater is their respect for you. With his wit and without his scholarship, Confucius would have been at best a Bernard Shaw, or a G. K. Chesterton, instead of a Thomas Aquinas. After all, this body of historic scholarship was to Confucius what "the American language" is to H. L. Mencken—within the scope of their respective personalities.

FIRST DISCOURSE

Confucius said:* When I enter a country, I can easily tell its type of culture. When the people are gentle and kind and simple-hearted, that shows the teaching of poetry. When people are broad-minded and acquainted with the past, that shows the teaching of history. When the people are generous and show a good disposition, that shows the teaching of music. When the people are quiet and thoughtful, and show a sharp power of observation, that shows the teaching of the philosophy of mutations (*Book of Changes*). When the people are humble and respectful and frugal in their habits, that shows the teaching of *li* (the principle of social order). When the people are cultivated in their speech, ready with expressions and analogies, that shows the teaching of prose, or *Spring and Autumn*.† The danger in the teaching of poetry is that people remain ignorant, or too simple-hearted. The danger in the teaching of history is that people may be filled with incorrect legends and stories of events. The danger in the teaching of music is that the people grow extravagant. The danger in the

* Without quotation marks in the original, it is impossible to decide where the exact words of Confucius end. See the appearance of a quotation from Confucius at the end of the third paragraph.

† These constituted the *Six Classics* of Confucius' days.

teaching of philosophy is that the people become crooked. The danger in the teaching of *li* is that the rituals become too elaborate. And the danger in the teaching of *Spring and Autumn,* is that the people get a sense of the prevailing moral chaos. When a man is kind and gentle and simple-hearted, and yet not ignorant, we may be sure he is deep in the study of poetry. When a man is broad-minded and acquainted with the past, and yet not filled with incorrect legends or stories of events, we may be sure he is deep in the study of history. When a man is generous and shows a good disposition and yet not extravagant in his personal habits, we may be sure he is deep in the study of music. When a man is quiet and thoughtful and shows a sharp power of observation, and yet is not crooked, we may be sure that he is deep in the study of philosophy. When a man is humble and polite and frugal in his personal habits and yet not full of elaborate ceremonies, we may be sure he is deep in the study of *li.* And when a man is cultivated in his speech, ready with expressions and analogies and yet is not influenced by the picture of the prevailing moral chaos, we may be sure that he is deep in the study of *Spring and Autumn.**

* The *Spring and Autumn* as we have it today is a chronicle of political events in the centuries preceding Confucius, written by the Sage himself. But the name *Spring and Autumn,* or *Ch'unCh'iu,* was a general name for chronicles of the different countries in Confucius' time. Several such *Ch'unCh'iu* were known to exist. The moral chaos in Confucius' time and the centuries preceding was unbelievable. Kings were murdered by their princes, and princes married their father's concubines, and there was a great variety of incestual relationships; all

The Emperor ranks in his position with the Heaven and the Earth, and therefore his moral function or significance is equal to that of the Heaven and the Earth in presiding over the course of the myriad things for their benefit. He shines with the sun and the moon, and casts his light over the Four Seas, not excluding the smallest objects. At the court, he discusses the ideal of moral manhood and the principles of social order. At home, he listens to the music of *ya* (classical songs) and *sung* (sacred anthems). When he walks on foot, we hear the jingle of jade hangings and when he mounts a carriage, we hear the music of "phoenix bells." His home life is decorous and his deportment is in accordance with good form. Thus through him the officials find their proper functions and the entire course of social life finds its order. The *Book of Songs* says, "The virtuous sovereign is immaculate in his external conduct and appearance, and being immaculate in his external conduct and appearance, he serves as the example for the country." When he gets willing obedience to his commands, he achieves what we call "harmony" in the nation. When the rulers and the ruled are kind and friendly to each other, he achieves what we call "an atmosphere of friendliness." When people are enabled to get what they want,

---

powerful barons or counts or dukes called themselves "kings" and there was a great confusion in the practice of religious worship. A very good picture of this social and moral chaos is given in *Faugcht* (Chapter XXX of *Liki*), where we get a glimpse of the social background that explains Confucius' offering *li*, or restoration of the feudal order, as actually the "panacea" for the social ills of his days.

without having to ask for it, he achieves what we call "confidence" in the nation. And when he removes the causes of unhappiness in his people, he achieves what we call "decent living" in the nation. "General harmony" and "an atmosphere of friendliness" are the means by which the rulers by force (*pa*) and the rulers by virtue (*wang*) rule their countries. With the determined purpose, but without these means, of ruling the country, they will not be able to attain their object.

Li, the principle of social order, is to a country what scales are to weight and what the carpenter's guide-line is to straightness, and what the square and the compasses are to squares and circles. Therefore, when the scales are exact, one cannot be deceived in respect to weight; when the guide-line is properly laid, one cannot be deceived in respect to straightness; when the squares and compasses are properly used, one cannot be deceived in respect to the right angle and the circular line; and when the sovereign is familiar with the principle of social order (*li*), he cannot be deceived by cunning and crooked manipulations. Therefore, a people who respect and follow *li* are called "a people with a definite principle," and a people who do not respect and follow *li* are called "a people without a definite principle."

Li is the principle of mutual respect and courtesy. Therefore when it is applied to worship at the temples, we have piety; when it is applied to the court, we have order in the official ranks; when applied to the home, we have affection between parents and children and harmony between brothers; when applied to the village, we have respect for order between the elders and the juniors. That is the meaning of Confucius' saying that "there is nothing better than *li* for the maintaining of authority and the governing of the people."

Therefore, the rituals concerning a court audience are for the purpose of defining the proper relationships between the rulers and the ministers. The rituals of exchange of visits by diplomats are for the purpose of maintaining mutual respect among the rulers of the different states. The funeral ceremonies and rituals of sacrifice are for the purpose of showing the gratitude of children and subjects. The ceremonies of "the village wine feast" are for the purpose of defining order and discipline between the elders and the juniors. The marriage ceremonies are for the purpose of defining the distinction between the sexes.

Li, or the principle of social order, prevents the rise of moral or social chaos as a dam prevents flood. Just as people who think that they can destroy an old dam because they think it is useless will certainly meet a flood disaster, so will a people who do away with the old principle of social order becasue they think it is useless certainly meet a moral disaster. It follows, therefore, that when marriage ceremonies are taken lightly or disregarded, then marital relationships become difficult and promiscuity will become rampant. When the ceremonies of the "village wine feast" are disregarded, then the sense of order and discipline between elders and juniors is lost, and cases of fights and encroachments will be common. When the funeral and sacrificial rites are disregarded, then the sense of gratitude in children and subjects toward their parents and deceased spirits will decay, and there will be many who turn against the dead in their conduct and indulge themselves. When the ceremonies of diplomatic visits are disregarded, then the relations between fealties and sovereigns will be threatened and the different rulers will become arrogant or licentious, and wars of invasion will arise.

Therefore the cultural work of *li* is imperceptible. It prevents the rise of indulgent conduct beforehand and leads people gradually toward virtue and away from vice without their knowing it. That was why the ancient great kings placed such an importance on *li*. That is the meaning of the passage in the *Book of Changes:* "The sovereign is careful at the inception of things. A difference of a hundredth or a thousandth of an inch at the start results in a divergence of a thousand miles at the end."

Chapter VII

SECOND DISCOURSE:
AN INTERVIEW WITH DUKE AI

(*Aikung Wen, Liki,* Chapter XXVII)

DUKE AI asked Confucius, "What is this great *li?* Why is it that you talk about *li* as though it were such an important thing?"

Confucius replied, "Your humble servant is really not worthy to understand *li.*"

"But you do constantly speak about it," said Duke Ai.

Confucius: "What I have learned is this, that of all the things that the people live by, *li* is the greatest. Without *li,* we do not know how to conduct a proper worship of the spirits of the universe; or how to establish the proper status of the king and the ministers, the ruler and the ruled, and the elders and the juniors; or how to establish the moral relationships between the sexes, between parents and children and between brothers; or how to distinguish the different degrees of relationships in the family. That is why a gentleman holds *li* in such high regard, and proceeds to teach its principles to the people and regulate the forms of their social life. When these are established, then he institutes different insignia and ceremonial robes as symbols of authority to perpetuate the institutions. When everything is in order, then he proceeds to fix the periods of burial and mourning, provide the sacrificial vessels and the proper offerings, and beautify the ancestral temples. Every year sacrifices are made in their proper seasons, in order to bring about social order in the clans and tribes. Then he retires to his private dwelling where he lives in simple contentment, dressed simply and housed simply, without carved carriages and without carved vessels, sharing the same food and the same joys with the people. That was how the ancient princes lived in accordance with *li*."

Duke Ai: "Why don't the princes of today do the same?"

Confucius: "The princes of today are greedy in their search after material goods. They indulge themselves in pleasure and neglect their duties and carry themselves with a proud air. They take all they can from the people and invade the territory of good rulers against the will of the people, and they go out to get what they want without regard for what is right. This is the way of the modern rulers, while that was the way of the ancient rulers whom I just spoke of. The rulers of today do not follow *li*."

Confucius was sitting in the company of Duke Ai, and the Duke asked: "What, in your opinion, is the highest principle of human civilization?" Confucius looked very grave and replied: "It is the good fortune of the people that Your Highness has asked this question. I must do my best to answer it. The highest principle of human civilization is government."

The Duke: "May I ask what is the art of government?"

Confucius: "The art of government simply consists in making things right, or putting things in their right places.* When the ruler himself is "right," then the people naturally follow him in his right course. The people merely follow what the ruler does, for what the ruler himself does not do, wherewithal shall the people know how and what to follow?"

The Duke: "Tell me more in detail about this art of government."

Confucius: "The husband and wife should have different duties. The parents and children should be affectionate toward each other. The king and his subjects should have rigid discipline. When these three things are right, then everything follows."

The Duke: "Can you enlighten me a little more on the

* The Chinese words for "government" and "being right" or "making right" have exactly the same pronunciation. The character for "government" is written with two components, "right" and a causative particle, the whole meaning "to make normal" or "to put things in their right places." This notion of *cheng* or "normalcy" has no adequate equivalent in English. It is implied in the English expressions like "when you have the *right* leadership" or *"right* kind of person," or *"right* course of conduct." Thus it is nearest to the English word "right" in such senses. It is associated also with the notion of "centrality" and "orthodoxy," with *sheh* or "heterodoxy" as its antonym. A man who is said to be *chen* is one "who wants to do what is right," and a man who is said to be *sheh* is one who is always thinking of devious means to obtain dubious ends.

method to carry out these three things, unworthy as I am?"

Confucius: "The ancient rulers regarded loving the people as the chief principle of their government, and *li* as the chief principle by which they ruled the people they loved. In the cultivation of *li,* the sense of respect is the most important, and as the ultimate symbol of this respect, the ceremony of royal marriage is the most important. The ceremony of royal marriage is the ultimate symbol of respect, and as it is the ultimate symbol of respect, the king goes with his crown to welcome the princess from her own home personally because he regards the bride as so close in relationship to him. He goes personally because the relationship is regarded as personal. Therefore the sovereign cultivates the sense of respect and personal relationship. To neglect to show respect is to disregard the personal relationship. Without love, there will be no *personal* relationship, and without respect, there will be no *right* relationship. So love and respect are the foundation of government."

Duke Ai: "I want to say something. Isn't it making the royal marriage a little too serious by requiring a king to wear his crown and welcome the princess from her own home?"

Confucius looked very grave and replied: "Why do you say so? A royal marriage means the union of two ruling houses for the purpose of carrying on the royal lineage and producing offspring to preside over the worship of Heaven and Earth, of the ancestral spirits, and of the gods of land and grains."

Duke Ai: "Excuse me for pressing the question, for if I do not persist, I shall not be able to hear your opinions on this point. I want to ask you something, but do not know how to put it. Will you please proceed further?"

Confucius: "You see, if Heaven and Earth (representing *yin* and *yang*) do not come together, there is no life in this world. A royal marriage is for the purpose of perpetuating the ruling house for thousands of generations. How can one take it too seriously?"

Confucius then said: "In the art of government, *li* comes first. It is the means by which we establish the forms of worship, enabling the ruler to appear before the spirits of Heaven and Earth at sacrifices on the one hand; and on the other, it is the means by which we establish the forms of intercourse at the court and a sense of piety or respect between the ruler and the ruled. It revives or resuscitates the social and political life from a condition of disgraceful confusion. Therefore *li* is the foundation of government."

Confucius then went on to say: "The ancient great kings always showed respect or proper consideration to their wives and children in accordance with a proper principle. How can one be disrespectful (or show disregard) toward one's wife since she is the center of the home? And how can one be disrespectful toward (or be lacking in regard for) one's children, since the children perpetuate the family? A gentleman is always respectful or always shows regard for everything. First of all he is respectful, or shows a pious regard toward himself. How dare he be disrespectful or have no pious regard for himself since the self is a branch of the family line? Not to show regard for one's self is to injure the family, and to injure the family is to injure the root, and when the root is injured, the branches die off. These three things, the relationship toward one's wife, toward one's children and toward one's self, are a symbol of the human relationships among the people. By showing respect for his own self, he teaches the people respect for their selves; by showing regard for his own children, he teaches the people regard for their children; and by showing regard for his own wife, he teaches the people regard for their wives. When a sovereign carries out these three things, his example will be imitated by the entire country. This is the principle of King T'ai (grandfather of King Wen). Thus harmonious relationships will prevail in the country."

Duke Ai: "May I ask what is meant by 'showing respect for one's self'?"

Confucius: "When the sovereign makes a mistake in his speech, the people quote him, and when a sovereign makes a mistake in his conduct, the people imitate him. When a sovereign makes no mistakes in his speech or his conduct, then the people learn respect for him without any laws or regulations. In this way the sovereign shows respect for himself, and by showing respect for himself, he glorifies his ancestors."

Duke Ai: "May I ask what you mean by 'glorifying one's ancestors'?"

Confucius: "When a man becomes famous, we call

him 'a prince' or 'a princely man,'* and the people gladly follow him and honor him, saying that he is 'a prince's son' (or 'son of a gentleman'). Thus his own father is called a 'prince' through him and his name is glorified."

Confucius went on to say: "The ancient rulers considered loving the people as the first thing in their government. Without loving the people, the ruler cannot realize his true self, and without realizing or taking possession of his true self, he cannot establish peace in his land; without peace in his land, he cannot enjoy life in conformity with God's law; and being unable to enjoy life in conformity with God's law, he cannot live a full life."

Duke Ai: "May I ask what you mean by 'living a full life'?"

Confucius: "Just follow the natural law of things."

* The term *chuntse* is difficult to translate, and has been translated by various translators as "the superior man," "the princely man," "the gentleman," "the sovereign," and "the ruler." It undoubtedly had two senses, one of the ideal "gentlemen" or "the superior man," that is, one who is cultivated in learning and character, as distinguished from "the common man" or "inferior man." The second sense is that of "the ruler" or "the sovereign." In the Confucian discourses the two senses constantly come together and merge imperceptibly into one another, so that the word represents in effect Confucius' ideal of the wise and good and cultivated ruler, quite similar to Plato's "philosopher-king." In general, there was undoubtedly a cultivated ruling class, as opposed to the illiterate common people, and Confucius gave this distinction of the superior man and the inferior man a moral meaning. The antonym to *chuntse* is *hsiaojen,* or literally "the small man," and this consequently also had two senses, the morally inferior and the "commoners," in the English sense.

Duke Ai: "May I ask why the gentleman lays such stress on the laws of God?"*

Confucius: "The gentleman lays such stress upon God's law, because it is eternal. For instance, you see the sun and the moon eternally following one another in their courses—that is God's law. Life in this universe never stops and continues forever—that is God's law. Things are created or produced without any effort or interference—that is God's law. When the things are created or produced, the universe is illuminated—that is God's law."

Duke Ai: "I'm stupid and confused. Will you make it clearer and simplify it so that I can remember?"

A change came over Confucius' countenance. He rose from his seat and said: "A great man simply follows the natural law of things. A good son simply follows the natural law of things. Therefore, a great man feels he is serving God when he serves his parents, and feels he is serving his parents when he serves God. Therefore, a good son lives a full life."

Duke Ai: "I am extremely fortunate to have heard these words from you, and I crave your pardon if I fail to live up to them hereafter."

Confucius: "The pleasure is mine."

* Two conceptions are clearly distinguished here. First, the laws of man, *jentao*, translated at the beginning of this interview, as "human civilization," which Duke Ai asked about and which Confucius interpreted as "government." The entire interview up to this point discusses government or the laws of man. Here the Duke begins to ask about the laws of God, because Confucius talks about living in conformity with God's law.

Chapter VIII

THIRD DISCOURSE: THE VISION
OF A SOCIAL ORDER

(*Liyun, Liki,* Chapter IX)

THIS is one of the most important chapters in *Liki,*
probably recorded by Tseyu, a disciple of Confucius.
The first section makes an important distinction between
a Confucian Utopia, the *tat'ung,* in which none of the
humanistic distinctions in *li* would be necessary, and the
second best type of culture, the culture of *li* or of a social
order, practical and attainable in the present world, the
hsiaok'ang, with which practically all the teachings of
Confucius about *li* are concerned. The fact that Confucius
did have a vision of a world of more or less perfect
human beings in which *li* would not be necessary, is
interesting and gives his teachings concerning the principle of attainable social order a quality of practical
common sense and an implied meaning of resignation to
the second best. To know that a world of moral perfection exists, but to go along bravely establishing a social
order with the imperfect human beings that we know we
are today, is the part of wisdom. This vision of the Con-

fucian Utopia has gained increased prominence among recent Chinese scholars who have somehow been influenced by reading of Western Utopias and Western idealism in general. Dr. Sun Yat Sen's favorite phrase, the one that he most frequently used when asked to inscribe an autograph for his friends, consisted of the four words *"t'ien hsia tat'ung"* or "the world of *tat'ung"* taken from this section.

The meaning of *li,* or the principle of social order, and its identity with a general body of social practices are quite clear and most completely developed in this chapter. *Li* is here seen to include folkways, religious customs, festivals, laws, dress, food and housing, such as are usually included under the term "ethnology." Add to these original existing practices a conception of a *rationalized* social order, and you have *li* in its most complete sense.

In the following translation, I have omitted several paragraphs which concern strictly the details of the ancient feudal order which Confucius was trying to restore. Interesting as these details are for the students of ancient Chinese philology and comparative religion, they do not fall within the scope of this book, which deals more with the broader significance of Confucian teachings. Confucius himself emphasized again and again the importance of being widely read and learned in all aspects of life without forgetting the importance of having a philosophic principle that runs through all these details of scholarship. Only one who is able to couple thought with scholarship is a really educated man, according to Confucius. The early Han scholars, occupied with philological research, did involve themselves in such details to the exclusion of central philosophic principles, while the Sung philosophers, influenced by the Buddhistic bent for philosophy and meditation, on the other hand neglected this philologic scholarship and even developed the habit of "reading a book without knowing exactly what it means." An extreme example of mere occupation with philologic details was the case of a later commentator who wrote a treatise of over 30,000 words on two words of the *Shuking*. The three books on *li* (*Chouli, Yili,* and *Liki*) contain of course a rich field of material for the study of ancient Chinese folkways, but they cannot possibly be covered or even suggested in this book. I have also supplied sectional headings for the convenience of the reader.

I. THE TWO ORDERS OF HUMAN SOCIETY

One day Confucius went to see the ceremony of *tsa* (a winter folk festival at the end of the year at which the people offered a general sacrifice to all the animals and inanimate creation and of course indulged in dancing). After the ceremony was over, Confucius took a walk. He stopped at a roadhouse on the side of the city gate (overlooking the suburb) and heaved a deep sigh. Confucius was sighing over the social conditions in his country Lu. Yen Yen (Tseyu) was with him, and asked Confucius, "Why are you sighing?" And Confucius replied, "Oh, I was thinking of the Golden Age and regretting that I was not able to have been born in it and to be associated with the wise rulers and ministers of the Three Dynasties. How I would have loved to have lived in such an age!"

"When the great Tao prevailed (*i.e.*, in the Golden Age), the world was a common state (not belonging to any particular ruling family), rulers were elected according to their wisdom and ability and mutual confidence and peace prevailed. Therefore people not only regarded their own parents as parents and their own children as children. The old people were able to enjoy their old age, the young men were able to employ their talent, the juniors had the elders to look up to, and the helpless widows, orphans and cripples and deformed were well taken care of. The men had their respective occupations and the women had their homes. If the people didn't want to see goods lying about on the ground, they did not have to keep them for themselves, and if people had too much energy for work, they did not have to labor for their own profit. Therefore there was no cunning or intrigue and there were no bandits or burglars, and as a result, there was no need to shut one's outer gate (at night). This was the period of *tat'ung*, or the Great Commonwealth.*

"But now the great Tao no longer prevails, and the world is divided up into private families (or becomes the possession of private families), and people regard only their own parents as parents and only their own children as children. They acquire goods and labor each for his

* *Ta* means "great" and *t'ung* means "common."

own benefit. A hereditary aristocracy is established and the different states build cities, outer cities and moats each for its own defense. The principles of *li* (or forms of social intercourse) and righteousness serve as the principles of social discipline. By means of these principles, people try to maintain the official status of rulers and subjects, to teach the parents and children and elder brothers and younger brothers and husbands and wives to live in harmony, to establish social institutions and to live in groups of hamlets. The physically strong and the mentally clever are raised to prominence and each one tries to carve his own career. Hence there is deceit and cunning and from these wars arise. (The great founders of dynasties like) Emperors Yu, T'ang, Wen, Wu and Ch'eng and Duke Chou were the best men of this age. Without a single exception, these six gentlemen were deeply concerned over the principle of *li,* through which justice was maintained, general confidence was tested, and errors or malpractices were exposed. An ideal of true manhood, *jen,* was set up and good manners or courtesy was cultivated, as solid principles for the common people to follow. A ruler who violates these principles would then be denounced as a public enemy and driven off from his office. This is called the Period of *Hsiaok'ang* or "The Period of Minor Peace."

II. THE EVOLUTION OF LI OR SOCIAL ORDER

"Is *li* so very important as all that?" asked Tseyu again.

"This *li,*" replied Confucius, "is the principle by which

the ancient kings embodied the laws of heaven and regulated the expressions of human nature. Therefore he who has attained *li* lives, and he who has lost it, dies. The *Book of Songs* says,

> See even the mouse has a *t'i* (body)
> And a human being has no *li*!
> A human being has no *li*—
> Why doesn't he go off and die?

Therefore *li* is based on heaven, patterned on the earth deals with the worship of the spirits and is extended to the rites and ceremonies of funerals, sacrifices to ancestors, archery, carriage driving, 'capping,'* marriage, and court audience or exchange of diplomatic visits. Therefore the Sage shows the people the principle of a rationalized social order and through it everything becomes right in the family, the state and the world."

"Can you explain to me, fully and completely, this *li*?" asked Tseyu once more.

Confucius: I wanted to see the ancient practices of the Hsia Dynasty (2205–1784 B.C.), and that was why I went to visit the city of Chi (where the descendants of the Hsia rulers lived), but I found there weren't enough surviving customs left. There I secured, however, a copy of the book *Hsiashih*. And I wanted to see the ancient practices of the Shang Dynasty (or Yin, 1783–1123 B.C.), and for this purpose I went to visit the city of Sung (where the descendants of the Shang rulers lived), but found there were not enough surviving customs left.

* The ceremony of putting a cap on a boy when he reaches maturity.

There, however, I secured a copy of *K'unch'ien* (a version of the *Book of Changes*).* With the help of these two books, the *Hsiashih* and *K'unch'ien,* I tried to study the ancient customs.

In the beginning, *li* (civilization) started with food or drink. People baked millets and pork, torn apart with the hand, on heated slabs of stone. They dug holes in the ground to serve as jars and drank out of the palms of their hands. They kneaded clay into drums and drum sticks. And yet this seemed to have been worthy materials for them to worship the spirits. When a relative died, they went up on the roof and cried aloud to the spirit, saying to him, "Ahooooooooo! So-and-So, will you please return to your body?" (If the spirit failed to return, and the man was really dead) then they used uncooked rice and baked meats for sacrifice, and they turned their heads toward the sky to "see at a distance" (*wang*) the spirit and buried the body in the earth. The material spirit then descended (to the earth), while the conscious spirit went up (to the air). Therefore the dead were buried with their heads toward the north, while the living had their houses facing the south. These were the early customs.

In the ancient times, the rulers did not have houses, and they lived in dug-out caves or in piled-up mounds in winter and on "nests" made of dry branches (on top of trees) in summer. They did not know the use of fire, but

* *K'un* symbolizes the earth or the female principle; *ch'ien* symbolizes heaven or the male principle. It is interesting to note here that the female principle is put before the male principle in the Shang version.

ate fruits and the flesh of birds and animals, drinking their blood, including the hair in it. They did not have hemp or cloth or silk and were clothed in feathers and animal skins. Later came the Sages who taught them the use of fire, and to cast metalware by pouring it into bamboo moulds and to mould clay into earthenware. Then they build terraces and houses with doors and windows, and began to bake and broil and cook and roast by means of a spit, and made wine and vinegar. They began also to use hemp and silk and weave them into cloth for the use of the living and sacrifices to the dead and the worship of the spirits and God.* These ancient practices were also handed down from the early times. Therefore, the black wine was kept in the inner room, the white wine was kept near the (southern) door, the red wine was kept in the hall and the heavy wine was kept still further outside. The meat offerings were then displayed and the round tripod and the square vessel were laid in order, and the musical instruments, the *ch'in, seh,* the flute, the *ch'ing* (musical stone sus-

* There was a religious cult of a Supreme Ruler, *Shangti,* the word used here and generally used today by Chinese Christians, while there was a different religious cult which worshipped as the Supreme Ruler "Heaven," or *T'ien.* The offerings used in the worship of *Shangti* and *T'ien* were different, and these two religions were practiced by different tribes. In Confucius' time, there was already a great confusion, as the two religions had got mixed up with one another, and Confucius himself said at several places that he was unable to reconstruct the practices at the worship of Heaven, and that if he did, it would be a simple matter to govern the country. Somewhere at the back of his head, he had a notion of aspiring to restore the ancient theocracy.

pended from a string and struck like bells), the bell and the drum were arranged in their places, and the sacrificial prayer to the dead and the answer from the dead* were carefully prepared and read, that the celestial and the ancestors' spirits might descend to the place of worship. All these practices were for the purpose of maintaining the proper status of rulers and subjects, maintaining the love between parents and children, teaching kindness between brothers, regulating relationships between superiors and inferiors, and establishing the respective relationships of husband and wife, to the end that all might be blessed by Heaven. They then prepared the sacrificial lamentations. The black or dark wine was used for sacrifice, and the blood and hair of the animals were used in offering, and the raw meat was placed in a square vessel. Burnt meat was also offered, a mat was spread out and a piece of coarse cloth was used for covering the vessels, and silk ceremonial robes were used. The different wines, *li* and *chien,* and baked and broiled meats were also offered. The sovereign and the queen made the offerings alternately, that the good spirits might descend and they might be united with the occult world. After the sacrifices were over, they then gave a feast to the guests, dividing up the dogs, pigs, cows and lambs at the offering and placing them in various vessels. The prayer to the dead declared the grati-

* The answer was read by a small child, known as *shih,* representing the deceased. This *shih* is a prominent figure in all sacrifices to the dead even in modern times.

tude or loyalty of the living, and the answer from the dead declared the continued affection of the deceased. This was the great blessing and accomplishment of *li*.

Confucius: "Alas! I have studied the practices of the Chou Dynasty (in which Confucius lived), but (the bad Emperors) Yu and Li have completely destroyed them. Where can I turn to except to the country of Lu?" (*Here follows a brief description of the prevailing chaos in the social and religious life of his time.*)

Therefore *li* is the great weapon or means of power of a sovereign, with which to expose malpractices and beginnings of disorder, offer sacrifices to the spirits, establish the systems of social life, differentiate the uses of love and duty. It is the means by which a country is governed and the sovereign maintains the security of his position. Therefore, if the government is not "right," then the sovereign's position is threatened, and when the sovereign's position is threatened, the powerful officials become arrogant and the minor officials begin to steal. We should then see criminals punished by severe sentences and the general morality of the people degenerates and there would be a general absence of standards. With a general absence of standards, the general social order would be upset; and with the upset of the general social order, the gentry would not be able to attend to their proper professions. And when the criminals are punished with severe penalties and the general morality of the people degenerates, then the people will not be loyal to the sovereign, or will go away to other countries. This is called "a sickly state."

(Here follows a description of the proper functions of the sovereign.)

III. LI BASED ON HUMAN NATURE

The reason the Sage is able to regard the world as one family and China as one man (what is true of human nature in one man is true for all), is that he does not make arbitrary rules, but on the other hand tries to understand human nature,* define the human duties and come to a clear realization of what is good and what is bad for mankind. It is through this that he is able to do so. What is human nature? It consists of the seven things, joy, anger, sorrow, fear, love, hatred and desire, all of which do not have to be learned (*i.e.,* they are natural instincts). What are the human duties? Kindness in the father, filial piety in the son, gentility in the elder brother, humility and respect in the younger brother, good behavior in the husband, obedience in the wife, benevolence in the elders, and obedience in the juniors, benevolence in the ruler and loyalty in the ministers—these ten are the human duties. What is good for mankind means general confidence and peace, and

* The Chinese terms for "nature," "emotions," "heart," "mind," "will," etc., overlap in their meaning, as compared with the corresponding English words. *Hsin* means "the heart" and "the mind." *Hsing* means "original nature," "instinct." *Ch'ing* means (in the above passage) "nature," "natural feelings," "emotions." *Chih* means the "will," "direction of the mind," "hope," "ambition," "aspirations." *Yi* means "idea," "intention." *Yu* means "desires." *Jen* means "moral character," "true manhood." *Chih* (another word) means "wisdom," "the intellect."

what is bad for mankind means struggle for profit, robbery and murder. Therefore how can the Sage, or ideal ruler, dispense with *li* in his efforts to cultivate the seven emotions and the ten duties, and to promote mutual confidence and peace and courtesy and discourage the struggle for profit and robbery? Food and drink and sex are the great desires of mankind, and death and poverty and suffering are the great fears or aversions of mankind. Therefore desires and fear (or greed and hatred) are the great motive forces of the human heart. These, however, are concealed in the heart and are not usually shown, and the human heart is unfathomable. What other principle is there besides *li* which can serve as the one all-sufficient principle to explore the human heart?

Therefore man is the product of the forces of heaven and earth, of the union of the *yin* and the *yang* principles, the incarnation of spirits and the essence of the five elements (metal, wood, water, fire and earth). Therefore man is the heart of the universe, the upshot of the five elemeents, born to enjoy food and color and noise. . . .

IV. LI BASED ON HEAVEN (OR NATURE)

The worship of Heaven is for the purpose of recognizing the supreme rulership of Heaven. The worship of the god of Earth is for the purpose of displaying the productivity of the earth. Worship at the ancestral temple is for the purpose of recognizing the ancestry of man. The worship of the mountains and rivers is for the purpose of serving the different spirits. The five sacrifices* are for the purpose of commemorating the origin of human occupations. Therefore there are priests at the temple, the Three High Ministers at the court, and the Three Elders at the College. The soothsayer stands in front of the king and the official historian at his back, while the priest in charge of divination and the blind music master and his assistants are scattered on his right and his left, while the king sits in the middle, maintaining calm in his heart, a guardian (or symbol) of the ultimate rightness of things.

Therefore when *li* is observed at the worship of Heaven, then the different gods attend to their duties. When *li* is observed at the worship of Earth, then things grow and multiply. When *li* is observed at the ancestral temple, then filial piety and affection prevail. When *li* is observed at the five sacrifices, then standards of measurements are established. Therefore the worship of Heaven, of Earth, of the ancestors, the mountains and rivers, and the five sacrifices are for the keeping up of the human duties and constitute the embodiment of *li*.

Therefore, this *li* originates in *T'aiyi* (Primeval Unity),† which was divided into the Heaven and the Earth, transformed into the *yin* and the *yang*, operating

* There are five different interpretations of these five sacrifices, one interpreting them as the worship of the five elements, another as worship of the door, the street, the one-panelled door, the kitchen and the central hall, etc.

† According to the *Book of Changes*, the phenomena of this universe are traced back to the action or interaction of the two principles, *yin* and *yang*, which are again traced back to the Primeval Unity.

as the seasons, and assuming shape as the different spirits. The will of the gods is expressed as destiny, and is controlled from Heaven.

Thus *li* must be based on Heaven, shows its action on the Earth, and is applied to the different human occupations, changing according to the seasons and fitted into the different crafts. In man, it emerges as the principle of livelihood and is shown in trade, labor, social intercourse, eating and drinking, and in the ceremony of "capping," marriage, burial and sacrifice to the dead, archery, carriage driving, and audience at court.

Therefore the duties of *li* are the main principles of human life, serving the purpose of promoting mutual confidence and social harmony and strengthening the social ties and bonds of friendship. They are the main principles for worshiping the spirits and feeding the living and sacrificing to the dead.* *Li* is a great channel through which we follow the laws of Heaven and direct to proper courses the expressions of the human heart. Therefore, only the Sage knows that *li* is indispensable. Therefore, to destroy a kingdom, upset a family or ruin a man, you must first take away from him this sense of li.

V. THE METHOD OF CULTIVATING LI

Therefore *li* is to man as the yeast is to wine; the superior man has a little more of it, and the inferior man has

* *Li* here is seen to be a definitely religious principle, and this explains the disproportionate emphasis given to funeral ceremonies in the Confucian system. The detailed descriptions of funeral ceremonies in the *Liki* are overwhelming.

a little less of it. Therefore the sage, or saintly ruler, cultivates the proper approach to duties and the order of *li,* as a means of controlling or regulating human nature. Therefore, human nature is the field cultivated by the Sage or saintly ruler. He ploughs it with *li,* sows it with the seeds of duties, weeds it by education and learning, harvests it with true manhood, and enjoys it with music. Therefore *li* is but the crystallization of what is right. If a thing is in accordance with the standard of what is right, new social practices may be instituted, although they were not known to the rulers of the past. The standard of right* is the following of each class of people in its proper course and true manhood become articulate. Those who have followed the right, observing the proper course and cultivating true manhood, will become powerful administrators. True manhood is the foundation for proper conduct and the embodiment of conformity with the standard of right. Those who have achieved true manhood become the rulers of man.

It follows, therefore, that to govern a country without *li* is like tilling a field without a plough. To observe *li* without basing it on the standard of right is like tilling the field and forgetting to sow the seeds. To try to do

---

* The Chinese word is *yi,* which in the above is seen to refer to the well-defined ten duties of human relationships. It is therefore the concrete embodiment of the general principle of *li. Li* and *yi* often form a phrase, difficult to translate, but rendered above as "the duties of *li."* The official Chinese interpretation of *yi* is that it means "what is right" or proper. The next following notion, *jen* is interpreted as "true manhood," embodying the Confucian ideal of the true man or the most complete man.

right without cultivating knowledge is like sowing the seeds without weeding the field. To cultivate knowledge without bringing it back to the aim of true manhood, is like weeding the field without harvesting it. And to arrive at the aim of true manhood without coming to enjoy it through music, is like harvesting and forgetting to eat the harvest. To enjoy true manhood through music and not arrive at complete harmony with nature is like eating and not becoming well-fed, or healthy.

When the four limbs are well developed and the skin is clear and the flesh is full, that is the health of human life. When the parents and children are affectionate, the brothers are good toward one another and the husband and the wife live in harmony, that is the health of the home life. When the higher officials obey the law and the lower officials are clean, the officials have regulated and well-defined functions and the king and the ministers help one another on the right course, that is the health of the national life. When the Emperor rides in the carriage of Virtue, with Mucis as his driver, when the different rulers meet each other with courtesy, the officials regulate each other with law, the scholars urge one another by the standard of honesty, and the people unite with one another in peace, that is the health of the world. This is called the Grand Harmony (*Tashun*). . . .

Chapter IX

ON EDUCATION

(*Hsuehchi, Liki*, Chapter XVIII)

I. THE NEED FOR EDUCATION

TO DESIRE to do right and to seek what is good
would give a person a little reputation but would
not enable him to influence the masses. To associate with
the wise and able men and to welcome those who come
from a distant country would enable a person to influence the masses, but would not enable him to civilize the
people. The only way for the superior man to civilize the
people and establish good social customs is through education. A piece of jade cannot become an object of art
without chiselling, and a man cannot come to know the
moral law without education. Therefore the ancient
kings regarded education as the first important factor in
their efforts to establish order in a country. That is the
meaning of the passage in the *Advice to Fu Yueh* (by
King Kaotsung of the Hsia Dynasty, now a chapter of
Shuking) which says, "Forever occupy your thoughts
with education." Just as one cannot know the taste of
food without eating it, however excellent it may be, so

without education one cannot come to know the excellence of a great body of knowledge, although it may be there.

Therefore only through education does one come to be dissatisfied with his own knowledge, and only through teaching others does one come to realize the uncomfortable inadequacy of his knowledge. Being dissatisfied with his own knowledge, one then realizes that the trouble lies with himself, and realizing the uncomfortable inadequacy of his knowledge, one then feels stimulated to improve himself. Therefore it is said, "The processes of teaching and learning stimulate one another." That is the meaning of the passage in the *Advice to Fu Yeuh* which says, "Teaching is the half of learning."

II. THE ANCIENT EDUCATIONAL SYSTEM

The ancient educational system was as follows: There was a primary school in every hamlet of 25 families, a secondary school in every town of 500 families, an academy in every county of 2500 families, and a college in the capital of every state (for the education of the princes and sons of nobles and the best pupils from the lower schools.) Every year new students were admitted, and every other year there was an examination.* At the end

* "Every other year" is the regular interpretation. The phrase *chung nien,* however, can mean "in the middle of the year" as well as "in the in-between year"' (or alternate years). According to *Chouli,* however, there was said to be a grand examination every three years.

of the first year, an effort was made to see how the pupils were able to punctuate their sentences and to find out their natural inclinations. At the end of three years, an effort was made to find out their habits of study and their group life. At the end of five years, they would try to see how well read in general the pupils were and how closely they had followed their teachers. At the end of seven years, they would try to find out how their ideas had developed and what kind of friends they had selected for themselves. This is called the Minor Graduation (*hsiaoch'eng*—from the lower grades). At the end of nine years, they were expected to know the various subjects and have a general understanding of life and to have laid a firm foundation for their character from which they could not go back. This was called the Major Graduation (*tach'eng*—from the higher grades).*

By such an educational system only is it possible to civilize the people and reform the morals of the country, so that the local inhabitants will be happy and those in distant lands will love to come to the country. This is the principle of *tahsueh,* or higher education. That is the meaning of the passage in the *Ancient Records* which

---

* According to *Neitseh* (Chapter XII, *Liki*), the age of entering school is given as ten. The studies of music, poetry, dancing, and archery begin at the age of thirteen. This seems to indicate a nine-year program from ten to nineteen, the last two years between the Minor and Major Graduations probably considered the "secondary education." At twenty, the college education begins. Men were supposed to marry at thirty and women at twenty, and at the latest twenty-three, "for special reasons."

says, "The ants are busy all the time" (*the importance of continuous study*).

In the college, the students begin to study the proper use of ceremonial robes and vegetable offerings at sacrifices, in order to learn the principle of respect or piety. They are made to sing the first three songs of *Hsiaoya*,* in order to learn the first elements of official life.

On entering the college, a drum is beaten before the students unpack their books, so as to teach discipline at their studies. The ferule or hickory stick is used in order to regulate their external behavior. No inspector is sent to the college except on the occasion of the Grand Sacrifice to the royal ancestors,† that the students may be left alone to develop themselves. The teacher observes but does not constantly lecture to them, so that the students have time to think out things for themselves. The young ones are supposed to listen and not to ask questions, so that they may know their own place. These seven things are the main methods of teaching. That is the meaning of the passage in the *Ancient Records*‡ which says, "At

* The third division in the present *Book of Songs*, being the classical songs of *Chou*. These first three songs were supposed to have been used at dinners given by the Emperor to his ministers.

† Accounts conflict as to this Grand Sacrifice. One interprets it as the annual sacrifice in summer; another interprets it as coming once every five years.

‡ There are numerous references to the *Ancient Records* throughout the Confucian classics and other writings of the Chou Dynasty. It is from these ancient records that the present *Liki* is made. Again, the "Small Tai" collection now usually referred to as *Liki* and consisting of forty-nine chapters or books, differs from the "Great Tai" collection, consisting of eighty-five chapters or books, only two chapters being

the college, those who already have an office make studies relative to their respective departments, while those who do not have an office study what they want to do afterwards."

III. EXTRA-CURRICULAR STUDIES

In the educational system of the college, there are regular studies in class and collateral studies when the students are in their own rooms. Without the practice of fingering, one cannot learn to play the string instrument smoothly. Without wide observation of things,* one cannot learn poetry easily. Without acquaintance with the different ceremonial robes, one cannot master the study of rituals. Without learning the different arts (like archery and carriage driving), one cannot enjoy study at school. Therefore in the education of the superior man (or the intellectual upper class), one is given time to digest things, to cultivate things, to rest and to play. In this way the students learn to feel at home at college and

---

common to both collections. A fairly early authority says that "Great Tai" re-edited the original collection of two hundred and four chapters or books and reduced them to eighty-five. The ancient records were therefore a miscellaneous collection of writings, both those prior to Confucius and those written by his disciples, handed down from teachers to disciples in the Confucian school. There are many references to passages in these "records" that are not found in our present version of *Liki*.

* The *Book of Songs* is full of the names of insects, fishes, birds, beasts and flowers and trees. There are commentaries of the *Book of Songs* which are but botanical and zoological studies.

establish a personal relationship with their teachers, enjoy friendship and acquire conviction in ideas. They then may leave their teachers without turning their backs on their studies. This is the meaning of the passage in the *Advice of Fu Yueh,* which says, "Respectfully keep at your studies constantly, and then you will have results."

The teachers of today just go on repeating things in a rigmarole fashion, annoy the students with constant questions, and repeat the same things over and over again. They do not try to find out what the students' natural inclinations are, so that the students are forced to pretend to like their studies, nor do they try to bring out the best in their talents. What they give to the students is wrong in the first place and what they expect of the students is just as wrong. As a result, the students hide their favorite readings and hate their teachers, are exasperated at the difficulty of their studies and do not know what good it does them. Although they go through the regular course of instruction, they are quick to leave it when they are through. This is the reason for the failure of education today.

IV. THE IDEAL TEACHER

The principles of college education are as follows: First, prevention, or preventing bad habits before they arise. Secondly, timeliness, or giving the students things when they are ready for them. Thirdly, order, or teaching the different subjects in proper sequence. Fourthly, mutual stimulation (literally "friction"), or letting the students admire the excellence of other students. These four things ensure the success of education.

On the other hand, to forbid them after they have already acquired bad habits would seem to make everything go against their grain and efforts at correction would be without success. To teach them after the young age is past would make their learning difficult and futile. To fail to teach the different subjects in their proper order would bring about chaos in their studies, without good results. To study a subject all alone without friends would make a student too narrow in scope, lacking in general knowledge. Bad company would encourage them to go against their teachers and bad pastimes would cause them to neglect their studies. These six things cause the breakdown of a college education.

With the knowledge of the reasons for success in education and the causes of its failure, the superior man is then qualified to be a teacher.

Therefore in his teaching the superior man guides his students but does not pull them along; he urges them to go forward and does not suppress them; he opens the way, but does not take them to the place. Guiding without pulling makes the process of learning gentle; urging without suppressing makes the process of learning easy; and opening the way without leading the students to the place makes them think for themselves. Now if the process of learning is made gentle and easy and the students are encouraged to think for themselves, we may call the man a good teacher.

There are four common errors in education which the

teacher must beware of. Some students try to learn too much or too many subjects, some learn too little or too few subjects, some learn things too easily and some are too easily discouraged. These four things show that individuals differ in their mental endowments, and only through a knowledge of the different mental endowments can the teacher correct their mistakes. A teacher is but a man who tries to bring out the good and remedy the weakness of his students.

A good singer makes others follow his tune, and a good educator makes others follow his ideal. His words are concise but expressive, casual but full of hidden meaning, and he is good at drawing ingenious examples to make people understand him. In this way, he may be said to be a good man to make others follow his ideal.

The superior man knows what is difficult and what is easy, what is excellent and what is deplorable in the things to be learned, and then he is good at drawing examples. Being good at drawing examples, he then knows how to be a teacher. Knowing how to be a teacher, he then knows how to be an elder. And knowing how to be an elder, he then knows how to be a ruler of men. Therefore, the art of being a teacher is the art of learning to be a ruler of men. Therefore one cannot be too careful in selecting one's teacher. That is the meaning of the passage in the *Ancient Records* which says, "The Three Kings and the Four Dynasties (Yu, Hsia, Shang and Chou) laid the greatest emphasis upon the selection of teachers."

In this matter of education, the most difficult thing is

to establish a respect for the teacher. When the teacher is respected, then people respect what he teaches, and when people respect what he teaches, then they respect learning or scholarship. Therefore there are only two classes of persons that the king dare not regard as his subjects: his teacher and the *shih* (child representing the spirit of the deceased at a sacrifice). According to the customs of the college, a teacher doesn't have to stand facing north even when receiving an edict from the king, which shows the great respect for the teacher.

V. THE PROCESS OF LEARNING

With a good student, the teacher doesn't have much to do and the results are double, besides getting the student's respect. With a bad student, the teacher has to work hard and the results are only half of what is to be expected, besides getting hated by the student. A good questioner proceeds like a man chopping wood—he begins at the easier end, attacking the knots last, and after a time the teacher and student come to understand the point with a sense of pleasure. A bad questioner does just exactly the opposite. One who knows how to answer questions is like a group of bells. When you strike the big bell, the big one rings, and when you strike the small bell, the small one rings. It is important, however, to allow time for its tone gradually to die out. One who does not know how to answer questions is exactly the reverse of this. These are all suggestions for the process of teaching and learning.

That type of scholarship which is bent on remembering things in order to answer questions does not qualify one to be a teacher. A good teacher should observe the students' conversations. When he sees a student is doing his best but is lost, then he explains it to him, and if after the explanation, the student still does not understand, he may as well leave the matter alone.

The son of a tinker naturally learns how to mend fur coats, and the son of a good maker of bows naturally learns how to make a bamboo *chi* (shallow pan made of woven sliced bamboo for holding grain), and a man breaking in a horse first puts the horse behind the carriage. A gentleman can learn from these three things the proper method of education. The scholars of ancient times learned the truth about things from analogies.

The drum itself does not come under any of the five modes of music, and yet the five modes cannot succeed in harmony without the drum. Water itself does not belong to any of the five colors, and yet (in painting) the five colors would lack brightness without the use of water. Learning itself does not come under any of the five senses, and yet the five senses cannot be properly trained without learning. The teacher does not come under the five degrees of clan kinship, and yet the five degrees of clan kinship would not love one another without the teacher.

The gentleman says, "A great personality does not (necessarily) fit one for any particular office. A great character does not (necessarily) qualify one for any particular service. Great honesty does not (necessarily) make a man keep his word. Great regard for time does not (necessarily) make one punctual." To know these four things is to know the really fundamental things in life.

In offering sacrifices to the river gods, the ancient kings always began with worshipping the gods of the rivers before worshipping the gods of the seas. A distinction was made between the source and the outlet, and to know this distinction is to know how to attend to the essentials.

Chapter X

ON MUSIC

(*Yochi, Liki*, Chapter XIX)

I. THE ORIGIN AND FUNCTION OF MUSIC

MUSIC rises from the human heart when the human heart is touched by the external world. When touched by the external world, the heart is moved, and therefore finds its expression in sounds. These sounds echo, or combine with, one another and produce a rich variety, and when the various sounds become regular, then we have rhythm. The arrangement of tones for our enjoyment in combination with the military dance, with shields and hatchets, and the civil dance, with long feathers and pennants of ox-tails, is called music.

Music is the form wherein tones are produced, because it takes its rise from the human heart when the heart is touched by the external world. Therefore when the heart's chord of sorrow is touched, the sounds produced are sombre and forlorn; when the heart's chord of satisfaction is touched, the sounds produced are languorous and slow; when the chord of joy is touched, the sounds produced are glowing and expansive; when the chord of anger is touched, the sounds produced are harsh and strong; when the chord of piety is touched, the sounds produced are simple and pure; and when the chord of love is touched, the sounds produced are sweet and gentle. These six kinds of emotion are not spontaneous, but are moods produced by impact from the external world.

Therefore the ancient kings were ever careful about things that affected the human heart. They tried therefore to guide the people's ideals and aspirations by means of *li,* establish harmony in sounds by means of music, regulate conduct by means of government, and prevent immorality by means of punishments. *Li,* music, punishments and government have a common goal, which is to bring about unity in the people's hearts and carry out the principles of political order.

Music rises from the human heart. When the emotions are touched, they are expressed in sounds, and when the sounds take definite forms, we have music Therefore the music of a peaceful and prosperous country is quiet and joyous, and the government is orderly; the music of a country in turmoil shows dissatisfaction and anger, and the government is chaotic; and the music of a destroyed country shows sorrow and remembrance of the past, and the people are distressed. Thus we see music and government are directly connected with one another.

The mode of C is the symbol of the king; the mode of D is the symbol of the minister; the mode of E is the symbol of the people; the mode of G is the symbol of the affairs of the country; and the mode of A is the symbol of the natural world.* When the five keys are arranged in order, we do not have discordant sounds. When the key of C loses its tonality, then the music loses its fundamental and the king neglects his duties. When the key of D loses its tonality, then the music loses its gradation, and the ministers become unruly. When the key of E loses its tonality, then the music is sorrowful and the people feel distressed. When the key of G loses its tonality, then the music is mournful and the affairs of the country become complicated. When the key of A loses its tonality, then the music suggests danger, and the

---

* Throughout the entire system of Confucian thought, symbolism plays a very important part. Confucius seemed to constantly think of the need of external symbols for the common people, something that the mind of the common man could grasp. As the crown is the symbol of the king's authority, so the sun was the symbol of the king and the moon the symbol of the queen, and the different sacrificial vessels and the insignia of rank and position should be symbols of divine and secular authority. Western musicians recognize the different emotional qualities of the different modes, such as the "Lydian" and the "Aeolian." But apart from this, in order to understand this musical symbolism, one should understand the cosmogony of the ancient Chinese, believing that all life is the result of interaction of the five elements and ultimately of the two principles of *yin* and *yang*. These principles govern both natural phenomena and human society, and the ideal of the Confucianists was to bring the conduct of human affairs into harmony with cosmic forces. Hence corresponding to the five elements of metal, wood, water, fire and earth, we have "the five colors," "five flavors" of food, "five tones" of the pentatonic scale, and "five degrees of kinship" in the family system, and "five directions" in the universe (East, West, South, North and Center). Each ruling Dynasty had a symbolic "direction," expressed by a symbolic color. For detailed discussions on the ancient Chinese musical system, see the highly interesting and competent work, *Foundation of Chinese Musical Art*, by J. H. Levis (Vetch, Peiping).

people suffer from poverty. When all the five keys lose their tonality and upset one another, we have a general discord, and the nation will not have long to live. The music of the states of Cheng and Wei is the music of countries in turmoil, coming very near to a general discord. The music of "In the Mulberry Field," upon the banks of River P'u (in Wei) is the music of a destroyed country, whose government is tottering and whose people are dispersed or live in constant insecurity, calumniating their rulers and pursuing their selfish ends without restraint.

Tones rise from the human heart, and music is connected with the principles of human conduct. Therefore the animals know sounds but do not know tones, and the common people know tones but do not know music. Only the superior man is able to understand music. Thus from a study of the sounds, one comes to understand the tones; from a study of the tones, one comes to understand music; and from the study of music, one comes to understand the principles of government and is thus fully prepared for being a ruler. It is therefore impossible to talk to a man about tones who does not understand sounds, and impossible to talk to a man about music, who does not understand tones. He who understands music comes very near to understanding *li*, and if a man has mastered both *li* and music, we call him virtuous, because virtue is mastery (or fulfilment).*

Hence, when we say that music is well cultivated in a

* Here is a pun, of which the ancient scholars were very fond. Both "virtue" and "mastery" were pronounced *teh*.

country, we do not mean that its music is elaborate or complicated; nor do the ceremonies of feasting have sophisticated flavors. As we hear the music of the *seh** at the *Chou* ancestral temple, with its red strings and perforated resonance board, and only one man singing and three men joining in the chorus, we feel a certain restraint in its sounds; and as we see the ceremonies at the royal feast, with black wine and raw fish and unsavored soup, we feel there is a restraint in the use of flavors. Therefore the ancient kings did not institute rituals and music for the mere purpose of satisfying the desires of our senses ("the mouth, the stomach, the ear and the eye"), but rather for teaching the people the right taste and the return to normality.

The nature of man is usually quiet, but when it is affected by the external world, it begins to have desires. With the thinking mind becoming conscious of the impact of the material world, we begin to have likes and dislikes. When the likes and dislikes are not properly controlled and our conscious minds are distracted by the material world, we lose our true selves and the principle of reason in Nature is destroyed. When man is constantly exposed to the things of the material world which affect him and does not control his likes and dislikes, then he becomes overwhelmed by the material reality

* A string instrument longer than the *ch'in*, with fifty (or later, twenty-five) strings and usually accompanying the latter, supplying the low tones. The music of both string instruments is characterized by extremely quiet and slow movements.

and becomes dehumanized or materialistic. When a man becomes dehumanized or materialistic, then the principle of reason in Nature is destroyed and man is submerged in his own desires. From this arise rebellion, disobedience, cunning and deceit, and general immorality. We have then a picture of the strong bullying the weak, the majority persecuting the minority, the clever ones deceiving the simple-minded, the physically strong going for violence, the sick and crippled not being taken care of, and the aged and the young and helpless not cared for. This is the way of chaos.

The people are therefore controlled through the rituals and music instituted by the ancient kings. The weeping and wailing and wearing of the dress of mourning, made of hemp and without hemming, are for the purpose of regulating sorrow at funerals. The bell, the drum, the shield and the hatchet (in dance and music) are for the purpose of celebrating peace and happiness. The marriage ceremony and "capping" ceremony for boys reaching maturity and the "coiffure" ceremony for girls reaching maturity are for the purpose of establishing distinctions between the sexes. The archery contests and feasting at the village are for the purpose of normalizing social intercourse. The rituals regulate the people's feelings; music establishes harmony in the sounds of the country; the government orders their conduct and the punishments prevent crimes. When rituals, music, punishments and governments are all in order, then the principles of political order are complete.

II. A COMPARISON OF RITUALS AND MUSIC, BOTH BASED ON
HARMONY WITH THE COSMIC ORDER

Music unites, while rituals differentiate. Through union the people come to be friendly toward one another, and through differentiation the people come to learn respect for one another. If music predominates, the social structure becomes too amorphous, and if rituals predominate, social life becomes too cold. To bring the people's inner feelings and their external conduct into balance is the work of rituals and music. The establishment of rituals gives a well-defined sense of order and discipline, while the general spread of music and song establishes the general atmosphere of peace in the people. When good taste is distinguished from bad taste, then we have the means of distinguishing the good from the bad people, and when violence is prevented by the criminal law and the good men are selected for office, then the government becomes stable and orderly. With the doctrine of love for teaching affection, and the doctrine of duty for teaching moral rectitude, the people will then have learned to live in a moral order.

Music comes from the inside, while rituals come from the outside. Because music comes from the inside, it is characterized by quiet and calm. And because rituals come from the outside, they are characterized by formalism. Truly great music is always simple in movement, and truly great rituals are always simple in form. When good music prevails, there is no feeling of dissatisfaction and when proper rituals prevail, there is no strife and struggle. When we say that by mere bowing in salute the king can rule the world, we mean thereby the influence of rituals and music. When the violent elements of a nation are kept quiet, the different rulers come to pay homage, the military weapons are locked up, the five criminal laws are not brought into use, the people have no worries and the Emperor has no anger, then truly music has prevailed. When the parents and children are affectionate toward one another, the juniors respect the elders and this respect is extended to all people in the country and the Emperor himself lives such an exemplary life, then we may truly say that *li* has prevailed.

Truly great music shares the principles of harmony with the universe, and truly great ritualism shares the principles of distinctions with the universe. Through the principles of harmony, order is restored in the physical world, and through the principles of distinctions, we are enabled to offer sacrifices to Heaven and Earth. We have, then, rituals and music in the material world and the different gods in the spiritual world, and thus the world will come to live in love and piety. Rituals teach piety under different circumstances, and music teaches love in varying forms. When this moral condition is established through rituals and music, then we have a continuity of culture through the rise of different wise rulers. The political events differ with (the rulers of) the different generations, and the rituals and music celebrating the events are given names appropriate to the different accomplishments of the rulers.*

* For an example of music celebrating a particular ruler, see Section 5.

Music expresses the harmony of the universe, while rituals express the order of the universe. Through harmony all things are influenced, and through order all things have a proper place. Music rises from heaven, while rituals are patterned on the earth. To go beyond these patterns would result in violence and disorder. In order to have the proper rituals and music, we must understand the principles of Heaven and Earth. . . .

Therefore the Sage creates music to correlate with Heaven and creates rituals to correlate with the Earth. When rituals and music are well established, we have the Heaven and Earth functioning in perfect order. The Heaven is high and the Earth is low, and we have there the established relationship between the king and the ministers. When the high and low are arranged in different ranks, we have the principle of social ranks. When we have the law governing action and reaction, we have as the result the distinctions between the great and the small. And when the myriad things are grouped and classified according to their natural class, we recognize the principle of diversity in animal life. Thus are brought about the symbolic constellations of the stars in heaven and the different shapes of mountains and rivers and things on earth. This shows that *li* proceeds upon the principle of distinctions in the universe.

When the gases on the earth's surface go up and the gases in the upper atmospheres come down, when the principles of *yin* and *yang* meet and produce friction and the heaven and the earth interact upon one another, and when quickened by thunder and lightning, aroused into life by the lashing of wind and rain, stimulated by the rotation of the seasons and warmed by the sun and the moon, things grow and prosper. This shows that music proceeds upon the principle of harmony in the universe. . . .

Music illustrates the primordial forces of nature, while *li* reflects the products of the creation. Heaven represents the principle of eternal motion, while Earth represents the principle of remaining still, and these two principles of motion and rest permeate life between Heaven and Earth. Therefore, the Sage talks about rituals and music.

III. MUSIC REVEALS MAN'S CHARACTER

When you see the type of a nation's dance, you know its character. . . .

Man is gifted with blood and breath and a conscious mind, but his feeling of sorrow and happiness and joy and anger depend on circumstances. His definite desires arise from reactions toward the material world. Therefore, when a sombre and depressing type of music prevails, we know the people are distressed and sorrowful. When a languorous, easy type of music with many long-drawn-out airs prevails, we know that the people are peaceful and happy. When a strong forceful type of music prevails, beginning and ending with a full display of sounds, we know that the people are hearty and strong. When a pure, pious and majestic type of music prevails, we know that the people are pious. Wsen a gentle, lucid and quietly progressing type of music prevails, we know that the people are kind and affectionate. When lewd, exciting and upsetting music prevails, we know that the people are immoral. . . .

When the soil is poor, things do not grow, and when fishing is not regulated according to the seasons, then fishes and turtles do not mature; when the climate deteriorates, animal and plant life degenerates, and when the world is chaotic, the rituals and music become licentious. We find then a type of music that is rueful without restraint and joyous without calm. . . .

Therefore, the superior man tries to create harmony in the human heart by a rediscovery of human nature, and tries to promote music as a means to the perfection of human culture. When such music prevails and the people's minds are led toward the right ideals and aspirations, we may see the appearance of a great nation.

Character is the backbone of our human nature, and music is the flowering of character. The metal, stone, string and bamboo instruments are the instruments of music. The poem gives expression to our heart, the song gives expression to our voice, and the dance gives expression to our movements. These three arts take their rise from the human soul, and then are given further expression by means of the musical instruments. Therefore, from the depth of sentiment comes the clarity of form and from the strength of the mood comes the spirituality of its atmosphere. This harmony of spirit springs forth from the soul and finds expression or blossoms forth in the form of music. Therefore music is the one thing in which there is no use trying to deceive others or make false pretenses. . . .

IV. ON CLASSICAL AND MODERN MUSIC

Baron Wen of Wei asked Tsehsia, the disciple of Confucius, "Why is it that I feel sleepy every time I listen to classical music in my official dress, and never feel tired when I listen to the music of (the states of) Cheng and Wei? Why is it that the classical music is like that and this new music is like this?"

"In the ancient music," replied Tsehsia, "the dancers move in formation forward and backward in an atmosphere of peace and order and a certain luxury of movement. The *hsuan* (a string instrument) the gourd and the *sheng* (a kind of mouth organ with bamboo reed-pipes, resembling bagpipes in principle) are held in readiness until the drum gives the signal for the start. The music begins with the civil dance movements and ends with the military dance movements, and there is a continuity of movement from the beginning to the end,* while the measure of the classical music prevents or

* There is some ambiguity in the text here. One interpretation gives "the drum" instead of "the civil dance movements," "the cymbals" instead of "the military dance movements," and "keeps the time with the clay drum" instead of "continuity of movement from the beginning to the end."

checks the dancers who are inclined to go too fast. After listening to such music, the superior man will be in a proper atmosphere to discuss the music and the ways af the ancients, the cultivation of personal life and the ordering of national life. This is the main sentiment or character of ancient music. Now in this new music, people bend their bodies while they move back and forth, there is a deluge of immoral sounds without form or restraint, and the actors and dwarfs dressed like monkeys mix (or mix with) the company of men and women, behaving as if they didn't know who were their parents or children. At the end of such a performance it is impossible to discuss music or the ways of the ancients. This is the main sentiment or character of the new music. Now you asked me about music, but what you are really interested in is just sounds. Music and sounds are of course related, but they are two different things."

"What do you mean?" asked Baron Wen.

"In the ancient times," said Tsehsia, "the forces of nature were in harmony and the weather was in accord with the four seasons; the people were good in character and the harvests were plentiful; there were no epidemics and no monsters of bad omen appeared. That was the time when everything was right. So then the Sages (or priests) arose and established social discipline in the relationships between parents and children and kings and their ministers. With the establishment of social discipline, the world was brought into order, and after the world was brought into order, the Sages set the right standards for the six pitch-pipes* and the five keys. People then began to sing songs and anthems to the accompaniment of *hsuan* string instruments, and these were called sacred music (literally "virtuous sounds") and sacred music was music. . . . But what your Highness is interested in is merely a jumble of lewd sounds."

"May I ask, where do the lewd sounds come from?" asked the Baron.

"The music of Cheng," replied Tsehsia, "is lewd and corrupting, the music of Sung is soft and makes one effeminate, the music of Wei is repetitious and annoying, and the music of Ch'i is harsh and makes one haughty. These four kinds of music are all sensual music and undermine the people's character, and that is why they cannot be used at the sacrifices. The *Book of Songs* says, 'The harmonious sounds are *shu* and *yung* and my ancestor listened to them.' *Shu* means 'pious' and *yung* means 'peaceful.' If you have piety and peacefulness of character, you can do everything you want with a country.

"All that a king needs to do is to be careful with regard to his likes and dislikes. What the king likes, that the people will do, and what the king does, that the people will follow. That is the meaning of the passage in the *Book of Songs* which says, 'It is very easy to guide the people.' "

In accordance with this idea, therefore, the sages (or priests) made the musical instruments, the *yao* (a small

* There were twelve pitch-pipes, the major and the minor, giving the full diatonic scale.

drum with two beads suspended on both sides and a handle—when the handle is rolled between the palms, the beads strike the drum itself), the drum, the *k'ung* and the *ch'ia* (varieties of square wooden drums with wooden tops with a hole in the center), the *hsuan* and the *ch'ih* (varieties of mouth organs, the *hsuan* being a broad oval-shaped clay pot with six holes and the *ch'ih* being made of bamboo with different pipes provided with reeds). These six instruments produce sounds used in sacred music. In addition, they are accompanied by the bells, the *ch'ing* (a stone slab suspended in a stand), the *yu* (a kind of bagpipe with 36 reeds) and the *seh* (a long horizontal string instrument with fifty strings), and with the dance with shields and hatchets (military dance) and with pennants of ox-tail and long pheasant tails ("civil dance"). This is the kind of music used at the worship of ancient kings and at the drinking ceremonies. It is the kind of music by which a sense of social order between the different ranks was established and the sense of discipline between elders and juniors and superiors and inferiors was taught to the following generations.

The sound of the bell is clear and resonant; its clarity and resonance make it especially suitable for serving as signals, such signals create an impression of majesty, and the impression of majesty inspires a sense of the military power. Therefore when the sovereign hears the bell, he thinks of his military officials. The sound of the musical stone is sharp and clear-cut; its sharpness and clear-cut quality tend to foster the sense of decision, and the sense of decision makes it easy for the generals to die in battle. Therefore when the sovereign hears the musical stone, he thinks of his military officers who died in battle at the border. The sound of the string is plaintive; its plaintive quality cleanses the soul, and the cleansed state of mind makes for a sense of righteousness. Therefore, when the sovereign hears the sound of the string instrument, the *ch'in* and the *seh* (both horizontal string instruments on a flat sounding board) he thinks of his righteous ministers. The sound of bamboo (corresponding to the Western wood-wind instruments) has a floating quality; its floating quality tends to spread everywhere and bring together the masses of the people. Therefore when the sovereign hears the sound of bamboo instruments, he thinks of his ministers of the interior. The sound of the big and small drums is noisy; its noisy quality tends to arouse and excite, and the excitement tends to prepare the masses for action. Therefore when the sovereign hears the sound of the big and small drums, he thinks of his great generals. It is seen, therefore, that in hearing music, the sovereign does not hear their sounds only, but also hears the significance proper to the different sounds.*

* In this section only five of the eight classes of Chinese musical instruments are commented upon. The other three classes are: the gourd, the clay instruments and the wooden instruments. Brass is conspicuously absent. The drum represents the "leather" class. The commentators emphasize that the simple sounds of the drum, the square wooden box and the clay pipes, being simple in character, are chosen for use in sacred music.

V. CONFUCIUS ON THE DIFFERENT MOVEMENTS OF THE INTERPRETATIVE DANCE MUSIC OF EMPEROR WU

Pinmou Chia was talking one day with Confucius, and they began to discuss music, and Confucius asked, "Why is it that at the beginning of this dance of Wu, the dancers stand a long time holding themselves in readiness before they begin, while the drum is being played?"

"Because it symbolizes the fact that Emperor Wu waited a long time and did not launch out on the conquest of the *Shang* Emperor (Chou, whom he overthrew) until he was assured of the support of the other rulers," replied Pinmou Chia.

"What is the meaning again of the singing and the sighing of the dancers, with the movements slowly and gradually growing in intensity?"

"Because Emperor Wu was still waiting to assure himself of the support of the other rulers."

"What is the meaning again of the dance and the stamping on the ground early in the dance?" asked Confucius again.

"Because it was a time to act."

"Why is it that the dancers then begin to squat on the ground, with their right knees touching the ground and their left knees lifted?"

"They should not squat on the ground in the Dance of Wu."

"Why is it that in between we hear the characteristic melody of the Shangs (the enemy)?"

"That melody doesn't properly belong in this music of Wu."

"Then what melody is it, if it doesn't belong in the music of Wu?"

"The masters of music have forgotten its original meaning. . . . If this weren't a later interpolation (*i.e.,* if it was the melody of Emperor Wu), then Emperor Wu must have been a cruel king."*

"I have heard this interpretation from Ch'ang Hung (an official at the Chou capital)," said Confucius, "which essentially agrees with yours."

Pinmou Chia rose from his seat and said, "We all understand the meaning of that long preliminary waiting. But, may I ask, why the delay and waiting of the dancers at the start, and such a long delay?"

"Sit down and I will tell you," said Confucius. "This music is a symbolic interpretation of the historical events. That the dancers stand in long lines with their shields like a solid wall (literally "like a mountain") symbolizes the events of Emperor Wu. That the dancers start to stamp the ground at an early part of the dance symbolizes the agitations or ambitions of Emperor Wu's great-grandfather, King T'ai. The dancers then squat

* Here it is apparent that the introduction of the melody of the enemy, showing a spirit of license and terrible cruelty, was originally in this interpretative tone poem in order to complete the picture. Nothing is known about this Pinmou Chia. He and Confucius were apparently fellow students of music, discussing the matter on a friendly footing, and from here on Confucius begins to give his own interpretation, which in two places contradicts Pinmou's interpretation.

down on the ground to symbolize the rule of peace by the Dukes Chou and Shao (brothers of Emperor Wu later assisting his son in pacifying the country and founding the governmental system of the Chou Dynasty, after the overthrow of the previous dynasty). Besides, the dancers of Wu start out in the first movement from the south facing north (advancing to the second position and symbolizing the setting out of his army, *according to the commentators*). In the second movement, the Shangs are defeated (advancing to the third position, *according to the commentators*). In the third movement, the dancers turn south again (taking the fourth position). In the fourth movement, the establishment of his rule over the Southern countries is symbolized (taking the second position again). In the fifth movement, the dancers divide themselves, signifying the rule of Duke Chou on the left and Duke Shao on the right (taking the third position again). In the sixth movement, the dancers return to their original positions again to symbolize the homage of the entire country to the Emperor.*
The advancing of the dancers in formation, with the players of the wooden resonance box at their sides and their breaking up into the spear dance facing four directions (or repeating the dance of spears four times, *according to another interpretation*) show the spread of

---

* According to *Shuking*, the flute music of *hsiao* (ascribed to Emperor Shun) consists of nine movements. Of this *hsiao* music Confucius said it was perfectly good and perfectly beautiful; but of the Wu music, he said it was perfectly beautiful but not perfectly good. He forgot the taste of meat for three months trying to study the *hsiao*.

the military power of Emperor Wu over China. The advance in two parallel columns with the players of the wooden resonance box at their side shows their easy victory. Their long waiting in formation symbolizes the waiting for the armies of the allied rulers to arrive.

"Furthermore, haven't you heard the story about wha Emperor Wu did at the suburb of the capital of th defeated dynasty? When Emperor Wu had defeated th Shangs and arrived at their capital, he made the descen dants of Huangti (the Yellow Emperor) rulers of Chi, made the descendants of Emperor Yao rulers over Chu, and made the descendants of Emperor Shun rulers over Ch'en. This was done before the campaign was finished, and after the campaign was finished, he made the descendants of Emperor Yu rulers over Chi (*different from the 'Chi' above*) and degraded the descendants of the Shang Emperors and put them in Sung. He also gave a posthumous rank to the tomb of Prince Pikan,* released Chitse from prison and allowed him to continue to live according to the customs of the Shangs, and restored his rank. The people were freed from the army service and the knights were given double salaries. After he crossed the Yellow River westwards, he set the army horses free to pasture on the south of the Hua Mountains and did not ride them again. He set the buffaloes free on the plains of the Peach Grove and did not keep

---

* Pikan was a good prince, and because he protested against the cruelty of Emperor Chou of Shang, his uncle, he was sentenced to death. The ancestry of the clan of Lins, my clan, is traced back to this prince on a purely legendary basis.

them again; and he had the chariots and armors smeared with blood and kept in the Imperial Treasury and did not use them again. The spears and shields were carried backwards (with the handles first) and wrapped in tiger skins, and the generals were made rulers over cities. This was called the disarmament (literally "locking up the arrow-bag."). So then it was made known to the world at large that Emperor Wu was not going to use his military weapons any more. The army was disbanded and made to take up the sport of archery in the suburbs. In the eastern suburb, the ceremony of archery contests was accompanied with the song *Lishou,* and in the western suburb, the ceremony of the archery contests was accompanied with the song *Tsouyu.** The practice of shooting to penetrate the target was discontinued. Ceremonial robes and audience tablets (held between the hands by the ministers when seeing the Emperor) were used and the knights were relieved of their swords. Sacrifices were made at the Grand Temple (the Mingt'ang or "Hall of Clear Virtue"), in order that the people might understand filial piety. The ceremonies of the court audience were established so that the different dukes might know how to show their homage. The ceremony of the Emperor tilling the field himself was established, so that the people might understand respect toward Nature. These five institutions were the five great cultural institutions of the world.

"At the Imperial College, the Three Elders and Five

---

* The poem *Tsouyu* is found today in the *Book of Songs.*

Superiors were maintained; the Emperor bared his left arm* to cut the sacrificial animal and gave it to these Elders; he held the pot of gravy in his hands, and presented it to them; he held the wine cup and made them drink (literally "gargle"); and he wore a crown and held a shield in his hand. These were done that the different dukes might be taught the general virtue of humility and respect. In this way the culture of the Chous was spread to entire China, and rituals and music prevailed throughout the country. Don't we understand now why at the beginning of the Dance of Wu, the dancers waited so long in formation (*ie.,* for the other rulers to follow Emperor Wu)?" . . .

---

* A custom used (originally, I believe) in archery for practical reasons, with the sleeve of the left arm rolled up, and later at sacrificial ceremonies.

Chapter XI

MENCIUS

(*The Book of Mencius,* Book VI, Part I)

IN THE study of the character of Confucian thought, it is important to have some ideas of its chief developments in Mencius, because of the clearer exposition of philosophic values in Mencius and because of their actual influence. Mencius represents the "orthodox" development of the Confucian school. The *Book of Mencius,* in seven books, each divided into two parts, is thicker than the *Analects* by almost one-third, and is incomparably better prose than the *Analects.* Mencius was an eloquent writer and speaker, good at debates, and the passages often consist of long and sustained discourses, and there are so many brilliant passages that it is difficult to make a selection in a volume devoted to Confucius.

Nevertheless, the ideas of Mencius represent such an important development of one side of Confucius' teachings, that it is impossible to get a fair conception of the Confucian ideas without reading something from Mencius. Hantse said, "The teachings of Confucius were broad and covered a wide scope, and it was impossible for any of his disciples to master the whole field. Therefore the early students of Confucianism developed each that side of his teachings which lay closest to his mental equipment. These disciples later on dispersed and settled in different countries and began to teach their disciples what they themselves had mastered, and the farther they were separated from the original source, the more divergent became their views or lines of study. Only Mencius studied under Tsesze, whose knowledge of Confucius' teachings came from Tsengtse. Since Confucius' death, only Mencius was able to carry on the orthodox tradition. Therefore, in order to study the teachings of the Sage, one must begin with Mencius." Hantse also said, "Mencius was the purest of the pure in the interpretation of Confucius; Hsuntse and Yangtse were on the whole pure, with certain adulterations."

I have selected for translation, a whole part of one of the Books of Mencius, in my opinion the most important and representative one. The most important ideas in Mencius are, the goodness of human nature, consequently the importance of recovering that original good nature, the recognition that culture or education merely consists in preventing the good nature in us from becoming "beclouded" by circumstances, the theory of nourishing what amounts to an equivalent of Bergson's *elan vital* (the *haojan chih ch'i*), and finally the declaration that all men are equal in their inherent goodness, and that since the Emperors Yao and Shun were also human beings, "any man could become a Yao or Shun."

Mencius also developed the distinction between the ruler by virtue (*wang*) and the ruler by force or cunning (*pa*)—roughly, the distinction between "a kingly ruler" and "a dictator." He further developed Confucius' idea of government by example into a well-defined system, and for the first time used the phrase "benevolent government" which Confucius never used. (*Jen* definitely means "benevolence" in *Mencius*. He was also probably the best historical scholar of his days and had definite ideas about taxation systems, agricultural systems and the feudal system. We do not get a clear idea of his theory of "benevolent government," developed from Confucius' government by moral example, but in this essay we find practically all his ideas about the goodness of human nature and the importance and method of finding one's "greater self." This essay is translated in full without omissions.

I. THE GOODNESS OF HUMAN NATURE

Kaotse said, "Human nature is like the willow tree, and righteous conduct or character is like a wicker basket (made of the willow branches). To make human nature follow benevolence and righteousness is like making willow branches into wicker baskets." Mencius said, "Now in making a wicker basket, don't you try to follow the nature of the willow branches (in bending them), or are you going to violate the nature of the willow branches? If you are going to violate the nature of the willow branches in order to make wicker baskets, then you are also going to violate humun nature in order to make it benevolent and righteous. Your teachings are going to mislead the entire world and ruin the teachings of benevolence and righteousness."

Kaotse said, "Human nature is like water in the gulley. You guide it toward the East and it flows eastwards, and you guide it toward the West, and it flows westwards. There is no distinction between goodness and badness in human nature, as there is no distinction between East and West in water." "It is true," said Mencius, "that the water has no preference for the East or the West, but doesn't it make a distinction between 'up' and 'down' or a 'higher' and a 'lower' level? Human nature follows the good as water seeks the lower level. There is no man who is not good, as there is no water which does not flow downwards. Now you can strike the water and it splashes upwards above your forehead, or you can force it up the hills. But is this the original nature of water and not just due to the circumstances? And you can make human nature turn to evil in the same way."

Kaotse said, "What is born in us is called our nature." And Mencius replied, "When you say that nature is what is born in us, do you mean that it is like saying that a white substance is called 'white'?" "Yes," replied Kaotse. "Then do you consider the whiteness of a white feather the same as the whiteness of white snow, or again, consider the whiteness of white snow the same as the whiteness of a piece of white jade?" "Yes," said Kaotse. "Then do you consider the nature of dogs the same as the nature of cows, or again consider the nature of cows the same as the nature of human beings?*

Kaotse said, "The desires for food and sex are born in us. Benevolence comes from within and is not something external, while righteousness is something external, and does not come from within." Mencius replied, "What do you mean by saying that benevolence comes from within while righteousness (or righteous conduct) is something external?" "When I see a tall man and call him tall," Kaotse replied, "it is not I who am tall (or that tallness is not within me), just as when something is white and I call it white, I observe its external white appearance merely. Therefore, I say righteous conduct is external." "Now," said Mencius, "the whiteness of a white horse in no way differs from the whiteness of a white person. But do you think that the tallness of a tall horse is in no way different from the tallness of a tall person? Now is the tall person or horse *right* (same word as *righteous*) or the man who calls it tall or regards it as tall *right* (*the right conception of 'tallness' is a subjective element belonging to the observer*). "But," said Kaotse, "I love my own brother, but I don't love the brother, say, of a man from the country of Ch'in. That shows that love comes from myself and is therefore regarded as something from within. On the other hand, I equally respect the elders of Ch'u as well as my own elders. That shows that what pleases me is the fact of their being elders, and this re-

* Mencius always considered the moral distinction or consciousness of good and evil as peculiarly human and often said that when a man lost that distinction, "he was not far different from the beasts."

spect (a virtue of righteous conduct) is therefore something external." Mencius replied, "But we love the roast pork of the Ch'in people as much as we love our own roast pork. That is so even with respect to material things. Then are you going to say that this love of roast pork is also something external?"

Baron Chi Meng asked Kungtutse, "What does Mencius mean by saying that righteous conduct is internal or comes from within?" The latter replied, "Righteous conduct is merely the showing of my inner respect. That is why it is considered to come from within." "If you have a person in the same village who is one year older than your elder brother, whom are you going to serve with respect?" asked the Baron. "Of course I will serve my elder brother with respect first." "But in offering wine at a feast, whom are you going to offer it to first?" "Of course I will offer wine first to the villager," was the reply. "Then you see you serve with respect one person, while you honor another person, which shows conduct is something external (depending on external circumstances) and not something internal." To this Kungtutse could not make a reply, and he told Mencius about it. Mencius said, "If you ask him whether he will serve with respect his uncle or his younger brother, he will say that he will serve with respect his uncle. Then you ask him, in case his younger brother is acting at a sacrifice as the representative of the deceased, then to whom is he going to show greater respect? He will then say he will show greater respect to his younger brother. Then you say to him, 'Where then is your respect for your uncle?' He will reply, of course, that in this case his younger brother represents that spirit in an official capacity. Then you can say to him, 'Exactly. In our every day life we serve with respect our own elder brothers, but on special occasions we honor the villager.' " When the Baron heard this, he said, "Now in one case you respect the uncle, and in the other case you respect the younger brother. That shows clearly respect is dependent upon external circumstances." Kungtutse replied, "You take hot soup on a winter day and take cold water on a summer day. Then would you also say that (our desire for) food and drink is also something external (though it differs with varying circumstances)?"

Kungtutse said, "Kaotse says that the original human nature is neither good nor bad. Some people say that human nature can be either good or bad; therefore when the Emperors Wen and Wu were in power, the people loved virtue, and when the Emperors Yu and Li were in power, the people loved violence. Again other people say that some natures are good, while other natures are bad, and that therefore even under the rule of Emperor Yao, there was a bad man Hsiang, and even with a bad father, Kusou, there was produced a good son, Shun, and there were the good princes Ch'i and Pikan with such a bad man as Chou for their uncle and king. Now if you say that human nature is (always) good, then are all those people wrong?" "If you let them follow their original nature," replied Mencius, "then they are all good. That is why I say human nature is good. If men become evil, that is not the fault of their original endowment. The sense of mercy is found in all men; the sense of shame is found in all men; the sense of respect is found in all men; the sense of right and wrong is found in all men. The sense of mercy is what we call benevolence or charity. The sense of shame is what we call righteousness. The sense of respect is what we call propriety. The sense of right and wrong is what we call wisdom, or moral consciousness. Charity, righteousness, propriety and moral consciousness are not something that is drilled into us; we have got them originally with us, only we often forget about them (or neglect or ignore them). Therefore it is said, 'Seek and you will find it, neglect and you will lose it.' This moral consciousness is developed in different persons to different degrees, some five times, some ten times and some infinitely more than others, because people have not developed to the full extent what is in them. The *Book of Songs* says, 'Heaven created the common people with laws governing their affairs. When the people keep to the central (or common) principles, they will love a beautiful character.' Confucius commented upon this poem, saying, 'The writer of this poem understood the moral law, and therefore he recognized that there were laws governing human affairs. Because the people keep to the central principles, therefore they have come to love beautiful character.' "

Mencius said, "In years of prosperity, most of the young people are well behaved, and in bad years, most of the young people turn to violence. This is not due to a difference in their natural endowments from Heaven, but because something has happened to lead their hearts astray. Take, for instance, the growing of wheat. You sow the seeds and till the field. The different plants are planted at the same time and grow from the same piece of land, and soon they sprout beautifully from the earth. When the time for harvest comes, they are all ripe, and although there is a difference between the different stalks of wheat, it is due to the difference in the soil, in the obtaining of moisture from the rain and the dew, and to differences in human care. Therefore, all who belong to the same species are essentially alike. Why should you doubt that this holds true also of human beings? The Sages belong to the same species as ourselves. As Lungtse has said, 'A man who proceeds to make a pair of shoes without knowing the feet measurements will at least not end up by making a wicker basket.' Shoes are alike because the people's feet are alike. There is a common taste for flavor in our mouths. Yiya (a famous gourmet) is but one who has discovered our common taste for food. If, for instance, one man's taste for flavors should differ from that of another man, as the taste of dogs and horses, who belong to a different species, differs from the human taste, then why should the whole world follow the judgment of Yiya in regard to flavor? Since in the matter of flavor the whole world regards Yiya as the ultimate standard, we must admit that our tastes for flavors are alike. The same thing is true of our ears. In the matter of sounds, the whole world regards Master

K'uang as the ultimate standard, and we must admit that our ears are alike. The same thing is true of our eyes. In regard to Tsetu, the whole world considers him a handsome man, and whoever cannot see his handsomeness may be said to have no eyes. Therefore I say there is a common love for flavors in our mouths, a common sense for sounds in our ears, and a common sense for beauty in our eyes. Why then do we refuse to admit that there is something common in our souls also? What is that thing that we have in common in our souls? It it is reason and a sense of right. The Sage is the man who has first discovered what is common to men's souls. Therefore, reason and the sense of right please our minds as beef and mutton and pork please our palates."

II. HOW OUR ORIGINAL NATURE IS DESTROYED

Mencius said, "There was once a time when the forests of the Niu Mountain were beautiful. But can the mountain any longer be regarded as beautiful, since being situated near a big city, the woodsmen have hewed the trees down? The days and nights gave it rest, and the rains and the dew continued to nourish it, and a new life was continually springing up from the soil, but then the cattle and the sheep began to pasture upon it. That is why the Niu Mountain looks so bald, and when people see its baldness, they imagine that there was never any timber on the mountain. Is this the true nature of the mountain? And is there not a heart of love and righteousness in man, too? But how can that nature remain beautiful when it is hacked down every day, as the woodsman chops down the trees with his axe? To be sure, the nights and days do the healing and there is the nourishing air of the early dawn, which tends to keep him sound and normal, but this morning air is thin and is soon destroyed by what he does in the day. With this continuous hacking of the human spirit, the rest and recuperation obtained during the night are not sufficient to maintain its level, and when the nights recuperation does not suffice to maintain its level, then the man degrades himself to a state not far from the beast's. People see that he acts like a beast and imagine that there was never any true character in him. But is this the true nature of man? Therefore with proper nourishment and care, everything grows, and without the proper nourishment and care, everything degenerates or decays. Confucius said, 'Keep it carefully and you will have it, let it go and you will lose it. It appears and disappears from time to time in we do not know what direction.' He was talking about the human soul."*

Mencius said, "Do not think that King (Hsuan of Ch'i) is lacking in wisdom or moral consciousness (as a man). Even in the case of the things that grow most easily in this world, they would never grow up properly if for one day of sunshine they get ten days of cloudy (or chilly) weather. He seldom sees me, and when I leave, the people who are the 'cloudy days' for him arrive. Even if what I say to him is taking root (literally 'sprouting')

* Elsewhere Mencius defines the "great man" as "one who has not lost the heart of a child."

in his mind, what can he do about it? Even in a trivial thing like playing chess, one cannot learn it unless he concentrates his mind on learning it. You let Chess-player Ch'iu, who is the best chess player of the country, teach two persons how to play chess. One man will concentrate his mind and energy on it and listen carefully to Chess-Player Ch'iu's explanations and advice, and another man will hear the same explanations, but his mind will be thinking of how a wild goose is going to pass by and how he is going to take a bow and shoot at it. Now although the second man studies under the same master, he will never be equal to the other man. But if you say that this man is lacking in original talent of intelligence, you know it isn't true."

III. THE HIGHER LIFE AND THE GREATER SELF

Mencius said, "I like fish, but I also like bear's paw, but if I can't have both at the same time, I will forego the fish and eat the bear's paw. I love life, but I also love righteousness, and if I can't have both at the same time, I will sacrifice life to have righteousness. I love life, but there is something that I love more than life, and therefore I would not have life at any price. I also hate death, but there is something that I hate more than death, and therefore I would not avoid danger at any price. If there is nothing that man loves more than life, then does he not permit himself to do anything in order to save it? And if there is nothing that man hates more than death, then why does he not always avoid dangers that could be avoided? And so there are times when a man would forsake his life, and there are times when a man would not avoid danger. It is not only the good men who have this feeling that there are times when they would forsake life and there are times when they would not avoid danger. All men have this feeling, only the good men have been able to preserve it."* A man's life or death may sometimes depend on a bamboo basket of rice and a bowl of soup but if you say to a starving man passing by, "Hey, Mister!" and off them to him in the most insulting manner, he would refuse to take them, or if you offer them to a beggar with a kick, the beggar would not receive them.

"What is a salary of ten thousand bushels to me, if I come by it against my principles? Shall I take this position because it offers me beautiful mansions and the

---

* In the Chinese text, Mencius used the word "heart," which I have translated here as "feelings" (elsewhere also as the "soul"), because of the limitations of this word "heart" in the English usage. The whole Mencian philosophy centers around "keeping the heart" and not "losing" it. At other places I have found it necessary to render the same word by "mind" or "intelligence." Of course the English word "heart" comes closest to what Mencius calls *hsin,* since it is primarily a matter of feeling and not of thinking. But the same word is used in Chinese to express the "mind" also, and it should be strongly emphasized that the Chinese language does not admit of a clear distinction of, or separation between, the head and the heart. That is not only grammatically, but also historically a true fact. Mencius, however, uses three important words, "the heart" (including the mind or intelligence), "sentiment" (which is interpreted as the heart in action), and "talent" (or innate capacity, which is more or less fully developed in individuals according to the circumstances).

service of a wife and concubines, or because I shall be able to help my friends who knew me when I was poor? If formerly I refused to accept the post in the face of death (or starvation), and now I accept it in order to have a fine residence, if formerly I refused to accept this post in the face of death, and now I accept it in order to have the service of a wife and concubines, if formerly I refused this post in the face of death, and now I accept it in order to be able to help my friends who knew me when I was poor, would that not be something totally unnecessary? This is called 'losing one's original heart.'"

Mencius said, "Charity is in the heart of man, and righteousness is the path for men. Pity the man who has lost his path and does not follow it and who has lost his heart and does not know how to recover it. When people's dogs and chicks are lost, they go out and look for them, and yet the people who have lost their hearts (or original nature) do not go out and look for them. The principle of self-cultivation consists in nothing but trying to look for the lost heart."

Mencius said, "Suppose there is a man who has a crooked ring finger which cannot stretch out straight. It isn't painful and it doesn't cause him any inconvenience. And yet, if there was someone who could straighten out the finger for him, he would not mind going as far as Ch'in or Ch'u because he is ashamed that his finger is not like that of other men (or not normal). Now a man is wise enough to be ashamed of a finger that is not normal, and yet he is not wise enough to be ashamed of his heart, when his heart is not normal. We say such a man has no sense of the relative importance of things."

Mencius said, "People know that if they want a lindera tree whose circumference is a fathom long to grow and live, they must take proper care of it. But as to their own selves, they do not know how to take proper care of them. Can it be that they love their selves less than they love a lindera tree? It is mere thoughtlessness."

Mencius said, "There is not a part of the body that a man does not love. And because there is not a part that he does not love, there is not a part of it that he does not nourish. Because there is not an inch of his skin that he does not love, there is not an inch of his skin that he does not take care of. The thing that determines whether a thing is good or bad depends only on his regard for it, or the value he places upon it. Now in our constitution there is a higher and a lower nature, and a smaller and a greater self. One should not develop the lower nature at the expense of the higher nature, or develop the smaller self at the expense of the greater self. He who attends to his smaller self becomes a small man, and he who attends to his greater self becomes a great man. A gardener who attends to thorns and bramble to the neglect of his lindera trees will be regarded as a bad gardener. A man who takes good care of his finger and suffers an injury to his shoulder blade is deformed. People look down upon the matter of food and drink because food nourishes our smaller self and does nothing to our greater self. If a man attends to his food, without forgetting about his greater self, then it may be said that the

food taken indeed does not only go to nourish any particular small part of the body (an inch of his skin)."

Kungtutse asked Mencius, "We are all human beings.
Why is it that some are great men and some are small
men?" Mencius replied, "Those who attend to their
greater selves become great men, and those who attend
to their smaller selves become small men." "But we are
all human beings. Why is it that some people attend to
their greater selves and some attend to their smaller
selves?" Mencius replied, "When our senses of sight and
hearing are distracted by the things outside, without the
participation of thought, then the material things act
upon the material senses and lead them astray. That is
the explanation. The function of the mind is thinking;
when you think, you keep your mind, and when you
don't think, you lose your mind. This is what heaven has
given to us (for the purpose of thinking or knowing
what is right and wrong). One who cultivates his higher
self will find that his lower self follows in accord. That is
how a man becomes a great man."

Mencius said, "There is the heaven-made nobility, and
there is the man-made nobility. The people who are
kind, righteous, faithful and love virtue without fail belong to the heaven-made nobility (or the nobility of God),
and the *kung, ch'ing,* and *taifu* (different ranks of
officials) belong to the man-made nobility. The ancient
people cultivated what belonged to God's noblemen and
they obtained without conscious effort the ranks of man-
made nobility. People today, on the other hand, cultivate
what belongs to this heaven-made nobility in order to

secure man-made honors (or man-made nobility), and after they have secured man-made honors, they forsake the things that make for heaven-made nobility. Thus they are led grievously astray and must soon perish after all."

Mencius said, "All people have the common desire to be elevated in honor, but all people have something still more elevated in themselves without knowing it. What people usually consider as an elevated rank or honor is not true honor, for he whom Chao Meng (a powerful ruling family of Chin) has honored, Chao Meng can also bring into dishonor. The *Book of Songs* says, 'I am drunk with wine, and I am filled with virtue.' This figurative expression means that a man is 'filled' with kindness and righteousness, and when he is so filled, he does not care for the flavors of delicate food. And when a man wears a mantle of fame, he does not care for the embroidered gowns."

Mencius said, "The five kinds of grains are considered good plants, but if the grains are not ripe, they are worse than cockles. It is the same with regard to kindness, which must grow into maturity."

Mencius said, "When Yi (a famous archer) taught people to shoot, he told them to pull the string on the bow its full length. The man who wants to cultivate himself must also develop himself to the full extent. A great carpenter teaches his apprentice to use squares and compasses. The man who wants to cultivate himself, must also have squares and compasses for his conduct."